Engaging the Curri
in Higher Educatio

CW00919981

SRHE and Open University Press Imprint

Current titles include:

Catherine Bargh *et al.*: *University Leadership*
Ronald Barnett: *The Idea of Higher Education*
Ronald Barnett: *Beyond all Reason*
Ronald Barnett: *The Limits of Competence*
Ronald Barnett: *Higher Education: A Critical Business*
Ronald Barnett: *Realizing the University in an Age of Supercomplexity*
Tony Becher and Paul R. Trowler: *Academic Tribes and Territories (2nd edn)*
Neville Bennett *et al.*: *Skills Development in Higher Education and Employment*
John Biggs: *Teaching for Quality Learning at University (2nd edn)*
Richard Blackwell and Paul Blackmore (eds): *Towards Strategic Staff Development in Higher Education*
David Boud *et al.* (eds): *Using Experience for Learning*
David Boud and Nicky Solomon (eds): *Work-based Learning*
Tom Bourner *et al.* (eds): *New Directions in Professional Higher Education*
John Brennan *et al.* (eds): *What Kind of University?*
Anne Brockbank and Ian McGill: *Facilitating Reflective Learning in Higher Education*
Stephen D. Brookfield and Stephen Preskill: *Discussion as a Way of Teaching*
Ann Brooks and Alison Mackinnon (eds): *Gender and the Restructured University*
Sally Brown and Angela Glasner (eds): *Assessment Matters in Higher Education*
James Cornford and Neil Pollock: *Putting the University Online*
John Cowan: *On Becoming an Innovative University Teacher*
Sara Delamont, Paul Atkinson and Odette Parry: *Supervising the PhD*
Sara Delamont and Paul Atkinson: *Research Cultures and Careers*
Gerard Delanty: *Challenging Knowledge*
Chris Duke: *Managing the Learning University*
Heather Eggins (ed.): *Globalization and Reform in Higher Education*
Heather Eggins and Ranald Macdonald (eds): *The Scholarship of Academic Development*
Gillian Evans: *Academics and the Real World*
Andrew Hannan and Harold Silver: *Innovating in Higher Education*
Lee Harvey and Associates: *The Student Satisfaction Manual*
David Istance, Hans Schuetze and Tom Schuller (eds): *International Perspectives on Lifelong Learning*
Norman Jackson and Helen Lund (eds): *Benchmarking for Higher Education*
Merle Jacob and Tomas Hellström (eds): *The Future of Knowledge Production in the Academy*
Peter Knight: *Being a Teacher in Higher Education*
Peter Knight and Paul Trowler: *Departmental Leadership in Higher Education*
Peter Knight and Mantz Yorke: *Assessment, Learning and Employability*
Mary Lea and Barry Stierer (eds): *Student Writing in Higher Education*
Ian McNay (ed.): *Higher Education and its Communities*
Elaine Martin: *Changing Academic Work*
Louise Morley: *Quality and Power in Higher Education*
Moira Peelo and Terry Wareham (eds): *Failing Students in Higher Education*
Craig Prichard: *Making Managers in Universities and Colleges*
Michael Prosser and Keith Trigwell: *Understanding Learning and Teaching*
John Richardson: *Researching Student Learning*
Stephen Rowland: *The Enquiring University Teacher*
Maggi Savin-Baden: *Problem-based Learning in Higher Education*
Maggi Savin-Baden: *Facilitating Problem-based Learning*
Maggi Savin-Baden and Kay Wilkie: *Challenging Research in Problem-based Learning*
David Scott, Andrew Brown, Ingrid Lunt and Lucy Thorne: *Examining Professional Doctorates*
Peter Scott (ed.): *The Globalization of Higher Education*
Peter Scott: *The Meanings of Mass Higher Education*
Michael L. Shattock: *Managing Successful Universities*
Maria Slowey and David Watson: *Higher Education and the Lifecourse*
Anthony Smith and Frank Webster (eds): *The Postmodern University?*
Colin Symes and John McIntyre (eds): *Working Knowledge*
Peter G. Taylor: *Making Sense of Academic Life*
Richard Taylor, Jean Barr and Tom Steele: *For a Radical Higher Education*
Malcolm Tight: *Researching Higher Education*
Penny Tinkler and Carolyn Jackson: *The Doctoral Examination Process*
Susan Toohey: *Designing Courses for Higher Education*
Paul R. Trowler (ed.): *Higher Education Policy and Institutional Change*
Melanie Walker (ed.): *Reconstructing Professionalism in University Teaching*
Melanie Walker and Jon Nixon (eds): *Reclaiming Universities from a Runaway World*
David Warner and David Palfreyman (eds): *Higher Education Management of UK Higher Education*
Gareth Williams (ed.): *The Enterprising University*
Diana Woodward and Karen Ross: *Managing Equal Opportunities in Higher Education*

Engaging the Curriculum in Higher Education

Ronald Barnett and Kelly Coate

Society for Research into Higher Education
& Open University Press

Open University Press
McGraw-Hill Education
McGraw-Hill House
Shoppenhangers Road
Maidenhead
Berkshire
England
SL6 2QL

email: enquiries@openup.co.uk
world wide web: www.openup.co.uk

and Two Penn Plaza, New York, NY 10121-2289, USA

First published 2005

Copyright © Ronald Barnett and Kelly Coate, 2005

A catalogue record of this book is available from the British Library

ISBN 0 335 21289 1 (pb)   0 335 21290 5 (hb)

Library of Congress Cataloging-in-Publication Data
CIP data has been applied for

Typeset by RefineCatch Ltd, Bungay, Suffolk
Printed in the UK by Bell & Bain Ltd, Glasgow

For Ben

Contents

Acknowledgements

We should like to acknowledge Gareth Parry, who was a joint director (with Ronald Barnett) on the ESRC-funded research project which acted as the spur to this book; the work of Svava Bjarnason, who served as the first project officer on the project, conducting many interviews with academics across the UK; the ESRC itself for supporting the project with a grant (Project R000236973); Caroline Pelletier, who conducted research that identified many contemporary curriculum developments across the UK; and Alison Phipps, who commented on a draft of Chapter 9. We should like to thank John Skelton, Chief Executive of Open University Press, and his successor, Shona Mullen, in the new incarnation of the OUP within McGraw-Hill: both have given this book project much encouragement and support.

We would also wish to record our appreciation of the publisher's referees for these titles, namely, John Cowan, Norman Jackson, Stephen Rowland, Geoffrey Squires and Melanie Walker. Each provided many helpful ideas and suggestions which we have raided shamelessly. Above all, however, we should like to thank the many academic staff in our six chosen institutions, all of whom gave generously of their time to allow us to interview them. We hope that on reading this volume they may feel that their time was well spent.

Introduction

Purpose

All around the world, higher education is expanding rapidly, governments are mounting inquiries into higher education, more institutions are involved in running courses of study and more money is being spent on higher education, not least by students themselves. Higher education is ever more important to increasing numbers of people. And yet, despite all this growth and debate, there is very little talk about the curriculum. What students should be experiencing is barely a topic for debate. What the building blocks of their courses might be and how they should be put together are even more absent from the general discussion. The very idea of curriculum is pretty well missing altogether.

In this book, we want to help to put this matter right. We believe that the time is right to raise explicitly questions about the character of courses in higher education. What considerations should be present in their design? What, indeed, does it mean to design courses in higher education? Are there considerations that should transcend the different disciplines or is each field of knowledge a law unto itself? Is the current state of knowledge in a discipline or field the only consideration in shaping a curriculum or are there other considerations? What place should skills have in a curriculum? Is there any place for a sense of students as human beings as distinct from being enquirers after knowledge or as possessors of skills? These are the kind of questions that we want to tackle here.

In posing these questions, it will be clear what this book is not. It is not a recipe book for curriculum designers. It does not *legitimize* a new breed of professionals in higher education, namely 'curriculum designers'. It does not offer hard-pressed lecturers, suddenly faced with the challenge of designing a course, an easily accessible manual for the task. It does not introduce a compendium of lists of skills (whether for employability or any other purpose) that the modern higher education curriculum should contain. It is not an explanation to employers as to what they can necessarily expect of graduates who come their way; nor is it a guide to students as to what they will find in their courses of study at university.

If it is none of these things, what then is this book about? Who will find any use for it? Will it, indeed, have any uses at all? What we would hope is that – in reading this book – our readers, whether they be lecturers, heads of department, students, staff members of learning and teaching agencies or members of national higher education bodies, would all have a deeper appreciation of both the significance of the curriculum and its complexities. We hope for even more than that, however, for we also hope to persuade our readers that there are some large and serious challenges facing curricula in higher education today in the twenty-first century and these challenges need to be addressed certainly urgently but also concertedly. Energies and effort need to be turned towards the curricula in a systematic fashion by all concerned. In this spirit, we offer sets of principles which may help those involved in the shaping of curricula.

Arguments

'Engaging the curriculum': the title of our book contains an ambiguity, an ambiguity that allows us a space to offer three arguments. *Our first argument* is that the idea of the curriculum has not seriously been engaged within higher education debate and policy formation and even in its practices. Curriculum design in higher education is not yet a properly reflective practice. As a result, the debate over higher education is not what it could be and the newly emerging curricula are often not what they should be. In developing our argument, we shall try to sketch out what it might mean for the curriculum to be engaged in those different regions of practice and pronouncement.

Our second argument hinges directly around the idea of engagement itself. We argue that if curricula in higher education are to go any way towards meeting the challenges that bear upon them, then the idea of 'engagement' offers a fruitful way forward. Curricula may 'engage' in all manner of directions and at different levels, with different speeds and force. We want to draw out what it might mean for curricula to be developed and sustained in such a way that they 'engage'.

If our first argument holds up, namely that the idea of curriculum is not yet seriously addressed in higher education, it follows that part of the task of prosecuting our second argument – that curricula in the twenty-first century might be understood and be deliberately designed 'to engage' – lies in establishing a framework within which the idea of engagement can be drawn out and here lies *our third set of arguments*. In its essence, the framework for which we argue is quite simple, consisting of just three dimensions that help to form curricula. The three dimensions are those of *knowing, acting* and *being*. We propose three sets of ideas in particular.

First, while these three dimensions are already present in every curriculum, the extent to which they are present explicitly varies considerably and, by extension, the extent to which these dimensions are brought into a coherent relationship with each other also varies. It follows that, for us, adequate curriculum design in the twenty-first century lies in doing explicit justice to all three dimensions by engaging them directly and deliberately and doing so in ways that bring knowing, acting and being into a clearly thought through and sustained set of relationships with each other.

Second, we want to distinguish between *curriculum-as-designed* and *curriculum-in-action*. Partly, this distinction arises out of our sense that a curriculum is as much an achievement as it is a task: an effective curriculum has to be brought off *in situ*. Partly too this distinction arises out of our sense that a curriculum is a matter of engaging students in our three dimensions (of knowing, acting and being).

Third, we suggest that curriculum design has too readily been understood as tasks of filling of various kinds (filling spaces, time and modules, not to mention minds). Instead, we propose that curriculum design should be understood as the imaginative *design of spaces as such*, spaces that are likely to generate new energies among students and inspire them, and so prompt their *triple engagement* – in knowing, acting and being.

Approach

Our approach is twofold. *On the one hand*, and drawing on a research project on the undergraduate curriculum in which we have been involved, we will try to offer an overview as to the extent to which curricula are changing, especially but not only in the UK, at the present time. We do not pretend this 'survey' part of our story to be exhaustive, although we hope that readers who are engaged in the sharp end of teaching in higher education will test our account against their own experience. *On the other hand*, what we want to do in the 'descriptive' part of our endeavour is set things up so that we can develop a plausible view as to the options open for curriculum change and even reform at the present time.

This framework will not be a blueprint; it will not include rules that can be followed straightforwardly in designing a curriculum. We shall, however, offer a set of principles that we consider any well-founded curriculum in the twenty-first century should heed.

There are two reasons for believing that curricula rules or templates are not what is called for. First, in a mass and diverse higher education system, curricula are intended to fulfil a very wide range of purposes and it would not be sensible to try to capture, in a single formula as it were, a common code that would specify in advance the elements of every programme of study. Second, and as a value position on our part, we deliberately want to leave open space for and, indeed, to encourage, creativity in curriculum design. Part of our contention, after all, is that the design of curricula has not been sufficiently addressed to the challenges that graduates will face (and not just in the world of work) so we wish to do all we can to prompt experimentation and fresh ideas.

It follows too that this more speculative and open-ended part of our story is bounded by time and, to a lesser extent, location. Our views as to what is possible for curriculum development have a forward-looking aspect, building as it does from our sense of challenges that are presented by the twenty-first century. In turn, we hope that the analytical framework we sketch out may have some durability attached to it for we intend it precisely as a relatively benign and open framework such that it is susceptible to an infinite variety of interpretations.

At the same time, even though this is a book that has its immediate home in the UK higher education 'scene', still we hope that the framework we develop may be felt to resonate with agendas and challenges that are cross-national in character if not actually fully global. Indeed, things will be going awry if that turned out not to be the case precisely because our framework contains a sense that we live in a global age, even if there remain determinedly local ideas of curriculum, of what counts as a worthwhile student experience and of what should pass for proper relationships between teacher and taught in higher education.

Let us come clean as to our purposes: while we intend that the framework we offer will be susceptible to an infinite variety of interpretations, our framework – hinged around knowing, acting and being – is also intended to engage the curriculum with the wider world and to assist in developing curricula that are likely to encourage students to develop so as to be accomplished human beings in the world that they are likely to face. Of course, that sentence begs some large questions: What *is* it to be an 'accomplished human being'? What features of 'the world that they are likely to face' are being picked out? Why, in any event, should it be thought that *all* curricula should be oriented towards the wider world in some way? Since this is an introduction, we can duck those questions for the time being, but we hope to give answers to them in this book.

What we will own up to here is the admission that, for us, the matter of the curriculum can only seriously be addressed as a large *project*. Designing a curriculum and bringing it off cannot be a purely technical matter but poses large questions of ultimate educational aims: in short, what is it to educate in the contemporary world? The matter of the curriculum also poses large and open questions of the framing of the context within which a curriculum might be designed. To what degree, if at all, might questions be permitted about what it is to be an effective human being in the contemporary world, of human identity, of ultimate ends, of relationships between human beings and their wider environment, and so on? Our view is that, whatever the answer, the questions do not just legitimately come into view but do so necessarily.

Either these matters can come into view deliberately or they will be present tacitly. Indeed, it is part of our argument that these matters have too often been contained tacitly and not even felt to be proper matters for debate. It is one of our purposes in this book, therefore, to bring into the open the large matters of educational aims and of what it is to *be* and to *become* in the contemporary world. Unless such matters are brought into the open, debate over curricula will be jejune and lacking a purchase, both in its understanding and in its practical implementation.

Fuzziness

In many debates today, a vocabulary of fuzziness abounds: along with 'fuzziness' itself are to be found such terms as 'fluidity', 'liquidity' and 'instability'. This is, for us, an appropriate language with which to approach curricula. The very idea of 'curriculum' is unstable, its boundaries uncertain. Is it just to be confined to the intended educational experience? Does it embrace the 'hidden curriculum'? To what extent should the idea be focused on the actual felt experience of the student? How far out of the laboratory, seminar room or lecture hall does it extend geographically? The library? The clinical setting? The study room?

These questions are legitimate and awkward: they are legitimate in that they ask of anyone concerned about the higher education to come clean and mark out the territory in which they are operating. They are awkward, however, in that the questions yield no definite answers. It is not just that all manner of answers are to be found in the literature as varying aspects are taken up and given prominence by different scholars; it is also that they call attention to the problematic nature of responsibility in this area. Just where do the responsibilities of lecturers, tutors and others 'involved' in the student experience begin and end? What too are the responsibilities of students towards bringing off the potential of their curricula? (Of course, the very construction 'their curricula' implies an ownership of the student towards the curriculum that she experiences which is precisely in question.)

Why do we make these points in an introduction? We do so for two reasons. *First*, as we have just intimated, for many scholars, a curriculum is nothing except as realized and its realization is dependent upon not just its reception among the students for whom it is intended but also their actual engagement with it. Much as we are in sympathy with this sentiment – that a crucial ingredient of a curriculum is its students and their 'negotiations' with and 'constructions of' their curriculum – our main focus is not students as such; and we explain our reasons for this focus in the book itself.

Second, we feel that we should be open and honest right at the start and, yet, on the grounds of elusiveness and permanent fluidity, we cannot be precise as to the territory that the book is in. One source of our inevitable imprecision lies in this question: where do issues of curriculum end and issues of pedagogy begin? Crudely, we might say that a curriculum is a set of educational experiences organized more or less deliberately and that pedagogy is concerned with the acts of teaching that bring off that curriculum. Here, pedagogy becomes a handmaiden to curriculum: curriculum sets out the aims and pedagogy looks to realize those aims in the most efficacious way. It is a means–end relationship: pedagogy is the means to the ends put up by the curriculum. But things aren't as simple as that nowadays.

For example, is problem-based learning a pedagogical device or would it count as part of a curriculum? To take another example, is the device of students working collaboratively in groups on particular tasks a curriculum or a pedagogical matter? That there is no simple answer to these questions is indicative of the fuzziness of the territory in which this book is situated. Problem-based learning could be considered to be *both* a matter of pedagogical interest and of curricula interest. This fuzziness is explicable: in the contemporary age, 'the student experience' and 'learning' have come to occupy the high ground of interest in public debate – such as it is – over learning and teaching. This has implications for our contemporary understanding of 'curriculum' for the term is widening in meaning to embrace pedagogical acts and to encourage such teaching styles as engage the student. So, even as we seek to wrestle with the idea of 'curriculum' in the context of higher education, the very concept of curriculum is subtly changing. This fuzziness offers both challenges and opportunities.

Significance

By 'significance' here, we mean the significance of the topic with which we are grappling. Its significance, we suggest, takes two forms. First, we contend that there can hardly be a more significant concept than 'curriculum' with which to understand higher education. Across the world, governments are enlarging their national systems of higher education so as to become 'mass' systems: 40 per cent and even 50 per cent or more of young adults are expected to experience higher education. Under these circumstances, therefore, attention to the curriculum becomes an urgent matter: it can no longer, if indeed it ever could, be a matter to which a blind eye is turned. Becoming clear about the purposes of the education all these students are to receive and translating those purposes into coherent sets of experiences is a tall order: matters of curriculum, accordingly, cannot be ducked if higher education is to be enabled to live up to its potential for educating those who experience it. In the context of higher education, curriculum simply *is* a significant matter.

But curriculum has a second kind of significance, one that we have already hinted at. It is that matters of curriculum have, in our judgement, been seriously underplayed in public debate about higher education. We shall say more about this later, but here we just flag the matter. There is – largely, if not entirely – a silence about curriculum as such. This too is a significant matter, there being an apparent reluctance or difficulty to develop a debate about one of the more important aspects, if not *the* most important aspect, of higher education. 'Hamlet without the prince' may be an apt metaphor in describing debate about higher education: the very concept that arguably should be at the very centre of that debate – namely, that of curriculum – is hardly anywhere to be seen.

If, then, we attach the idea of significance to our endeavours here, it is in the twofold sense that the topic has a significance for the well-being and effectiveness of higher education *and* that the topic has been underplayed and even neglected. As systems move to being more inclusive of students, more diverse across institutions, and more imaginative in their course offerings, and as the world in which graduates will live becomes ever more complex, this neglect can continue only at the expense of higher education and the wider society.

Against this background, it might be felt to be a worthwhile exercise simply in bringing into view the idea of curriculum in higher education. Be that as it may, we are taking the opportunity offered by this book to develop a particular view about curricula in higher education in the twenty-first century; a view that advances a sense of curricula as a space wider perhaps than is normally understood. Indeed, it is precisely part of our argument that curricula, insofar as they are thought about whether tacitly or explicitly, are normally understood in terms that are far too narrow. Part of the motivation for this book lies in a wish on our parts to widen the general understanding of the concept of curriculum to embrace a sense of the student's self and self-understanding; of the student as a person of *being and becoming*. We contend that such a vocabulary is essential if curricula in higher education are to be adequate to the tasks that they face, that of assisting individuals to develop the human wherewithal to prosper in the twenty-first century.

It follows from these initial reflections that we construe our task as necessarily not just multidisciplinary in character, but also, as it might be termed, multi-textual. We draw on our own study which sought to illuminate understandings of curricula and curricula practices in a number of subjects in a range of institutions. That evidence is brought to bear on a story which we develop that in turn draws upon sociological, philosophical and cultural perspectives.

We mention all this not because we wish to parade our credentials but rather to suggest that any serious attempt to understand the contemporary efforts of lecturers, course teams, curriculum designers and others who are grappling with curriculum matters has to be nuanced. The matter before us is complex and deserves an openminded approach. If a higher education curriculum is a set of intentions and activities intended to advance human learning to a high level such that it is adequate to the challenges facing human being and society, then we need all the ideas that may be forthcoming. This book is just one offering in that spirit.

There is, it has to be admitted, a further kind of significance at work here in this book. It is simply that this matter is of personal and professional significance for both of us. For each of us, teaching is of some personal significance: it is partly through teaching that we understand ourselves professionally. We enjoy teaching, are often awed by its responsibilities and gain much – personally and intellectually – from it. Unashamedly, therefore, what we have to say in this book often derives from our own experience as university teachers.

But our intimate involvement with teaching, with wanting it to be all that it might be, has led us to understand the challenges of teaching as possessing a scope that is not often acknowledged (though see Oakeshott 1989). In particular, we have become convinced from our own experience that the student experience will not be all that it might be unless detailed attention is given to the curriculum. In some senses, then, this is a book that has an autobiographical character and it is a book that represents our own values and beliefs *as* university teachers.

Plan

Our book has three parts. *In Part 1*, we sketch out the context that for us bears upon the design of higher education curricula. Here, we try to identify recent and current ideas of the curriculum embedded in practices and policies. We also go on to point to key features of the wider world in which graduates will have their living and their being and which, therefore, suggest the need for a reshaping of curricula.

In Part 2, by drawing on our empirical study, we develop a schema by which curricula can be understood and we offer some observations on the directions in which curriculum is moving. We suggest that conceptions of curricula in higher education have been widening from a base in knowledge to embrace action and we go on to suggest that a concern with a third dimension, that of human being as such, can also just be detected in contemporary developments.

We applaud this continual widening of curricula, but also suggest that those three dimensions have been and are being construed too narrowly, even as they imply an already widening curriculum. Knowledge has tended to be just that, knowledge without a knowing subject; and action has been confined to talk of 'skills' independently of those skills being deployed in a zone of willed action by a self-conscious human being. A curriculum for the age of instability in which we now are will, we contend, need to do some justice to all three dimensions of knowing, acting and being, although what their precise configuration might be in different subjects and even in different institutions will have to be worked through on the ground. There is room for all kinds of curriculum practices within our schema. If it is at all prescriptive, it is so only at a meta-level. The hard work of determining a proper balance between the three dimensions and of bringing them off in curricula practices lies in front of all concerned.

In Part 3, we build on our findings by examining the idea of curriculum as a form of engagement. Here, we develop our distinction between curriculum-as-designed and curriculum-in-action and we draw out our idea of curriculum as the design of spaces for the student's development in knowing, acting and being. We then go on to explore what it would mean to institute systematically our conception of curricula – as founded on knowing, acting and being – both at the very local level of teaching and learning and also across institutions.

We observe, for example, that the idea of 'learning and teaching strategies' is bound to fall short of its potential unless they become '*curriculum, learning and teaching strategies*'; but that idea presents challenges of a near intractable kind. If the world is especially complex, then the challenges of bringing off the kind of curriculum we are proposing must themselves be complex in character and must pose considerable challenges to academic professionalism. This is not to say that the challenges of curriculum in the contemporary age cannot be adequately met, but that we should become understanding of the nature of the challenges before us.

Part 1

The Possibility of Curriculum

1

Curriculum: a missing term

What's in a term?

The term 'curriculum' does not appear in the index of the report of the UK's most recent National Committee of Inquiry into Higher Education (the 'Dearing Report', NCIHE 1997). Nor is there any mention of 'curriculum' in the 2003 UK White Paper on 'The Future of Higher Education'. Does this matter? After all, the term did not appear in the index of a much earlier report, the report of the committee appointed by the UK prime minister in the early 1960s (the 'Robbins Report', 1963). It would appear that those who produce major reports on higher education, especially those having the backing of the state, are disinclined to deploy the term curriculum. A term that speaks of matters that lie right at the heart of higher education is hardly, in the UK at least, to be seen or heard in the framing of public debate on the future of higher education itself.

It could be said that the appearance or otherwise of a single term (such as curriculum) is neither here nor there. What matters is that the ideas that attach to a term such as curriculum are seen to be present in the key texts and in the debate. It is certainly the case, to anticipate some of our argument to come, that there are elements of the idea of curriculum in both Robbins and Dearing. Robbins, for example, was concerned with matters of 'breadth' and 'depth' and urged that studies broader than those associated with the UK's honours degree should find their way into undergraduate programmes of study (paras. 258–269). Dearing took up those themes (Chapter 9) but quickly passed on to questions of skills, to which it gave much more attention: what kinds of skill should courses of study promote and how should we understand their internal relationships?

It could reasonably be argued, therefore, that even though the term 'curriculum' was not in evidence in their reports, both reports were in fact interested in curriculum matters, were keen to promote particular kinds of curricula and the ingredients of the idea of curriculum are well to the fore in their analyses and prescriptions for higher education. As well as being

concerned with matters of finance, institutional structures, research, participation and other large policy matters, far from being neglected, the reports
put curriculum matters in the shop window as well. In the policy debate,
therefore, curriculum matters are very much alive.

We disagree with this analysis and we want to put a counter view. Our view
is that the absence of the term 'curriculum' from these reports is not happenstance. It represents a systematic disinclination to engage seriously with
matters concerning higher education as an educational project. The lack of
an explicit reference to curriculum as such allowed both reports to frame a
debate about curriculum matters that was narrow and reflected interests
driving those reports.

Crudely, we can say that the Robbins inquiry was representative of the
academic community, albeit a liberal and relatively enlightened wing of that
community. Accordingly, it was natural in looking substantially to increase
and widen participation in higher education that the Committee would draw
attention to the specialized nature of the honours courses currently enjoyed
then by a small proportion of the population in an elite system. Correspondingly, we can say that the Dearing inquiry was much more representative of
the state, which was in turn concerned about the contribution that higher
education could make to the UK's position in the global economy. Accordingly, it was natural that the Committee should raise issues about the skills
that higher education should be developing in order to fill that wider end
beyond higher education itself.

The higher education policy debate in the UK, therefore, has by no means
been devoid of an interest in curriculum matters, but this is not the same as
an interest in curriculum as such. Two kinds of interests are apparent in the
public debate, steered as it is by the agencies of the state. First, there has
come to be a framing of the curriculum largely as a matter of skills. Knowledge and, to a lesser extent, understanding are typically granted a place, but
for the most part the forms of development expected of students are to be
understood mainly as various forms of skills, as means to ends beyond themselves. Second, important but peripheral matters loom into view: on the one
hand, participation and access; on the other, standards and quality. Courses
are to be understood through their capacities to extend life chances *and*
through the outcomes that attach to them from state-sponsored evaluations.
Curricula are to be understood, therefore, as much through their contribution to policy agendas that lie on the margins of curricula, as through the
internal elements that actually work to produce the student's experience.

There is an avoidance, therefore, of the term curriculum and it is pervasive
in the public debate. For example, the debate as to the 'learning society' is
notable for the extent to which curriculum is a missing term. That debate has
been framed through ideas such as entitlements, rights, democracy and citizenship on the one hand (the softer versions of the learning society) and
economic regeneration, skills, professional development and systems articulation on the other (the tougher version). Vehicles for furthering the hopes
of the learning society include learning accounts, packages made available

via computer-based systems and credit accumulation. Again, other than the formation of skills, whether 'basic skills' or advanced skills, the idea of the curriculum is barely to be seen. This is, of course, an extraordinary state of affairs: that there can be a national debate about the 'learning society' in which many kinds of interests and stakeholders can be seen to have a voice and yet the idea of curriculum can gain no real foothold at all in that debate.

It might be countered that, even if public debate and governmental documents fail to refer explicitly to 'curriculum', at least educational texts produced from within the academic community can be presumed to evince a readiness to embrace the concept. Such a presumption would be over-optimistic.

First, there are hardly any modern books at least produced from within the UK that explicitly focus on the curriculum in higher education. Geoffrey Squires wrote two books on the curriculum some two decades ago (1987) while Harold Silver and John Brennan (1988) jointly produced a book in the context of the UK's then 'binary' system of higher education, but otherwise there is little to be found. It might be felt that texts on learning and teaching would pay explicit attention to the curriculum but such references are limited in the extreme. Where such books do focus on curriculum matters, they are contained within a discussion more oriented towards improving teaching, for example, Paul Ramsden's (1992) *Learning to Teach in Higher Education*, or students' learning, such as John Biggs's (2003) *Teaching for Quality Learning at University*. For substantive texts on the curriculum, we have to look either to school education, for example, Michael Young's (1998) *The Curriculum of the Future*, or to the USA such as the (1990) reader edited by James Sears and J. Dan Marshall, *Teaching and Thinking about Curriculum*. Outside the USA, with rare exceptions, substantial treatment of the curriculum in higher education is thin on the ground.

How should we understand this void? Is the pretty well total absence of curriculum as a term – either in the policy domain or in the intellectual literature – significant or not? Should we read that absence as a consensual taken-for-grantedness, a general belief that curriculum so obviously matters that it requires little direct attention? Or is this void deserving of a more systematic explanation? We contend that its absence is explicable: simply put, there is little in the way of a constituency – *at the moment* – for whom an interest in the idea of curriculum would be an attractive proposition.

Curriculum as such is hardly in anyone's interests. The state's contemporary interest in the 'knowledge economy' and 'skills' on the one hand, and the interests of both the state and the academic community in research on the other hand, point such debate as there is around curriculum matters away from 'curriculum' as such. Besides, talk of curriculum in higher education harbours for some a sense of an imposed or a national curriculum that would limit academic freedom.

To raise questions about curriculum as such would also bring into view matters of the purposes of higher education, the framing of the student experience and the kinds of human being that higher education might seek to develop in the twenty-first century. These are complex matters which, in turn, usher in issues of values, the nature of human being, the relationships of individuals and society and the challenges facing mankind in the twenty-first century. Implicitly, too, the raising of such matters would draw into view the uses – and the limitations – both of knowledge and skills (the key concepts deriving from the interests of the dominant groups in the contemporary debate). These are not matters that a public debate can easily accommodate. Their inclusion would be bound to produce messiness, dispute, value conflict and added uncertainty. Much better therefore, or so it may seem, to contain the debate and keep it within apparently manageable limits. Besides, opening the debate might run counter to the immediate though separate interests of the major stakeholders. Skills, knowledge, and even research and 'learning and teaching', might then be found to constitute an inadequate construction of curriculum matters. In turn, too, the ensuing debate might turn out to be difficult for the major stakeholders to contain.

   We may judge, therefore, that the absence of the term curriculum is not just a matter of vocabulary; not just a matter of a missing term. Its absence is indicative of systematic interests at work for which the term curriculum would pose difficulties. But in this void society itself is impoverished since large and important questions go virtually unasked, at least within the public debate, as to the future and proper character of higher education. In reinstating the term, 'curriculum', therefore, we are – in this book – hoping to assist in redrawing the boundaries of the public debate over higher education. The idea of curriculum goes to the heart of what we take higher education to be, of what it might be and should be in the twenty-first century.

Professional leanings

Of late, there has been much talk about professionalizing higher education and those who work in it. Strikingly, again, an overt concern with curriculum as yet hardly appears to be a significant factor. Key terms in that debate are 'learning' and 'teaching' from one quarter and 'standards' and 'benchmarking' from another quarter, but of 'curriculum' virtually nothing is heard. Two camps are seen, not exactly jousting with each other; rather, they are like knights who ride past each other, on either side of a divide, without ever engaging with each other. The one camp, largely from within the academic community, structures its discourse around terms such as 'learning', 'teaching', 'development' and 'enhancement'. Sometimes, these terms become almost the battle cries of developments by quasi state agencies. For example, in the UK we have seen the establishment of an Institute for Learning and Teaching in Higher Education (ILTHE) and its rapid replacement by a Higher Education Academy, the formation of a complex Learning and Teaching Support Network (LTSN) and the encouragement to institutions to develop their own *learning and teaching strategies*. The other camp, orchestrated largely from outside the academic community, structures its discourses around such terms as 'standards', 'benchmarking' and 'quality'.

Of course, these camps find themselves in each other's territory from time to time, and some individuals have a foot in both camps. Inevitably, the initiatives of some state agencies reveal a degree of hybridity. We see, for example, the Teaching Quality Enhancement Fund, a phrase in which the term 'quality' is technically redundant (since it is difficult to see how teaching could be enhanced without its quality also being improved). The inclusion of the term quality, however, resonates with the more managerial discourse of explicit standards; in other words, management for accountability *and* enhancement in the one phrase. The new Higher Education Academy (in replacing the ILTHE) may also be judged to be the outcome of a confluence between accountability and developmental influencies. On the one hand, we see the hand of the state at work, in driving forward the establishment of the Academy; on the other hand, we see, within the new Academy, indications of collaborative working across the academic community. The Higher Education Academy, accordingly, is a kind of *hybrid agency*.

Linkages between different camps in this field can also be seen in the vocabulary in use. The term 'skills', for instance, acts as a kind of linguistic bridge between the camps: on the one hand, *some* academics are happy with the idea of developing their teaching skills and the term 'skills', therefore, can sit more or less within a discourse of professional development. On the other hand, 'skills' offers for external parties a means of calibrating the progress, as it were, that the academics are making in improving their effectiveness and efficiency as teachers in higher education. Here, the term 'skills' can do duty within a discourse of professionalism understood as a willingness to subscribe to and be measured by explicit standards that stand outside of the tacit values of academic life.

Astonishingly as, on reflection, it may seem, this debate and these developments, oriented as they are in the direction of improving the student experience, systematically fail to raise, let alone engage with, the idea of curriculum. Despite the national seminars, the books, the new journals, the funded initiatives, the appointment of pro-vice-chancellors (for 'learning and teaching' or for 'academic development'), the new interest in the 'scholarship of teaching' and the establishment in universities of 'educational development centres' or centres for 'learning and teaching' or 'academic practice', the idea of curriculum pretty well goes entirely unremarked. New discourses emerge supposedly concerned with the professionalism of lecturers beyond their research function and yet the idea of curriculum is hardly ever pursued. We may conclude that our earlier surmise that none of the parties have an interest in getting the idea of curriculum onto any of the agendas is here confirmed.

Missing tricks

In the process, tricks are being systematically missed. For example, the 'benchmarking' statements produced under the aegis of the UK's Quality Assurance Agency (QAA) could have addressed the matter head-on. Those statements are intended to:

> *provide a means for the academic community to describe the nature and character-istics of programmes in a specified subject. They also . . . articulate the attributes and capabilities that those possessing such qualifications should be able to demonstrate.*

(QAA 2000)

It is true that many if not most of the groups did in fact voice their views on curriculum matters, but it was done in a sideways manner, as an unrequired fallout of a task oriented towards 'learning outcomes'. Almost all of the benchmarking statements, for example, structure the programme specifica-tion for their subject around skills, which are listed in a concluding table (knowledge and understanding skills; generic intellectual skills; personal transferable skills).

Almost inevitably, the groups often found themselves reflecting on the general purpose of a degree course in subject X or subject Y as they saw it, but they came at those considerations *ab initio*. No attempt was made by the QAA to develop, with the assistance of say a group of cross-subject academics, even the beginnings of a vocabulary, let alone some principles in which curriculum matters *in general* could be raised with any profundity or seriousness. In one sense, this reluctance was understandable: 'It was not the intention of the QAA to identify something like a national curriculum in terms of the content of a degree in a given subject. This remains a matter of academic freedom' (Politics and International Relations Benchmarking Statement 2000: 1). But the result is that an opportunity to open up a debate about curriculum in higher education has been missed and emerging assumptions about programmes of study are going largely unexamined.

We may judge, therefore, that the professionalization of the academic community is tipping into a skills, standards and outcomes model of curriculum rather than a reflexive, collective, developmental and process-oriented model. It is a model overly concerned with the skills levels of stu-dents and with the effectiveness of programmes in driving up those skills. In turn, the tacit dominant conception of teaching coming through the debates is that of teaching being itself understood simply as a set of skills, perhaps even wide ranging, perhaps even to include course design alongside student support. Such skills can of course be developed discretely and therefore be a matter of 'staff development', but the key point is that this is a means–end view of professionalism. The ends are known; all that is problematic are the means, and these are to be construed as sets of skills.

The point deserves just a little emphasis. Professionalism can be under-stood as a collective determination on the part of a social group to maintain its own reflexivity, in part by keeping under review its own ends. What is the profession in business for? What, in general terms, is it trying to do? What, in a broad-brush sense, are the values that it seeks to uphold? It is this self-governing conception of professionalism that is in danger of being implicitly repudiated in what is becoming a lurch to a more performative sense of professionalism in academe. In the current view of professionalism in teaching, aims are reduced to outcomes, processes are reduced to skills, and systematic reflection and even critique are reduced to knowledge or what is already known.

Under these conditions – of a turn towards a performative professionalism – it is hardly surprising that again the idea of curriculum is not on the agenda. For to bring into view the idea of curriculum would be precisely to raise questions over ends and over the main constituents of a student's learning experience and their relative weightings and relationship. Is the dominant element in a curriculum to be skills? If so, are they to be specific or generic? If generic, which generic skills are to be developed? Is there anything more to a curriculum than skills? Presumably, knowledge; but then, what place does understanding have? Is that the full description of a curriculum? What of personal qualities and dispositions? What of the social character of a curriculum?

Even just to put down these bald and brief questions is to reveal the complexity of the terrain that would open up if the notion of curriculum were seriously to take hold. The questions too would generate further questions: are there, in fact, *any* generic skills? Are not all skills relative to context? Higher education is supposed to be a site of critical thought, but is critical thought a task or an achievement? Is it a relationship between an individual and a text or a relationship between an individual and a community? There was, once upon a time, a nice conundrum facing those in higher education who were interested in pedagogical issues: does a lecturer teach her subject or her students? The question captures a nice tension in higher education between dominant interests respectively in students as persons and in students as recipients of a tradition.

The point of reminding ourselves about questions of this order is to indicate their absence from the contemporary debate as to professionalism in teaching *and* to point up that the professionalism on offer is a truncated form of professionalism. As stated, this is a performative professionalism, in which the ends are not so much taken for granted as barely being allowed to come into view at all. In the process, we witness a sliding away from the possibility of a professionalism that is willing to raise complex and awkward questions about its own purposes to a professionalism that is willing simply to demonstrate its capacity to fulfil efficiently and effectively a set of roles already cast for it. We are not there yet, but that is a prospect and one that this book seeks to combat.

Curriculum strategies

In the UK, as we have just noticed, the funding councils have been asking every institution of higher education to develop its own 'learning and teaching strategy'. This initiative, we may note, is itself just a part of a larger initiative, the *Teaching Quality Enhancement Fund*, through which is being put in place a number of strategies at individual, institutional and subject levels. In addition to institutional learning and teaching strategies, the England and Wales Funding Council has orchestrated the setting up of both an interlinked national set of subject centres, aimed at encouraging and supporting learning and teaching initiatives within subjects, and a scheme for recognizing teaching excellence of individuals, a *National Teaching Fellowship Scheme*. There is also a *Fund for the Development of Teaching and Learning*, which has been coordinated from a centre with a base in one of the universities. This is a powerful and unusual tranche of initiatives at national level: few countries have witnessed such a broad and systematic programme.

Despite the range of this programme, and despite the number of initiatives embedded within it, strikingly again the idea of curriculum is notable for its absence. The dominant sense is that learning and teaching are almost independent of curricula. It is true that one of the initiatives in this programme hinges precisely around subjects, namely the *Learning and Teaching Support Network (LTSN)*. In that Network, some 24 subject centres are coordinated by a Generic Centre and so projects are emerging both at subject level and at the national level. The discourse of the LTSN is one in which curriculum as such is muted. There is much talk of the sharing of 'good practice', of innovation in learning and teaching and the development of skills. Just occasionally, we see in the literature emanating from the subject centres mention of 'curriculum design and management', but it is presented as a technical matter as if again the ends of curricula and its general components were largely known and agreed, and all that was in question were the fashioning of innovative teaching approaches to reach those ends. (An important qualification to this observation lies in a project on *The Imaginative Curriculum* conducted by the LTSN Generic Centre. (See the Appendix for some other examples of initiatives related to curriculum development.)

A corresponding absence in relation to the idea of curriculum is apparent in the National Teaching Fellowship Scheme, which seeks to reward demonstrative performance in teaching evidenced especially through manifestly efficient and effective student learning. Within the description of the Scheme there is set out the 'characteristics of excellent teaching' that 'an excellent teacher' might demonstrate. Within an eight-point list, while there is mention of 'innovation in the design and delivery of learning activities' and 'the ability to organize course materials and present them effectively and imaginatively', there is no mention of the excellent teacher being imaginative in the design of curricula. But learning activities and course materials gain their point precisely in the context of curricula intentions, which in turn require reflection as to the purposes of a course of study. Again therefore, we see an orientation towards the more performative aspects of teaching and an avoidance of the more reflective moments.

We wish, however, in supporting our claim as to the absence of 'curriculum' in contemporary debate in the UK, to focus our attention on the Funding Council's initiative aimed at securing learning and teaching strategies from institutions. At least there we see explicit reference to the idea of curriculum.

In its invitation of July 1999 (HEFCE 1999a), the Funding Council set out its expectations of institutions that they should form their own learning and teaching strategies. It backed up that invitation both with funding and guidance, much of which has emerged out of commissioned studies of the ways in which institutions have sought to develop their strategies and of contents. The 'invitation' statement was the first time in which the Funding Council had formally placed the term – *'learning and teaching strategy'* – in the public domain and, reasonably enough, that statement contains both a 'definition of a learning and teaching strategy' and pointers on the 'content and structure of the strategy'. There is no mention of 'curriculum' in the definition that is offered of a learning and teaching strategy:

> 39 *An effective learning and teaching strategy will outline what an institution wishes to achieve with regard to learning and teaching, how it will do so, and how it will know when it has succeeded.*

None of the ensuing four paragraphs under that definition mention 'curriculum'. However, the term 'curriculum' does appear in the paragraphs on the 'content and structure of the strategy', appearing under 'national priorities' that 'institutions may wish to address':

> 46c *Promoting innovation in the curricula, particularly activity to increase the employability of graduates . . . including work experience and developing key skills.*

Curriculum, therefore, turns out to be a vehicle for realizing taken-for-granted ends (such as employability): the matter of the curriculum is not seen as posing questions as to the ends of higher education.

The term 'curriculum' also appears in an annex (Annex D), which reports on the components being found at that time in emerging institutional learning and teaching strategies:

> 10h **Curriculum**: *changes it is envisaged that the institution will need to make in its pattern of course provision.*

There is a double strangeness here. The idea of 'need' is itself strange: under what circumstances will an institution 'need' to make changes to the pattern of its course provision? Could it be because it considers that it is being required to move its curricula more in the direction of 'employability', 'work experience' and 'key skills'? Therefore, is this 'need' one expressive of a situation of some compulsion, with constraints being placed upon institutions, or is it a matter of a need felt by institutions? The second strangeness arises out of the reference to the 'pattern of course provision' in institutions. If by 'pattern of course provision' is meant simply pattern of the subjects in which courses are placed or the levels of the awards to which they lead, then we are hardly in the presence of curriculum matters as such. Perhaps it meant some kind of general institutional policy that courses might embed more overtly 'key skills' or might be based on, say, problem solving or might be more evidently linked to the world of business and commerce. Perhaps it is one of these or none of these; the matter here is not clear.

The meaning of the phrase 'pattern of course provision' becomes more evident in the accompanying *Guide to Good Practice* (HEFCE 1999b), a commentary on the emerging approaches being taken by institutions in developing their learning and teaching strategies. In its single paragraph on curriculum (para. 50), it is noted that such strategies 'often specify the changes it is envisaged that institutions will need to make in their pattern of course provision': we see here precisely the same wording as in the principal document. Perhaps recognizing that the phrase is not entirely clear, the authors go on to note that 'some institutions state only what new courses they intend to develop and offer. That is a curriculum strategy; not a learning and teaching strategy.' We agree that the mention of new courses does not amount to a learning and teaching strategy, but neither surely does it amount to a curriculum strategy.

The authors go on in more positive vein to offer some examples of 'curricular implications of a learning and teaching strategy'. These include:

- 'developing learning skills to support the development of an "independent learning strategy" '
- 'requiring all course descriptions to specify key skills among learning outcomes and introducing more work-based provision, to support an "employability strategy" '.

That there might be such implications of a learning and teaching strategy is hardly to be doubted but as the only two implications *and* in their both identifying curriculum with skills, they surely amount to a thin conception of 'curriculum'.

In these documents, then, we are being pointed on the one hand to learning skills and a learning approach on the part of the student and on the other hand to an employability strategy looking to the inculcation of key skills. There is nothing here, for example, about the forms of knowledge and understanding that might be sought for in a knowledge society and nor is there any indication of the kinds of personal qualities and attributes in a changing world that a learning and teaching strategy might encompass. This is a conception of curriculum that is focused on outcomes and on skills. It is a nice instance of our earlier claim that policy-driven conceptions of curriculum understand curricula in terms of their capacity to deliver skills for the economy. There is nothing wrong in this *per se*, but in itself it betokens a techno-economic conception of curricula, as means to particular ends outside of themselves.

In a more recent HEFCE Guide to Good Practice (2001), 'curriculum' as such is barely if at all mentioned. What we do see, however, are a number of case studies of good practice in support of learning and teaching strategies, some of which are clearly concerned with curriculum matters and fall within the dominant concerns of skills development and employability. For example, one case study focuses on 'Enhancing student employability' while another is that of 'Focusing a strategy around student skills'.

Two case studies are of *prima facie* interest in that – from their titles – they point to work that extends beyond a skills and outcomes conception of curriculum. The first is entitled 'Implementing a strategy concerned with graduate attributes' and takes as its starting point 'the specification of the attributes of a "Leicester graduate" '. One of these attributes is that of 'team working skills' and the reader is then provided with the University's guidelines as to what it would mean for the development of such skills to be part of any degree programme. That description, which runs to one and a half pages of A4 text, focuses on the 'minimum outcomes' set out in five team working skills, the 'learning opportunities' to achieve those outcomes and the management processes that might assure their achievement. The second case study of *prima facie* significance here is entitled 'Developing student-centred learning and lifelong learning'. The strategy that the University in question has adopted includes targets concerned with project work (to be included in all undergraduate programmes), programme specifications defining skills and knowledge, and the embedding and articulation of key skills, work-based learning and the enhancement of student learning through communications and information technology. *In other words, in the rare moments where we might sense an orientation towards large educational ends, where ideas such as facing complexity and criticality in a world of uncertainty might have had an airing, we find ourselves confined again to a skills/outcomes conception of curriculum.*

In all of this work – the national policy statement on learning and teaching strategies, the supporting guides to good practice and the examples presented in those guides of relevant curriculum developments in institutions – a number of features are evident. First, curriculum is given some but very little attention as a relevant topic in its own right. Second, curriculum appears quite extensively in tacit form. Third, in that tacit form, we see that the concept of curriculum developing is a performative concept, hinged significantly around learning outcomes, and these understood in terms of students' skills, especially those oriented towards employability.

Our point in making these observations is not to imply that such elements should not find their way into a curriculum. It is rather that the curriculum implications of a 'learning and teaching strategy' are being framed in an unduly narrow way, particularly since embedded in this initiative is an unduly narrow understanding of curriculum itself.

Curriculum by stealth

Our argument in this chapter has been fourfold:

- There is no substantial debate about curriculum in the context of higher education as such (at least in the UK).
- There is, nevertheless, a discourse developing and, indeed, a considerable effort in driving through curriculum change, both nationally and institutionally.
- Especially in the absence of a serious debate about curriculum *per se*, the tacit idea of curriculum that is developing is unduly narrow. It is also dominated by a determination to see curricula framed in terms of economically productive skills.
- Students as such are only minimally implicated in this dominant conception of curricula. They come into play only as potential bearers of skills producing economic value rather than as human beings in their own right.

In short, we are witnessing the march of a certain view of curriculum by stealth. This situation is not quite the worst of all worlds but it is a situation with disturbing features.

First, the concept of curriculum that is emerging is, as stated, unduly narrow. Focusing, as we have seen, on skills and knowledge, the emerging concept of curricula neglects more intractable dimensions of human development such as human qualities and dispositions. As a result, higher education is itself facing the prospect of being transformed in ways that run counter to key ideas – such as criticality and personal autonomy – that are strongly identified with the long-standing sense of a university education. We are being pointed towards a sense of curricula that is reductive in character: students are being reduced to the status of bearers of value beyond themselves.

Second, being left largely unexamined, the tacit conception of curriculum that is emerging reflects the interests of the dominant players, the academic community on the one hand and the state and employers in the labour market on the other. Other voices, including the voices of students, are less evident.

Third, academic life, which prides itself on its reflectiveness and powers of self-critical thought, is failing to subject these developments to any searching critique. There is no sense that the transformations taking place are either advancing or possibly even undermining the traditional value background of the university.

Fourth, there being little in the way of a collective debate and inquiry into the curriculum as such, the discourse in this domain of academic life is thin. Curriculum is ultimately about choices in the higher forms of human development: all bets should be on, and a rich vocabulary, with lots of ideas, terms and concepts, *should* be developing.

Last, the current discourse may even be undermining its own tacit intentions. Those tacit intentions, we may judge, are to do with driving up the value of higher education to the economy on the one hand and to derive greater cost effectiveness on the other. But the modern world may be such as to require human qualities and dispositions that are not easily caught in a language of skills and outcomes. Admittedly, human qualities and dispositions are intractable and not necessarily amenable to straightforward assessment. Yet there may be qualities that are both especially beneficial in a changing and complex world and that higher education can be adept at developing and, with the appropriate attention and effort, could be more adept still.

In short, the turn that the current 'debate' over curriculum has taken may be judged to be self-defeating. Not only is it likely to lead to efforts that fall short of what is required even for capability in the disciplines, but it is also likely to lead to curriculum approaches that run counter to the understandings and practices that are necessary if higher education is to be in any way adequate to the contemporary world.

Conclusion

'Curriculum' is, or should be, one of the major terms in the language of higher education. Through curricula, ideas of higher education are put into action. Through curricula, too, values, beliefs and principles in relation to learning, understanding, knowledge, disciplines, individuality and society are realized. Yet these profoundly important matters are hardly ever raised. It is as if there is a tacit agreement that these are not matters for polite company. Curricula are practised and even, on occasions, discussed at least at a local level, but a proper public debate about curriculum never gets off the ground.

Curricula are changing; that is not in doubt. But at a local level, when a new course is being designed, there is – as we shall see – evidence to suggest that discussion is limited both to academic matters (which topics are to be included and what approach is to be taken?) and to technical matters, such as credit weightings, assessment approaches, the integration of any work-based learning elements and, more occasionally, pedagogical matters (for instance, as to whether a curriculum might be shaped more around problem-based learning). The larger and first-order matters that such questions should raise are hardly ever voiced. Questions as to the relative pedagogic responsibilities of teacher and taught, what it is to be 'critical', the balance between work and wider life aims, and even the relationship between staff's research and scholarship on the one hand and their presence in the curriculum on the other hand: there is much less evidence that matters such as these gain a hearing.

As we have seen, the paucity of a serious debate about curriculum has not led to a void so far as curriculum reform and development are concerned. What has happened is that we have curriculum change being effected – in the UK, at least – by stealth. In the economicizing of the curriculum, it may be that we are in the midst of one of the most profound changes being wrought in higher education, and yet these changes are taking place without public debate and considered collective reflection by the academic community.

The idea of curriculum raises questions at different levels. It is the higher order questions that are being overlooked. Perhaps the key question raised by the idea of curriculum is: what is higher education for? Or, more precisely: in which directions should a student's experience be pointed? Or, more precisely still: what kinds of human development are being promoted through a curriculum, what are the elements in the curriculum that are assisting that development and what are their relative weightings? Answers to these questions, *of some kind*, are always to be found in all curricula. Those answers, however, tend to be hidden in their underlying presuppositions. It is, therefore, to an understanding of the presuppositions inherent in different kinds of curricula that we next turn.

2

Understanding the curriculum

Introduction

The avoidance of issues to do with curricula in public debate, policies and practices leaves us on unsettled ground. We have argued that, in the absence of explicit understandings of the curriculum, we are in danger of being steered towards inadequate or overly narrow conceptualizations of curricula that do not do justice to the complexities of the world that students and teachers face. Yet we need to go further in this analysis if we are to arrive at a better understanding of how the curriculum as such has been shaped by, and is an integral part of, the higher education system.

Are there, then, other conceptions of curricula to which we could turn? What do we already know about the higher education curriculum? In comparison with research and theories at the compulsory level, or school curriculum, particularly in the UK, the higher education curriculum remains largely unknown. The UK school curriculum has long been the subject of research in the area of curriculum studies (for example, Lawton 1975; Stenhouse 1975; Kelly 2004). A prescribed national curriculum has also resulted in a standardized and public curriculum that is easily accessible for empirical investigations. Understanding the higher education curriculum, in contrast, is somewhat more difficult.

However, various conceptualizations of curricula have been part of the educational landscape for some time, but tacitly so. These tacit notions of curricula have emerged from different voices within higher education and as such exhibit varying concerns. Therefore, whatever conceptualizations of curricula we can tacitly identify will not necessarily form a coherent picture. Sometimes, these notions of the curriculum overlap and at other times some conceptions of curricula are more dominant than others.

This chapter will offer a broad overview of some of the key concerns that have emerged about higher education. While our focus is the UK, we believe these debates are resonant in other contexts. We shall also look to important contributions made by educational theorists that implicitly reveal certain conceptualizations of university curricula. The tacit notions of curricula that we identify below are not intended to provide an exhaustive overview of various approaches to understanding the higher education curriculum. Some of them may also seem to be only tangentially related to curricula as such (although this reflects our contention that curriculum matters are largely absent from the literature). What they do reveal is that issues of curricula are intertwined with the social and historical contexts of universities and the wider world in which they are situated. In other words, the curriculum is shaped within certain social contexts. We start with a few examples of key debates from the recent history of higher education that can inform us about ideas of curricula within it.

Curriculum as outcome

It is prudent to start here by further expanding on developments we discussed in the previous chapter: the implementation of the Quality Assurance Agency's (QAA) subject benchmarks and programme specifications. These are arguably the closest we have come to an explicit formulation of the purposes of curricula in the UK. What the QAA (as the agency contracted by the government to assure quality of teaching in higher education institutions) has presented are statements of the 'general academic characteristics and standards of honours degrees' in 46 subject areas. Each statement sets out the aims of degree programmes, or the general competences that graduates in each subject area should attain. The programme specifications require all course designers to indicate how their curriculum can be referenced and measured against these benchmarks. Although the word 'curriculum' actually appears rather infrequently in the statements and specifications, they are the first attempt to identify standards across the curriculum, and as such represent the highest level of (indirect) central guidance for curriculum designers in the history of UK higher education.

Subject benchmarks are, then, an explicit formulation of the intended outcomes of courses with appropriate reference points enabling comparisons to be made across courses. The impact of the implementation of benchmarks and specifications for curriculum design has not been fully evaluated, but has arguably required a reorientation of curricula towards the outcomes of each course. Standards, after all, can only be upheld if the end result represents the required outcome. Benchmarks, therefore, require an outcomes-based approach to the learning process, which presumes that learning outcomes can be made explicit in such a manner that enables their achievement to be measured (Jackson 2002). They are indicative of what we are identifying here as a curriculum-as-outcome approach.

There are a number of issues arising from benchmarks and specifications in terms of what these new requirements reveal about contemporary notions of the curriculum and of higher education itself. First, the benchmarks and specifications can be seen as a response not only to a diverse and mass higher education system, but also to globalization. The higher education system has expanded, the diversity within the system has led to new and complex forms of stratification, and universities are operating within a global context requiring new forms of engagement with the wider world. The UK government has become a key stakeholder in safeguarding the standards of its higher education system worldwide, with a twin agenda to account for public funds and to uphold the reputation of UK degrees. These drivers are similar in other higher education systems across the world (Room 2000), although the UK was arguably the first to develop a robust national infrastructure for the identification of standards.

On the one hand, it is suggested by the QAA that the benchmarking statements are to be merely guides or starting-off points for course planners. On the other hand, we can see signs within these requirements for specified end points of a tightening or closing down of possibilities for curricular development. Furthermore, the state's concerns with skills and the knowledge economy, as noted in the previous chapter, loom large within the benchmarking statements, seeking as they do to identify the value of degrees through the skills they impart. Benchmarking seems to require forms of accountability and specificities in a complex world in which the labour market has become a key indicator of success. They are an attempt to impose an external agenda and order on an expanding curricula that had become difficult to measure in terms of its value.

An outcomes-based approach towards a more transparent curriculum, as we see in the QAA model, has been a recent development for some subject areas. Many of the professional subject areas, on the other hand, are more accustomed to developing curricula in relation to external requirements. Engineering programmes, for example, have been required for some years to evaluate their outputs in response to the standards set by other external agencies, such as the UK Engineering Council, the UK Engineering Professors' Conference, and the US Accreditation Board for Engineering and Technology. These increasing requirements for transparency are undoubtedly placing extra administrative burdens on curriculum designers, as course standards may need to be held accountable to up to four separate external agencies (Houghton 2002).

There is a certain irony here, then. While the approach of an outcomes-based model of curricula has been one of simplifying and making transparent the curricula of a diverse and mass higher education system, an unintended consequence has been the introduction of greater administrative complexities. Course leaders must adapt to this language of outputs and standards, must learn to work with the requirements of identifying learning outcomes and specifying course objectives, and in the process must produce seemingly endless new reams of documentation about their courses. The resulting 'programme specifications' may satisfy the administrators, but are they enhancing the students' learning experiences? We do not have the answer to that question yet, but it seems fair to say that the increasing amounts of administrative demands on academics and support staff have made their working lives much more complicated.

There is one other point relevant to our discussion here about the move towards a model of curriculum as outcome that we have identified in this section. The QAA subject benchmarks, as the name suggests, have been developed within specific subject areas, as have the requirements of other external agencies. To a large extent this is understandable, given that the higher education curriculum has traditionally been bounded by divisions between the different subject areas. However, the implications of these sub-ject-based demands on the potential for new developments in interdisciplin-ary areas are not yet known. We could see this development as a further closing down of possibilities for new forms of curricula, or for raising cross-subject curriculum issues. At the very least, the subject benchmarks could discourage the efforts of course planners to develop interdisciplinary courses that span different subject areas.

The curriculum-as-outcome approach is therefore maintaining the sub-ject-based character of much of UK higher education. The requirements of the QAA and other external agencies that standards be identified and assured *within* subject areas enables the boundaries around the subjects to be maintained. Whether or not this fairly rigid, subject-based approach to curriculum development is appropriate has barely been questioned in the UK higher education system, with its long history of single-subject degree programmes.

Curriculum as special

Subject benchmarks are more of a guide or starting point for curriculum designers than they are detailed prescriptions of curriculum content. Given the complexity of the higher education curriculum, a central agency can only perhaps be expected to steer lightly. Yet there may be other reasons for this indirect approach to central curricular control. If we re-examine two of the UK's most highly visible pronouncements on higher education in the twentieth century, it becomes apparent that there have been historical pre-cedents to the QAA's attitude towards the curriculum. As we noted in the previous chapter, both the Robbins Report (1963) and the Dearing Report (NICHE 1997) reveal certain attitudes towards higher education, and both preferred to maintain a distance from those educators who develop curricula. The issues raised in these reports deserve further examination.

The Robbins Report (1963) mainly commented about the curriculum through a concern with tensions between breadth and depth of knowledge. This small section of the report reveals a reluctance to interfere in the activ-ities of the academics, who were then the guardians of knowledge. The hands-off approach is evident: 'We know of no argument that would justify the imposition of external control from the centre' (1963: 231). In other words, when it came to the details of curricular development, academics knew best. Robbins (1963) recommended that external representations from those on the outside should be carefully considered by universities, but in the end the choice was to be made by the disciplinary specialists on the inside. Indeed, the reverence with which academic knowledge was held by Robbins is apparent in this description of university educators: 'It is good that they [universities] should be free to make their own experiments and to develop the subjects most congenial to their leading spirits' (1963: 233).

Presumably Robbins held academics in such high regard that he trusted the 'leading spirits' to experiment without error. It would seem that academic freedom, at least so far as the content of curricula was concerned, had been earned and should be preserved. These sentiments set a precedent, in that they constructed boundaries around the world of academic knowledge and left it to the experts to decide its form and function. The freedom of the academic experts was such that some of the 'new' universities established in the 1960s were reknowned for their innovative curriculum design. The University of Sussex, in particular, was founded with the plan to create a 'new map of learning' (Briggs 1964), with the emphasis on interdisciplinary approaches to undergraduate study. The 'leading spirits' were free to experiment.

When Dearing (NCIHE 1997) reported some decades later, a similar regard for academic freedom in curricular matters was evident. Again, a reluctance to engage directly and to intervene with issues of curricula was demonstrated. The Dearing Report picked up on Robbins's concern with breadth and depth, and encouraged all institutions to review their programmes for ensuring a better balance between the two. This time, however, there was a recognition that breadth could be a positive attribute of a degree programme. Yet breadth was only desirable insofar as it enabled specialists to 'understand their specialism within context' (1997: 132). Disciplinary specialization was still considered to be a goal of a university education. A common thread between Robbins and Dearing is this commitment to guarding the core of academic knowledge, and perhaps a presumption in favour of its 'specialness' that allows only indirect guidance from the centre. The knowledge fields, or disciplines, are accorded much authority within the curriculum.

We would not wish to suggest that there needs to be more direct control over curriculum content, nor that the power of the knowledge fields has been damaging to higher education. What we do wish to encourage is a questioning of this situation: how the state's indirect guidance of the curriculum tacitly reveals certain presumptions and values, and how the knowledge fields or subject areas within curricula become shaped in turn by these concerns. To better understand these forces at work, we can look to insights from theories within the sociology of education that have attempted to understand academic knowledge.

Curriculum as culture

For many educators, the academic disciplines are at the core of all academic activity and the main role of curricula is to transmit the knowledge that students are to master. The disciplines have been a subject of study in their own right and have been written about, debated and pondered over throughout the modern history of education. The study of disciplines has been a study of different academic cultures.

The term 'culture' can be ambiguous. Here we are not referring to those aspects of the curriculum that shape the culture of a society, although this notion of culture has been pertinent to discussions about the role of higher education (Readings 1996). Indeed, universities have been viewed as repositories of culture – albeit an elite form of culture – in terms of their role in transmitting the knowledge and ideas deemed to have value in society. Rather than trying to delineate here the notion of a common core culture that universities help define, protect and transmit, we are instead turning to the idea that curricula are formed by many different cultures that exist within universities. These cultures are distinctly shaped by disciplinary values, norms and rules of communication.

In a well-known study (Becher 1989; Becher and Trowler 2001), the knowledge fields have been conceptualized as disciplinary territories, the boundaries of which are marked out within the university curriculum by the various tribes within them. It is the tribal members who identify the boundaries and distinctions between the various territories, and form collective identities through the cultures of the disciplines. On this analysis, two dimensions of academic tribalism stand out in particular: whether disciplines are 'hard' or 'soft' and whether they are 'pure' or 'applied'. Putting these two dimensions across each other forms a grid which, as it were, structures the territory of academic life. The curriculum might then be seen as a kind of map of a territory situated within that grid space, and the knowledge fields as the academic cultures and subcultures to which members belong.

For many who write about higher education, the idea of academic tribes and territories has been appealing. Yet sociological studies of academic knowledge often point to the challenges of empirically studying these cultures. For example, Bourdieu (1984), in his groundbreaking study *Homo Academicus*, suggested that academics will resist attempts to turn their enquiring gaze back onto themselves. Undoubtedly there has been some reluctance of academics to examine their own practices critically. Yet there may be other reasons behind this reluctance that are related to the special character of the disciplines themselves.

As the study of academic cultures has pointed out, it is those within the academic disciplines who establish and maintain the boundaries around disciplines. Only through their deep immersion in disciplinary communities can they identify who the contributing members are and where the boundaries lie between and around the relevant specializations. Disciplines, in this sense, require not just cultural membership, but *enculturation* or *initiation* into their communities (Peters 1964; Oakeshott 1989). A curriculum-as-culture approach, as we are describing it here, is shaped by these disciplinary communities in ways that are difficult for outsiders fully to understand.

Here we are emphasizing the character of *disciplines* over *subject areas*. At first glance, the connotations of the two terms – 'discipline' and 'subject' – may be felt to be broadly similar and point to similar approaches to curricular design. However, as Parker (2002) has pointed out, a discipline requires *immersion*; it is to be engaged with and mastered. It has a kind of hardness to it, requiring 'discipline' for its mastery. On the other hand, a subject is more inclusive towards those who choose to study it, more easily commodified into curricular packages, with a knowledge base that is more readily identifiable and defined through taught units and assessed outcomes. A 'subject' sits in a pedagogic and curriculum space. It is interactional and shaped by human hopes and intentions. Looked at in this way, we can distinguish between *disciplines* that require a long-term socialization into tacit values developed through immersion in academic communities, and *subjects* that can provide intended developmental outcomes, which themselves are increasingly determined by *external* agendas such as employability.

We have, in the UK at least, moved towards the latter framework of a subject-based approach to curricular development, apparent in such developments as the subject benchmarks and quality assurance mechanisms based on the subject areas. Are we then witnessing a shift away from curricula based on disciplinary specialization and towards curricula organized around the acquisition of competencies within subject areas? If so, it is worth considering how the processes of disciplinary specialization and the reproduction of disciplinary communities have been seen to operate. These processes have been described as being about the reproduction of boundaries; between the disciplines themselves and, in turn, between social divisions more generally.

Curriculum as reproduction

The term 'hidden curriculum' is a key aspect of the *curriculum as reproduction*. It has often been used to describe the non-explicit rules of the game that students must negotiate when they encounter curricula. In this sense, there is a 'public face' of curriculum set out in course handbooks, textbooks and lecture notes. This is the curriculum that is presented and given to the student, but there is another and hidden curriculum that students must learn if they are to achieve success: a kind of rulebook in which the rules are written between the lines (Snyder 1973).

The term 'hidden curriculum' has become a shorthand for expressing a belief that the system seems to benefit some students more than others. It suggests that something else is going on beyond what can be seen on the surface in classrooms and textbooks. It is not just that some students are better able to decipher the rules of the hidden curriculum and thus achieve success, but that this hidden curriculum acts as a deliberate form of gate-keeping by ensuring that only certain types of students will be able to use it to their advantage. This reflection suggests that curricula serve to reproduce divisions in society. As such, we could see here a sense of *curriculum as social reproduction*.

This notion of curriculum as social reproduction has been used to try to explain why, for example, working-class students end up in working-class jobs. Although this became a contentious political debate in the UK as well as the USA (mainly through the 1970s work of Bowles and Gintis), it prompted some sociologists to attempt to untangle the inner workings of curricula in order to see how this process of reproduction was occurring. Basil Bernstein was one of the most influential theorists and he generated virtually a new language for analysing the interactions that take place between students and teachers.

Bernstein (1971, 1990) produced a theory for analysing all pedagogical encounters, be they in schools, universities, or in doctors' surgeries. Anywhere that people interact in a way that is instructional is open to a Bernsteinian analysis. So, although his theories seem to provide a detailed means of examining curricula, this was only part of the story. What can we take from Bernstein to help us in producing a framework for understanding and analysing the higher education curriculum?

Bernstein proposed that all educational interactions (or pedagogical relationships) are bounded by certain rules. These rules govern what is taught, how it is taught, and how it is assessed. Every pedagogical encounter varies in the strength of its *classification* and *framing*, in which 'classification' refers broadly to the strength of boundaries within and across curricula, and 'framing' refers to the strength of the boundaries within pedagogical relationships. Strongly classified subject areas are often found in the hard sciences, for example, where the knowledge content of the curriculum has firm boundaries and is segregated in a hierarchical structure. Weakly classified subjects may be characterized by interdisciplinary approaches to curricula and/or through porous boundaries between subject areas. On the other hand, strongly framed classroom interactions include the traditional lecture format, with students listening and taking notes. In contrast, other types of courses can be weakly framed, as students take on different and more ambiguous roles in the classroom.

The language of classification and framing has provided a means by which to examine, in detail, the educational processes and transactions in the classroom or lecture theatre. The curriculum, though, is only part of the message that is relayed to students when they enter higher education. Bourdieu's (1990) concept of *habitus* recognizes this as well, and has been used to explore how the higher education culture is more accessible to some people than others. Bourdieu suggests that students need to acquire a form of cultural capital in order to succeed in higher education. The university *habitus* is a place and a form of being, but it is largely hidden from view, with rules and forms of communication that become implicitly understood and socially internalized by those with the necessary capital. This is a tacit notion of curriculum as reproduction: social divisions, mainly in terms of the social classes, are maintained and reproduced in higher education through the gatekeeping functions of the hidden curriculum.

Although these notions offer an insightful means by which to analyse educational processes, they are not exactly theories of the curriculum *per se*. They do, however, open up an insight into curricula that suggests all may not be what it seems on the surface, and it is necessary to ask probing questions about the content of curricula and the ways in which it is delivered. There is an underlying message in relation to these concepts of education processes, in that the hidden rules and boundaries of curricula are a pervasive and powerful feature of higher education. Exposing these tacit rules can reveal the power of the knowledge fields and the sometimes exclusionary processes of educational transactions.

Curriculum as transformation

Political debates over the role of higher education have generated theories about its potential to empower and transform the lives of students. The literature concerned with empowerment begins from a similar starting point, from the premise that higher education has excluded certain groups, and recognizes that some people have been disadvantaged within the system. The analysis of universities as social institutions in which discrimination, power relations and exclusionary practices are part of the *habitus*, has been a marginal but important contribution to studies of higher education. In contrast with theories of reproduction, theories of empowerment seek to challenge this culture of inequality.

The transformative potential of higher education has tended to be identified with pedagogical strategies rather than the curriculum. Arguably, it is in the classroom and in face-to-face encounters with students that a transformation of the culture is most visible and viable. Both feminist and critical pedagogical theories, as examples, have traditionally looked to the student–teacher relationships for possibilities of a higher education of empowerment.

From the 1960s, much of the early literature in these fields grew out of Friere's criticisms of 'banking' education (Freire 1970), whereby students are passive recipients of the lecturer's knowledge. The early theories were arguably based on somewhat simplistic notions of power relations in which the implicit goal was to transfer power from the teacher to the student. They also developed an analysis of education as a social institution in which social actors are differentially located within positions of power. From the 1980s, feminist and critical pedagogies were influential in the margins of higher education, particularly in adult education, and around the growing fields of women's studies and cultural studies. Theories of power relations in the classroom became more complex (Ellsworth 1989; Gore 1993), and shifted towards an understanding of the more subtle processes of power relationships within the classrooms.

Theories of the empowerment of students, as they developed from the 1960s, have broadly reflected the social movements of the time. The women's movement of the 1970s, for example, was strongly connected to the feminist literature on pedagogies. Most of the political and social movements challenging the *status quo*, however, lost impetus through the 1980s. As they declined, theories of the potential of education to transform and empower students were marginalized. So are they now outdated and, in any case, merely a matter of pedagogical strategies? What relevance do they have for contemporary curriculum design?

First, these theories sought to uncover educational processes at work on a tacit level in the classroom, in the same way as we can uncover tacit processes at work within the curriculum. For example, the educational experiences of a student of physics will be bound by certain rules of behaviour in the classroom, such as limiting their interruptions of a lecture. Their encounters of the curriculum will be bound by other rules, such as having to acquire a level of specialization in mathematics before proceeding to the higher levels of physics. These are insights into tacit educational processes, bounded by certain rules of behaviour and through boundaries around and hierarchies within knowledge fields. The curriculum as it has been designed may be framed by tacit rules and underlying power structures, but the pedagogic experiences of that classroom operate in parallel ways.

Second, the transformative approach to understanding the potential of education to empower individuals has shifted in response to the social context of the times. Throughout the 1990s, for instance, theories of power relations in higher education became removed from their association with political and social movements, and became more identifed with other frames of reference. In particular, the field of cultural studies and certain post-structuralist theorists developed new approaches to the analysis of power in higher education (Giroux and McLaren 1994). Power itself is now seen as a more complex and shifting dimension, rather than as a zero-sum property in which the greater the power of the teacher, the less the power of the students.

In addition, the idea of a curriculum that can be transformative has taken a new turn and has been associated with a different set of values that reflect more current concerns. Interestingly, this new transformative model of higher education that has been proposed looks to the ways in which the 'educational experience enhances the knowledge, ability and skills of graduates' and in these terms can be empowering for students (Harvey and Knight 1996: 8). This approach aligns itself with the outcomes and employability agenda, suggesting that transformation comes through an education that adds value to students' lives.

This new take on the curriculum as transformation is becoming ever more pervasive in the twenty-first century. It is reflected in many of the drivers of curricular change in the UK, but it also features predominantly elsewhere, for instance, within the new National Qualifications Framework in South Africa (Moore 2000; Breier 2001). In South Africa, the proposed framework is intended to be 'educationally transformative' through a value-added approach that is outcomes oriented and aligned with the 'global trend in higher education towards the production of flexibly skilled graduates' (Moore 2000: 184). We can, therefore, see echoes of this new understanding of transformative education in wider trends, such as the influence of the higher education marketplace and the idea that students have become consumers of their education in order to increase their value within the labour market.

Curriculum as consumption

As the higher education system has expanded, the state has guided universities into the market and has encouraged them to respond to its demands. The economic base of this growing system has shifted towards the people who benefit from it, and students in turn are being recast as consumers of their education. As universities now compete with each other for lucrative student populations, contemporary curricula are now guided increasingly by consumer demand. Universities advertise their courses in ways that seemed unimaginable when institutions in elite systems relied almost solely on reputation.

Students are becoming discerning consumers of higher education. The cost of a degree is high: most students will graduate with significant debts even if, as most do, they seek employment throughout their degree in order to help finance their studies. Faced with this prospect, they will select their course carefully. Many make their decision on a financial basis, choosing a course that leads to secure employment and maximizes the return they receive from their investment in education.

What impact do these changes have on the curriculum? Many academics now perceive their courses as products to be sold to niche markets. Courses are designed to offer the kinds of skills and knowledge that attract students who anticipate having to compete in the labour market. Modularization has become a key signifier of consumption, as programmes are repackaged and even rebranded for students to choose amongst. Universities have taken on something of the character of supermarkets or shopping malls, producers of commodities that offer a lifestyle choice to their customers (Gokulsing 1997). This development of curricula as consumption in a mass higher education system is a key driver of contemporary curricular change.

The marketization of higher education and its effect on curricula have yet to be fully understood. On the one hand, some of the arguments against a 'pick-and-mix' style of modularized and commodified curricula have seen it as an indication of a general decline in the social purposes that universities can fulfil. Should education be viewed as a product that can be bought, just like any other product on the market? Many academics have therefore resisted modularization and guarded the core of their specialist degrees, and through this we can see the extent to which the power of the knowledge fields is maintained in universities.

On the other hand, however, the curriculum has become increasingly influenced by outside interests. Higher education stakeholders – including the government, industry, students – all have a greater say, either directly or indirectly, in the types of curricula that universities offer. Consumers of education can thus be seen as having more power, and designers of curricula are aware that they must find products that will sell.

Curricula are therefore pulled in different directions. The desire to maintain the depth of a university education, to preserve the disciplines and to produce disciplinary specialists are often set against external demands for a 'useful', functional curriculum product. The tacit notion of curricula as consumption reveals some of the challenges of contemporary curricular design. It also reveals how social values have shifted towards the marketplace, which is seen by some as in itself offering the potential for empowering students or transforming higher education. In turn, curricula have been adapted to and shaped by these new demands.

The liberal curriculum

In spite of the current shifts we have identified towards an outcomes-based, employment-related and market-oriented curricula, it would be odd not to recognize a rather different conceptualization of liberal education. Liberal education is worth briefly considering here for several reasons:

1 It has a long history and, particularly in the USA, it has often been employed as a cornerstone of curriculum development.
2 It is a powerful concept that helps set out the purposes of higher education.
3 We may find ideas within the notion that are worth hanging on to as we pursue our schema of curricula in this book.

The concept of a liberal education has a long history, adapted throughout the centuries to address changing concerns within education systems, remaining largely focused on the education of the whole individual. Goodlad (2000) reviews this history from Plato and the 'Hellenic ideal' of a liberal education, to present-day initiatives in curricular development at one UK, scientific-based institution. Throughout its history, notions of a liberal education have been evoked to counter those forms of university education that have been perceived as too narrow and unbalanced. These imbalances were noted through the stark distinctions that arose at various times and in different contexts between the worlds of the practical and the academic, the sciences and the arts, and the dividing lines between doing and knowing. As a result, different ideas as to what might be meant by a 'liberal' education emerged (Peters 1964). Liberal could point to an expansion of the mind, to curricula processes that were relatively open or to pedagogies that required a personal engagement.

Contemporary examples of attempts to foster a liberal education are not in shortage. Developments in the US higher education system have promoted particular forms of liberal education which are worth touching upon. In the USA, liberal education has at times been associated with a balanced general education which is thought integral to the education of all university students (Boyer 1987; Howard 1991; Nussbaum 1997). A practical insight into a liberal education as it has been fostered within one institution comes from Alverno College in Wisconsin, which has widely publicized its pursuit of a balanced education, or an 'ability-based learning program' (Alverno College 2000). Turning to the personal characteristics that an Alverno College curriculum seeks to develop in its students, we find three goals that, for us, have a particular significance:

• a sense of responsibility for learning and the ability to continue learning
• the ability to assess critically one's own performance
• an understanding of the application of knowledge in different contexts.

In keeping with the aims of a liberal education, the Alverno College programme sets out developmental goals that include the 'facility for social interaction' and the development of a 'global perspective', 'effective citizenship' and 'aesthetic responsiveness'. This approach is an 'effort to redefine education in terms of abilities needed for effectiveness in the worlds of work, family, and civic community' (Alverno College 2000).

Here we must emphasize that these are considered to be general goals of the curriculum, not subject-specific competencies or narrowly defined, employment-related outcomes. In this sense, they offer a broad conceptualization of what it might mean to educate citizens for their roles in society. This is not to suggest that ideas about liberal education are entirely absent in the UK. Rather, we wish to draw attention to the contrast between the ways in which curricula are largely being framed in the UK and approaches in other contexts that ask larger questions about the role of curricula in higher education.

Conclusions

In this identification of various tacit notions of curriculum, we have seen how the higher education curriculum has often been a site of contestation and debate. Yet there are underlying points emerging that should be recognized in a search for a framework for curriculum. These include a set of ideas:

1 *The curriculum reflects the social context in which it is located:* curricula are created within a wider social order and, as such, an understanding of the curriculum cannot easily be accomplished without recognition of the social world in which it has been shaped.
2 *The hidden curriculum is pervasive and powerful:* all curricula require processes of understanding and complying with rules, some of which are explicit, but many of which remain tacit. There is a certain degree of

inevitability about these processes. Therefore, an understanding of how these processes operate is essential for an understanding of contemporary curricula.

3   *The power of the knowledge fields:* the subject areas or knowledge fields that constitute the foundations of the curriculum have a powerful hold on changes to the curriculum. Academic knowledge has had a special, almost untouchable, place in the universities that has resisted outside attempts to interfere.

We have briefly reviewed tacit notions of curricula in order to help to bring to the foreground what has largely been a missing term in debates about higher education. In doing so, we have seen that there are different ways of thinking about the role of curricula in higher education. We have also seen that curricular changes often occur without a public debate about the direction of those changes. As the world we live in becomes increasingly complex, it is now time to highlight the role of curricula and consider the future direction of curricula. To do so, we need to consider the types of challenges we face in the twenty-first century.

3

Higher education for an age of uncertainty

An uncertain world

Problem-based learning, work-based learning, learning in the community, peer-assisted learning, collective learning, modularization: these are just some examples of attempts to develop curricula and pedagogies for a changing world. But what, precisely, are they responses *to*? What are the challenges of 'change' that they are attempting to address? Are the challenges to which they are addressed the right challenges or are there, perhaps, other and even larger challenges that are as yet only dimly recognized?

That curricula *should* bear witness to change as such is widely agreed, at least beyond the academic community. Government reports, leaders in the world of work and others in the wider society urge that the world is one of change. Often, the observation is a preliminary remark to the suggestion that students should be better prepared for the world of change that they are going to encounter. Terms such as 'skills', 'adaptability', 'flexibility', 'self-reliance' and 'learning how to learn' are frequently used at this point. The implication – and often it is asserted outright – is that curricula in higher education have insufficiently taken account of the character of the wider world and need to be redesigned so that they address the challenges that it brings.

The texts in question, however, whether they are reports or speeches, are notoriously vague on the matter of change itself. That the world is changing and changing faster than ever are simply stated, as if the character of the changing world was self-evident. But the ways in which the world is changing are far from self-evident. Even less self-evident are the implications for curricula in higher education. The world has always been changing, after all. Are there then particular features of contemporary change that are especially significant? Even if there are, just why should they be taken on board in the design and development of curricula? Higher education surely cannot be expected to meet all of the challenges facing human beings. It may be that some of the challenges to learning and development should fall on organizations, or on individuals as they make their way through life, as part of the 'learning society'. There are, therefore, some large questions to be addressed in understanding what is meant by the idea of curricula for a changing world.

The terms that we have just picked out above provide some clues, but there are different stories coming through those terms. We hear much about the redundancy of knowledge in the sense that – as we are told – knowledge acquired by undergraduates quickly becomes out of date; a situation that befalls the hapless graduate even at the point of his or her graduation. Presumably, it is this reflection that leads some to suggest that higher education should develop the capacity among students to 'learn how to learn' (NCIHE 1997; para. 9.18). If knowledge, in some disciplines at least, is being rapidly overtaken, then what is required of curricula is that they enable students to go on learning under their own steam.

This approach to curriculum has certain implications. One implication is that it implicitly condemns the view that says that if knowledge is changing fast, then the best way forward is to ensure that students acquire as much of it as possible. In contrast, the idea of 'learning how to learn' looks to a parsimonious approach to curriculum design. Far from packing a curriculum with pure knowledge, knowledge as such might even be jettisoned and, instead, time and effort can be used in imaginative ways of stimulating students' capacities for learning for and by themselves. Such an approach to curriculum design might presumably embrace research processes, the structure of disciplines and their purposes and values. In this way, students could come to understand what it is to be involved in the process of knowledge creation as well as simply the capacity to go on learning through life. Pushed to its limit, the 'learning how to learn' idea could be said to herald the *redundancy* of knowledge as such as a component of curricula.

Just one fly in the ointment is that the notion of 'learning how to learn' is fraught with ambiguity. Does it refer to, say, skills of information acquisition and information processing or are there other skills implied here? Is it singular or plural? Is 'learning how to learn' a generic skill or does it take varying forms in different contexts? Is the idea of 'learning how to learn' even internally coherent? Presumably it implies that learning how to learn can lead to a particular form of knowledge, namely 'knowing how to learn'. But is there such a form of knowledge? Even if there is, perhaps the phrase is actually calling up a larger human attribute, which is the more diffuse human disposition of being prepared to engage with strangeness?

'Learning how to learn', however, is by no means unique in its ambiguous and yet far-reaching nature. Those other terms that we noted – 'adaptability', 'flexibility' and 'self-reliance' – also speak to broad and large dimensions of human capability. How do we understand such terms? They are not isolated terms, but indicate the emergence of a discourse, a new vocabulary that is associated with shifting challenges to higher education itself; challenges that arise out of yet wider challenges as to the nature of the contemporary world and what it is to live effectively in that world.

If the contemporary world is faced with particularly new kinds of change, perhaps that newness lies neither in technological change nor even in its pace of change. Perhaps the change in question is the challenge to human beings as such. This surely is implicit in the discourse exemplified by the terms 'adaptability', 'flexibility' and 'self-reliance'. The world in general, and work more particularly, seems to call for not just change in individuals but the development of internal personal powers and qualities that promote continuing readjustment (Hassan 2003). The self, as we may put it, has to be continually remade in this milieu *and* the self has be ready to become another self.

We glimpse, therefore, the emergence of three intertwined stories as to the ways in which curricula in higher education might move in the future as a means of coping with a changing world. First, a story of *skills* in the sense of particular capabilities suited to meeting definite 'needs', especially in the world of work; second, a story around *information processing* and *problem solving*, that is, new relationships to and with knowledge; third, a story around *the powers of remaking the self*. All of these approaches stem from a sense of a relationship between individuals and the world but, in moving across the three stories, the relationship becomes increasingly complex. In the end, the world is seen as changing in fluid and unpredictable ways such that only a continual capacity for remaking the self is going to offer any possibility of closing the gap between the challenges presented by the world and what it is that the individual brings to bear.

Responsibilities

In a changing world, an age of 'liquid modernity' as it has been called (Bauman 2000), the design of a curriculum invokes two kinds of responsibilities. First, there are the tacit responsibilities of the students. Should the curriculum be developing among students responsibilities towards (a) a discipline and its standards; (b) the world of work; (c) the wider society; (d) the student her- or himself? It may be said that it is all of those, but then large and possibly intractable problems arise. It is not at all clear that developing responsibilities in those four domains are easily compatible with each other. Acquiring a deep understanding of and commitment to the tacit norms of a discipline, learning the challenges of contemporary work, gaining an immediate sense of what 'citizenship' might mean and developing the powers of self-critique: these aims call up large and quite possibly different curriculum projects for they look to developing the self in different directions.

The second set of responsibilities falls on curriculum designers themselves. How do lecturers and others in universities who find themselves in positions of responsibility towards curricula understand those responsibilities? To what extent do their actions in the shape that they impart to the curriculum (their 'theory in action') match their words in describing what they are trying to do (their 'espoused theories', Argyris and Schön 1974)? If those in universities talk of their curriculum intentions in terms of the challenges of work or broader social or personal considerations, what might that mean? What responsibilities befall them in giving shape to those ideas and hopes?

Responsibilities then fall on both students and tutors in the context of the curriculum in a changing world. But a key question arises: what are the *relative* responsibilities of both student and tutor in realizing those ideas and hopes? The answer to this question turns on our basic conception of curriculum itself. Is a curriculum a set of educational processes that is simply presented to a student? If so, then the realization of the hopes invested in a curriculum falls purely on the tutors and the host institution. If, however, a curriculum in higher education is much more a set of experiences that a student inhabits, experiences that arise out of the student's interactions with his or her 'learning environment', then the responsibilities that attach to realizing a curriculum fall significantly on the student as well.

We take the view that while the student is implicated in realizing a curriculum, a curriculum *can* be understood, in significant part at least, as the set of organized processes and materials that, intentionally and unintentionally, are put before the students by their educators. ('Materials' here is to be understood in a generous way to include discursive materials – as we might term them – such as propositions, theories and concepts within knowledge communities.) To focus on the curricular intentions of educators is not to deny the crucial significance of the student's responses to that curriculum. In the end, the student's experience is precisely marked out by the curriculum as experienced as distinct from the curriculum as presented. To return to one of Pierre Bourdieu's terms, the *habitus* of the student is constructed in significant measure by the student him- or herself. But the curriculum as presented by lecturers and tutors has to be counted as providing the context within which the student's experience takes its shape. The curriculum as presented both opens up educational possibilities on the one hand and limits educational possibilities on the other. It contains choices, whether explicit or tacit, that constrain the educational experience available to the student.

Accordingly, while a full account of curriculum would be bound to include the student perspective as such (and we devote Chapter 10 to the matter), focusing on the intentions of the key staff involved is, we suggest, a worthwhile exercise in itself. 'Curriculum' has to be understood, in part, as a set of *intentional* purposes and strategies and it constitutes a valid quest to inquire into the intentions of academic staff who bear the major responsibility for curriculum design.

Indeed, we would go further in contending that since the primary responsibility of curriculum design rests with staff and not with students, any study of the curriculum must take as its point of departure a study of the staff concerned. Students are clearly important in determining the character of the curriculum, especially in higher education which is characteristically a transaction between teacher and taught, but students' *formal* responsibility towards the curriculum is less than that of the staff. Staff have both the formal responsibility and the power to shape curricula in ways that students do not have.

Admittedly, this distinction between the curriculum as presented and the curriculum as experienced cannot be held entirely watertight. On the contrary, in understanding the curriculum as presented, we also have to take account of the curriculum as experienced. As a matter of fact, those designing curricula are increasingly thinking about the student experience. Course proposals often include descriptions of the intended teaching approaches and the kinds of learning experiences that a course team is hoping to elicit among the students.

It follows that the idea of the process of curriculum design subsisting in a timeframe in which a curriculum is first designed and then put into action has to be abandoned. Good curriculum design is partly in action, in the pedagogy, in the daily shaping of the student experience. That is why talk of 'aims' and 'objectives' can be misleading for they may encourage precisely a sense of the kind of sequentialism involved in aiming at a target; once one has let go the arrow, there's no further action. In effective curriculum design, however, one is never off duty. The curriculum is not so much being 'delivered' as being enacted in a nuanced way, with interplays and imaginative offerings. A curriculum is in part a *curriculum-in-action* and, therefore, curriculum design is itself *design-in-action* (a point to which we shall return).

Being successful

What counts as success in the world? What counts as success in the education of students? The dominant way of thinking in relation to these questions is surely clear: success in the world is what works in the world and individual success is that of high achievement in the world of work. Correspondingly, success in the education of students lies in an education that is felt to contribute substantially to this worldly success. 'Employability', proportions of students entering 'the labour market' and economic 'rates of return' for different kinds of degree awards: these are the indicators and the language of this account of success.

This orientation towards the world of work has long been present in higher education policy making. It was evident even in the Robbins Report (1963). Indeed, it was 'the instruction in skills suitable to play a part in the general division of labour' that constituted the very first of the report's four objectives (coming first if only because the objective 'is sometimes ignored or undervalued'). Over the last 40 years, this objective has become increasingly pronounced in policy framing. In the UK it has, for example, been carried into the national evaluation exercises, such that the rates of employability (as measured by the 'first destination data') constitute a signal performance indicator.

This 'vocational' turn in policy framing (Salter and Tapper 1994) may be seen as a wider attempt on the part of the state to steer the higher education system towards playing its part in developing the skills base for a 'high skills' economy within the larger global economy. But as implied, we consider that this way of looking at success is now not just an aspiration on the part of the state, or even a matter of policy implementation, but is now part of the cultural framing of higher education. That is to say, the relationship of higher education to the wider world is being defined in significant measure in terms of success in work.

This seems to part of the message of Robert Reich's (2000) book *The Future of Success*: that success comes to be understood in terms of salary and influence achieved in the world of work. Reich shows too that complex societies in the present 'networked' age offer different ways of succeeding. The lone financial adviser may enjoy higher levels of income, status and influence than the chief executive of a large corporation. The general point is that the rewards that accompany success, seen in these terms, are now so considerable and growing so rapidly that there is developing a skewed structure of success within society. To them that hath shall continue to be given very much more.

This emerging structure of success is part of the context of higher education. The curriculum becomes an allocator of opportunities to succeed. In this context, questions arise as to the forms of human development, or *subjectivities*, that any particular curriculum offers. Is success a matter of personal or collective endeavour? Is it likely to nurture the intellectual but also, and equally importantly, the personal and practical human capital that is likely to make for success in this emerging milieu? Is success in the world ultimately the test of an effective curriculum? To the last question at least we are prepared to say yes, but only insofar as 'success in the world' is understood in a way larger than success in the workplace.

Success of course is never assured; in a fragile world it cannot be. The educational fragilities of success are at least fourfold. *First*, the educational and professional biography, built up with some effort over perhaps 20 or more years, may turn out not to be entirely appropriate after all. Individuals, having gained a degree with a particular profession in mind, may later find themselves suddenly made redundant and may be unclear if and where they might find a new occupation.

Second, in higher education especially, there is a gap between an educator's intentions and the students' realizations of those intentions. A genuine higher education has to allow for the student to take on the expected cognitive and personal states in his or her own way. A set of stated 'learning outcomes' can be less understood as a blueprint for their faithful reproduction and more as a guide to a set of educational hopes and efforts. Educational transactions in higher education *have* to have significant elements of *educational risk*, as we might put it.

Third, an external body engaged in evaluating a department's teaching may emerge with a somewhat critical judgement overall that may be considered surprising by the peer community. In turn, such a judgement may have an impact on the student's learning opportunities. Accreditation might be withdrawn or resources might be diverted away from the department concerned. In short, quality systems produce a turbulence that often has unforeseeable consequences.

Fourth, uncertainty characterizes the educational infrastructure within which those educational processes are conducted. During a student's programme of study, key staff may leave, taking their intellectual capital with them. There might be an academic restructuring, bringing individual staff newly into contact with each other. Key resources may change, not only 'hard' physical resources but less tangible resources: the industrial company in which a student was going spend her placement moves or even goes out of business and the set of learning opportunities that had been so carefully set up over a period of time is no more. The student's learning environment, then, is characterized by many kinds of fragility.

Therefore, effort and goodwill may be necessary but they cannot be sufficient to ensure success in a world of fragility, uncertainty and risk (Stehr 2001). ('Fragility' speaks of a tendency to dissolve; 'uncertainty' reminds us that the world of tomorrow may not resemble that of today; and 'risk' underlines the difficulty of computing the opportunity costs in such a fluid age.) As our examples have indicated, matters of fragility, uncertainty and risk are not purely those of physical or systems infrastructure; they are not even, in a straightforward sense, matters of human infrastructure. They are, in addition, matters of *conceptual and ontological fluidity*. Indeed, what counts as success in the world and, by extension, in curricula is contested.

Accordingly, curricula in an age of uncertainty are being presented with ever-widening challenges. Curricula in higher education are both achievements and tasks. As *achievements* they represent the fruits of hard thinking, effort and typically collaboration among a group of staff, simply in the design, planning and organization that enables any course simply to get off the ground. As *tasks* they represent the continual effort that goes into ensuring that the educational processes are conducted professionally and to high quality standards.

Success in curriculum matters can never be assured, therefore. It is as if the rope ladder that one is on is not only known to be fraying but is even showing increasing signs of disintegrating altogether. Empirically, tutors go on, course teams go on. Extraordinary effort is put in day after day. Yet, it is surely understood that the curriculum, as an educational project, has little security attached to it. Much is precarious. In what follows, we shall reveal the state of that precariousness, but we also hope to be able to help put matters on a more reliable basis.

Knowing, acting and being

From our discussion so far, both in the last chapter and this one, there is emerging a foundational question for those who are responsible for framing curricula in higher education. It is simply this: what are the challenges of a changing world? To pose this question is itself to make a statement. It is to say that the claims of the wider world offer a valid set of considerations in the framing of a curriculum in higher education. That reflection may be felt to be uncontroversial, but it is significant. *First*, its being acknowledged as part of the relevant context is a recent acknowledgement, its emergence being perhaps of the order of the last 50 years. *Second*, and here we chance our arms, that question ('What are the challenges of a changing world?') has never been *generally* accepted as an overarching question for systematically framing curricula in higher education. A question of this kind may have been present for the design of particular courses or even for developments in the teaching of certain subjects (for instance, in the development of problem-based learning in medical education), but it has not, we suggest, been accepted as a generally valid way of approaching curriculum design.

If this question ('What are the challenges of a changing world?') has emerged in our review as a key contextual question, our discussion so far is also beginning to imply three challenges by way of response: they are the challenges of knowing, acting and being. A brief commentary on each is surely in order.

First, a changing world does not rule out knowledge as such, but it poses questions as to what kinds of knowledge are going to be fruitful in a changing world. It may be that formal propositional knowledge has not yet had its day, but if it is to be retained within higher education curricula it needs to be rethought and repositioned alongside other more practical and personal forms of knowledge. In a curriculum for the twenty-first century, what matters is the student's own engagements with knowledge – in other words his or her *knowing*.

Second, a changing world both calls for action but renders action problematic. How is action to be evaluated when there are multiple frames of reference to hand? Is it in its effects or the individual's intentions? Action, therefore, deserves attention in its own right. It can no longer, if indeed it ever could, be seen as an adjunct of knowledge, an arena in which knowledge is simply put to work. Again though, it is the student's own actions that are important: not action in a dessicated sense as might appear on the pages of a course proposal but action *in action*; the student's involvements in and her interpretations of her own actions – in short, her *acting*.

Third, as we have seen and as employers are increasingly noting, a changing world calls for certain kinds of human capacity and dispositions and for self-awareness and self-confidence. The self is implicated in a changing world. No longer can the wider norms and practices be endorsed: individuals have to work things out for themselves in their own situations. Individuals have to become selves, strong, careful, open, resilient and critical selves. Students' *being*, willy-nilly, comes into play.

Knowing, *acting* and *being*: these then are the three challenges of a changing world that curricula in higher education have to address. Different responses will doubtless be forthcoming across both institutions and subjects, as we shall see, but we contend that three challenges are universal and there is, as a result, a responsibility on all those at the sharp end in higher education to ensure that curricula with which they are associated are supplying responses of some kind to these three challenges.

These challenges open up possibilities for universities to do even more justice to their hopes of educating. For example, if 'higher learning' is that form of learning that is appropriate to higher education, it has now to be interpreted as referring to a composite of especially challenging forms of learning that are appropriate to a changing world. A further challenge opens up, therefore, of trying to delineate what 'knowing', 'acting' and 'being' might look like that could be said to constitute a higher learning in these terms.

A challenge too lies in trying to say something about the relationships between these domains of higher learning – of knowing, acting and being. The very way in which we have sketched out these terms in the last few passages hints at real and necessary relationships between them: for example, talk of knowing rather than knowledge itself calls up suggestions of self and action coming into play in the epistemological domain. The more general reflection is that forms of human being adequate to a changing world would have to find *some* levels of integration between knowing, doing and being. Whether it is possible to say anything that has general applicability across all subjects as to what integration among these three domains would look like remains before us.

Curriculum as an art form

We are suggesting, then, that curricula in higher education in the twenty-first century can be understood as intended educational processes that give expression to three domains – of knowing, acting and being. Yet this suggestion may give rise to a false impression. It may give rise to a sense that the construction of curricula is mainly a matter of determining what part should be accorded to each of the three dimensions and their interrelationships. This *is* part of our intentions, but there is the prospect of things going awry here. For that way of construing matters – of dimensions playing their own part and standing in determinate relationships to each other – may give rise to a tacit sense that curricula are to be constructed and even engineered. On this conception of curricula design, nothing need be left to chance; all can be window-tunnelled out of risk and indeterminacy.

Such an approach is understandable for it arises out of the limitations of language, for example, of terms such as 'design', 'construction', 'dimensions' and even 'domains' and 'relationships'. It resonates with talk of 'outcomes', 'objectives' and even 'alignment'. This is an *engineering sense of curriculum*, a sense that with sufficient pre-planning and organization problems can be foreseen and overcome in advance. Risk can be largely removed, or at least significantly diminished. This is not our view, however.

Far from being engineered, even as a flexible structure, in a fluid age a curriculum has to be open-ended. This open-endedness is not that our kind of curriculum bends with the wind and that its structure has been computed in advance to tolerate such disturbances; rather this open-endedness comes of genuine human engagements with the material environment, with the conceptual and symbolic environment and with other human beings. Such engagements take on an art form in the sense that, even though a performance or work of art builds upon thousands of previous corresponding experiences, still there are aspects at play that cannot be caught fully in advance or held in a template (Schön 1987). The tolerances and even the disturbances have to be achieved *in situ*, in the felt constraints and possibilities of the particular context.

Curricula as design, it is apparent then, moves at different levels. One lies in the possible drawing up of something of a generic schema or template for a group of courses, perhaps even across a whole discipline (the kind of task undertaken in the UK's *subject benchmarking* exercise). A further level lies in the *prior* drawing up of the curriculum for a particular course or programme of study, probably by a course team: What are the specific educational intentions behind this course? How might they be brought off? How much is to be presented to the students? What might the students be asked to inquire into by themselves? How much space might be accorded to the students? What kinds of relationships might be developed between the different elements? These are questions that curriculum as *design-in-advance* must face. No matter how helpful any template or discipline guide, hard work lies ahead in working out and addressing the exigencies of the context of a particular course – of its institutional and material resources, interests and capacities of the teaching team, and the likely general level of immediate competencies that the students will bring to the party. Out of these contextual considerations are likely to spring innovations in the course aims and the identification of the various curriculum elements.

A further mode of design lies in *design-in-action*, in the working out of the curriculum week by week and day by day. The pedagogical device, which is sometimes adopted, of identifying with the students what they have gained from the last teaching session they have experienced is an example of such design in action: Does the original design need any adjustment mid-term? Are more skills or techniques required? Is some further understanding of key concepts in order? Are the students lacking in self-confidence? The curriculum has to be constructed daily and reconstructed if need be.

But the curriculum is also designed, in a sense, on a day-to-day basis by the student him- or herself. Even if silently, even if in resistance, let alone in a creative or positive disposition, especially in higher education, a student will exploit the spaces available to her to inject her own orderings of the experiences opened up to her. Personal priorities will be set by the student. In our schema, the student may choose the level of commitment that she will give to the three separate calls of knowing, acting and being (quite apart from more discrete discriminations she may make within any of those domains; whether, for instance, she chooses to spend time acquiring the skills associated with a bibliographic database rather than particular skills more closely associated with a knowledge field). Students working together, and given encouragement and space to work together, are likely to impart more substance to this student-led design-in-action.

An implication of this analysis is that a curriculum represents the imaginative design of spaces in which desirable processes of personal and interpersonal development are likely to occur. This design is an interactive venture and a venture through time: it involves staff and students acting together and through the course of the curriculum.

A curriculum, then, is always a *curriculum in process* (cf. Stenhouse 1975). It is dynamic and in flux and is also a site of contested interpretations. A curriculum is fluid and is not – cannot – be caught by any schema or template. To some degree, this consideration is a necessary follow-on from one of our starting points: if we live in a fluid age, curricula themselves can hardly be thought to be exempted from such fluidity. But the fluidity of curricula also arises from the educational intentions appropriate to higher education in such an age. For curricula in higher education have now to be charged with the responsibility of encouraging the formation of human wherewithal that is adequate to an age of fluidity. Dispositions and capabilities appropriate to fluidity can hardly be forthcoming if curricula themselves are not also characterized, at least to some extent, by fluidity.

Conclusion

Curricula as art forms, fluidity, fuzziness, open-endedness, contestability, indeterminacy, processes of engagement: it is terms such as these that begin to suggest themselves as part of a vocabulary that does justice to the 'design' of curricula in a fluid age. Some are now calling on concepts and theories of complexity to assist our understanding of curricula (Tosey 2002; Jackson 2004). We are happy to sign up to any such declaration provided that that complexity is understood as characterizing the framing and acting out of curricula as well as the forms of human capability that curricula are intended to develop.

In saying this, we are implicitly being critical of much of the contemporary thinking about curricula in education (that is, including but not being confined to higher education). It is understandable that in an age of formal accountability, of pressure on budgets and of the felt need to be producing overt and demonstrable outcomes, such thinking as there is about curricula seeks precisely to formulate a template for 'programme specifications' that has universal application, and to call for aims, objectives and outcomes to be clearly specified. That way lies economy, reliability and even, it might be felt, effectiveness. But the wish for security in advance, as it were, can only reduce the possibility of emerging with a curriculum that is adequate to the patterning of human beings that is appropriate to an unforeseeable and highly challenging world. In an age of risk, curricula themselves have, in part, to become curricula of *risk*: they have to contain a degree of unpredictability and openness.

In this chapter, we have introduced our idea that knowing, acting and being can form the key dimensions of curricula, precisely in the context of an unforeseeable and challenging world. We now turn to firming and developing that embryonic schema and to do so especially through an examination of another contemporary schema.

4

Framing curriculum

Introduction

In our three preceding chapters:

1 We have noted that there is a policy vacuum in relation to curricula: despite the arrival of mass higher education systems across the world, by and large the nature of the curriculum as such is not something that has much concerned governments.
2 We have examined current ideas of the curriculum (such as they are), observing that, on the one hand, current ideas of curricula in higher education are rarely spelt out but held simply tacitly and, on the other hand, whether spelt out or not, current thinking about and understandings of the curriculum are inadequate when set alongside the fluidity, indeterminacy and contestability of the modern world.
3 We have sketched out the social context that in our view bears upon curricula. The key questions here are: what kind of world is it that curricula in higher education are preparing students for? What kinds of capability, therefore, in general terms might curricula be fostering? Our view is that the modern world is characterized by heightened levels of complexity *and* uncertainty. Fluidity, fuzziness, instability, fragility, unpredictability, indeterminacy, turbulence, challengeability, contestability: these are some of the terms that mark out the world of the twenty-first century.

In this chapter, and building on that background, we want to address the following question: what, if anything, can be said in general about designing curricula in higher education?

Building blocks?

A question that might easily form as discussion of curriculum matters gets underway is this: what are the building blocks of a curriculum? It will already be apparent that – on our emerging view – such a question should be treated carefully. If it is intended to invite consideration as to the features that a curriculum should possess, then the question has value. But the question then, it will be noticed, takes on a metaphorical form: it encourages reflection on the structural characteristics of a curriculum. The question, though, runs the risk of setting up misleading presumptions if it is taken somewhat literally; if, that is to say, it is taken to imply that the task of forming curricula is essentially that of placing alongside each other, perhaps with some cement, separate blocks of experience.

It might be assumed that a proper approach to the shaping of curricula might be found in the sentiment 'Let's have a block of that here and a block of that there'. Even at this early stage in our explorations, it is clear that this way of thinking about curricula has to be extinguished as a general approach. This is not to say that, *for some purposes*, curricula cannot be helpfully caught in diagrams formed of, say, boxes or even circles with lines between them showing their interrelationships. Indeed, we shall be offering some of those ourselves. But it is to say that any such diagram has to be interpreted with caution if it might imply that a student's curriculum experiences can be disentangled in a neat fashion.

Of course, those diagrammatic building blocks – whether boxes, circles, triangles or any other shapes – can overlap, even in a diagram. The diagram can be drawn so as to imply close interrelationships and even fluidities: the lines may be dotted, or run over each other; the arrows may fly in multiple directions. Even a three-dimensional configuration may be implied. But there remains still the possibility of a fundamental error arising even at the outset, namely that any one moment in a student's curriculum experience may and even *should* develop but a single capability and that teaching, therefore, becomes a matter of determining – at any one instant – which capability is to be stretched.

At this stage, all we want to do is flag our concern that such an assumption, which we believe to be endemic not just to the design of curricula but also to teaching in higher education, is grossly out of kilter with the challenges of our times. If the world heaps upon us, at any one instant, multiple and competing challenges of action, knowing and being – as so we have begun to argue it does – then a curriculum that is going to be adequate to that world has itself to be understood as inherently *multi-textual* (Kress and van Leeuwen 2001). This statement may sound ambitious or jejune or plain unrealizable. In fact, it is evident daily in higher education, at least wherever higher education lives up to its self-rhetoric about, for example, the development of a student's critical abilities.

Even as she writes an essay, with her fingers on a laptop computer and largely hidden in a carrel in the library, the student is willy-nilly engaging in all three modes of human being, of knowing, acting and being itself. In making an authentic first-hand knowledge claim of her own, the student is saying this is where I stand (if only at this moment). Not only is the student entering the realm of knowing, but the claiming to know involves both a deliberate act and a commitment that draws her into a fresh state of being. Critical thought, therefore, of the kind long espoused by western universities, invokes all three domains of knowing, acting and being, and does so simultaneously. In accepting the challenge of embarking on a course of study, a student enters into a set of curriculum experiences that are synchronous in nature: the student may be presented with much, with several invitations all at once and, in turn, may respond in multiple dimensions all at once.

In relation to curricula, therefore, the idea of building blocks is better treated metaphorically. Even to talk of the elements of a curriculum as forming a 'seamless whole', or of the elements 'percolating' the curriculum, or of ingredients 'mixing' with each other, while going some way towards pointing up the fluid character of curriculum; it does not quite meet the bill. Such talk still implies that a curriculum is separate from the student's responses and offerings whereas, on our evolving conception, the student is a key actor within the curriculum. That has to be the case, after all, if the curriculum is to be – as we believe it should be – an educational vehicle for the student's own journey of *becoming*, of the student coming into a certain kind of being, who has some chance of prospering in a world of simultaneous, unpredictable and contending challenges.

A contemporary schema

Let us follow through on these general observations by examining a schema that has been recently proposed by Neville Bennett, Elisabeth Dunne and Clive Carré in their (2000) book on *Skills Development in Higher Education and Employment*. The schema takes the form of five overlapping blocks (Figure 4.1) and a significant part of the book is given to showing how different curricula emphasize some blocks and neglect or even omit entirely other blocks.

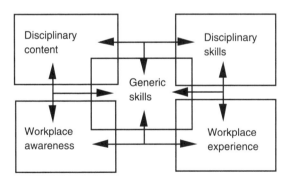

Figure 4.1   A contemporary schema (from Bennett, Dunne and Carré 2000)

There are a number of features about this schema that immediately stand out:

1   *Curricula may be considered to be a composite of three domains:* disciplines, work and generic skills.
2   *There are interconnections between the elements of the schema,* such that each of the main domains are interrelated: the domains of the disciplines and of work are interconnected and they are both connected to the domain of 'generic skills'.
3   *The connections flow in all directions:* no one domain is more important than other domains.
4   *There are overlaps between the domains:* no one domain is discrete, with neat boundaries separating it from other domains.
5   *The skills of disciplines can be understood as separate from disciplinary content* and students' capabilities in each may be separately developed.
6   *Generic skills are to be found in each of the other domains,* or at least generic skills can be exemplified and realized in each of the other domains.

This schema possesses several qualities that we would endorse:

• fluidity across the curriculum as a whole
• interconnectiveness among the elements
• a sensitivity to the inner complexity of any one major element.

These three properties, we suggest, should characterize any curriculum in any subject in any institution of higher education.
The schema, however, also possesses properties that raise some issues. For example, there is a reminder contained in the schema that we would also endorse: namely that a deep understanding of a field of knowing is not only a matter of mastering a body of knowledge but also a matter of getting on the inside of a form of life and so acquiring a set of relevant skills. But the implication contained in the schema that 'disciplinary content' and 'disciplinary skills' can be separated is problematic. There are three points that we would make.
First, it is through the requisite skills that one's understanding of a knowledge field is developed and revealed. *Second,* the skills only have point *in* their own field of knowledge. *Third,* and even more fundamentally, the intellectual becoming that awaits those who seriously wish to enter a field of knowledge is to accept a calling to enter a way of life with its own forms of going on. This is not to say that those forms of going on do not change. Indeed, they do and it is a hallmark of a genuine higher education that students are enabled to feel that they can be part of a community that is continuing to modify those ways of going on.
'Disciplinary content' and 'disciplinary skills', therefore, take in each other's washing. They have to be understood as shorthand expressions for the concepts, expressions, theories, dominant figures, major texts and signal achievements that constitute a field of knowing on the one hand, and for the forms of argument, mastery of technologies, research methods and forms of scholarship that constitute the field's 'skills' on the other. But while these two modes of living in a discipline may sound separable, in practice, the two

dimensions are intertwined. In learning within a discipline, I may ask myself: do I use this term or that term? Insofar as there is a genuine choice, the 'solution' is not easily classifiable as either a matter of 'content' or 'skill'. It is a matter of judgement in which both one's understanding of the discipline's 'content' and its 'skills' are brought nicely together.

There are two other features of the Bennett, Dunne and Carré schema that we wish to pick up. The first is that it gives a significant place to 'work'. This makes sense on at least two levels. On the one hand, many if not the majority of courses in higher education are designed explicitly if not with a particular occupation in mind, then with a cluster of cognate occupations in mind; for example, professions allied to medicine, engineering sciences and the built environment. On the other hand, courses are also taught with an increasing recognition, as we have noted, that students are looking towards their careers on graduation and are hoping that in some way at least their course of study will offer them some kind of preparation for the world of work. One indicator of quality in the UK is that of employability, since institutions of higher education are now required to make public their statistics on the employability of their graduates as part of a heightened transparency about the quality of institutions' programmes of study.

However, to cast the world of work, *a priori*, as playing a major role in a general schema for curricula in higher education is surely to cede too much on that front since it cannot be assumed that there is a clear link between a course of study and the world of work. For many courses, those linkages will be significant and will come to be explicitly present sooner or later in the framing of a curriculum. Forms of clinical experience may make their appearance only laggardly but they cannot be avoided if a course of study is intended to enable its students to advance on the path of becoming 'tomorrow's doctors' (GMC 2003). But links with the world of work may be tenuous and may even be non-existent; even a hint of the world of work may justifiably be absent from a set of course aims and objectives. That graduates find themselves typically in work following their graduation says nothing about the character of those work environments: employability indices in themselves can only be weak indicators of programme quality (Harvey 2001; Yorke 2001).

This is not to suggest that the wider world does not have claims on those who design curricula. Our position is already clear that the wider society has a legitimate claim to supply considerations that should be present in the design of curricula, but the claim cannot be built around work. *Work cannot offer a universal category with which to structure curricula.* There can be no moral imperative that work should be built into the framing of curricula unless it could be argued that work is a necessary condition of what it is to be human. Such an argument would at the very least be controversial and it is not one that we wish to make.

Yet, even if it *could* be shown that work is a necessary condition of what it is to be human, there could still be no absolute injunction that work as such should enter into curriculum design. After all, the students themselves – we are thinking especially of 'mature' students already in work – may have opted to come onto courses in higher education precisely to come into a non-work environment and to have access to experiences quite other from those of work. There can be no justification, therefore, for according work a privileged place in curriculum design (Arendt 1977; White 1997).

What we do want to urge is the tautology that being human is a necessary condition of what it is to be human. Whatever else they may do, students are going to be – and already are – members of a wider world, a world marked out by change, uncertainty and conceptual challenge. What it is to be and to act effectively in such a world supplies challenges of a universal kind. There is a responsibility on curriculum designers to build in such considerations – in relation to being and acting in the world – that obtain not only in relation to the category of work. Work, therefore, does not have to appear in any general schema for curricula in higher education, but a sense of acting and being in the wider world *do* have to appear.

Lastly, the Bennett, Dunne and Carré schema does not merely include, but affords a central and commanding position to 'generic skills'. For these authors, skills are 'generic' where they 'can potentially be applied to any discipline, to any course in higher education, to the workplace or indeed to any other context' (2000: 32). Here, the term 'potentially' is ambiguous. Is it intended to imply that there are skills that could be applied to all of those domains (it is just a matter of will as to whether those applications are actually made) *or* is it intended as a kind of hypothetical (such skills may or may not exist, but if they do exist they would take on this wide-ranging character)? Certainly, the authors' evidence indicates that many, both in the academic world and the world of work, either consider that such generic skills do exist or speak in such terms. There is a discourse in favour of such generic skills. But we suggest that caution is in order: it by no means follows from there being present a discourse in favour of generic skills that such skills are actually available.

So far, then, as our emerging general schema is concerned, our view of 'generic skills' is straightforward: we are agnostic on the matter. We do not feel drawn to offer a view, and for two reasons. On the one hand, there remains insufficient evidence as to the existence of generic skills. On inspection, so-called generic skills turn out to be heavily context-dependent. For example, what it is to communicate effectively – 'communication skills' – in one profession may be entirely different in another profession. Indeed, forms of communication may be counter-opposed to each other in that they are mutually exclusive in the same setting (compare political communication; communication in the operating theatre; communication in the primary school; communication by a church leader in a religious controversy).

On the other hand, driving forward an agenda of 'generic skills' may even be counter-productive, for such an agenda may diminish the possibilities of imaginatively creating curricula that are going to be likely to engender the kinds of human being appropriate to the twenty-first century. A limited number of generic skills are likely to be identified which, in turn, come unduly to constrain both curricula and the resulting student experiences.

This discussion, therefore, confirms us in our emerging view that the framing of any one curriculum should contain the properties of fluidity, interrelationships between elements and a sensitivity to the inner complexity of any one domain. These properties are to be found in the Bennett, Dunne and Carré schema and, to that extent, it is a helpful offering. But the separation of 'disciplinary content' from 'disciplinary skills', the emphasis that it gives to the workplace, and the assumptions that it makes about 'generic skills' are all problematic. Instead, we urge a more parsimonious approach. After all, if a schema is going to have any chance of being applicable to subjects, institutions and course aims across a diverse mass higher education system, any undue multiplication of elements will be bound to give rise to hostages to fortune. While there is much more to be said about each of the elements in our emerging triad – of knowing, acting and being – we suggest that it has both a *prima facie* robustness and a universality that may just enable it to survive, at least in our explorations that lie ahead.

Curriculum as engagement

In Chapter 2, we surveyed a number of contemporary and recent conceptions of curriculum. However, those several ideas are by no means exhaustive and we want to introduce an idea of curriculum that we shall pursue through this book, an idea of curriculum as engagement. We believe that curriculum as engagement offers an idea that may do justice to the challenges we have been sketching out. We can best show how this might be the case by tracing the idea through the three moments – or building blocks – of knowing, acting and being, which we have already introduced.

Knowing

We want deliberately to talk of knowing as distinct from knowledge for three reasons. *First*, we want to insert into curriculum construction a sense that knowledge has an active, indeed, dynamic component; knowledge is never static but, in the western tradition at least, is always in a state of flux. *Second*, that state of flux comes about partly because knowledge is socially developed. It comes about through hard effort, as a result of human minds being placed into contact with one another and through the ensuing interchange. There is a necessarily human, indeed collaborative, element to knowledge: there can be no knowledge unless minds are engaged with each other in acts of knowing (Vygotsky 1978; Bakhtin 1981).

Third, an act of knowing is just that: an act. It calls for will, an act of identity and a claim to ownership. An act of knowing is, therefore, a particularly personal act: in claiming to know, individuals mark themselves out, project themselves, and claim themselves to be here rather than there. An act of knowing is a positional and personal act. *Further*, an act of knowing calls for a determination to engage with – in Popper's terminology – a Third World of ideas that have been publicly attested and stand, thereby, external to the human mind (Popper 1975). Again, therefore, an act of knowing calls for a public act in which the individual shows herself, proclaims herself, to stand in such and such a place.

These human – personal and social – characteristics of knowledge have in the past, we believe, all too often been overlooked by those who construct curricula. Instead, knowledge in university curricula has come to be conceived, we suggest, as consisting of a corpus – of ideas, proposition, theories, concepts – that stand outside students. In this conception of curriculum, a curriculum is simply understood as a syllabus; it is nothing other than a syllabus. This is a *shopping list* conception of curriculum, a view that the spelling out of a curriculum is nothing else than the listing of its essential knowledge contents. On this view, accordingly, the student's task is to understand and assimilate the corpus. (This has not always been the case: the idea of Bildung, for example, reflects a sense that a genuine inquiry after knowledge can impart human virtues, and that ultimately epistemology and culture coincide (Løvlie et al. 2003).)

It is sometimes fashionable, especially for those who wish to emphasize that knowledge is constructed rather than fixed, to talk of 'constructivism' or even 'social constructivism' and/or 'epistemological constructivism'. Others may point up pedagogical implications that flow from such considerations, invoking ideas and approaches such as 'experiential learning', 'problem-based learning', 'reflective practice', 'clinical reasoning' and 'learning communities'. Talk of ideas and approaches such as these are presumably intended to convey a sense of knowledge as having a pragmatic element, finding its anchor in 'situated learning', in real-life situations. Yet others may wish to urge that higher education has been overly interested in formal – Mode 1 – knowledge and has been insufficiently concerned with forms of knowledge production that arise through the solving of problems in action: such Mode 2 knowledge should, the argument may run, be therefore finding its way overtly into the curriculum (Nowotny et al. 2001).

We are in sympathy with all of these viewpoints. However, to launch off down any of those routes now runs the risk of missing the key point that we want to make at this juncture; namely that a proper understanding of the relationship between student and 'knowledge', at least in the context of higher education, has to be one of personal engagement. A 'knowing' is necessarily a personal knowing: *knowing* is a personal relationship between the person and the intellectual field in question. Such personal engagement can often be enhanced through collaborative endeavours, through collaborative engagement by students acting and working together. That collective engagement may be valuable in its own right but is ultimately justifiable through the personal development that it sponsors.

We use the term 'personal' deliberately for it is the student as a person that has to do the engaging. Whether some forms of knowledge might prompt such 'engagement' more than others, whether some pedagogies might encourage 'engagement' more than others, and whether such engagement might be understood as a form of 'construction' (whether of the components of the knowing or even of the student's 'self'), is immaterial here. What matters ultimately is the sense of immediate personal encounter and of an individual wrestling and interlocking with the material at hand – that material, the knowledge corpus, being itself always in flux.

Acting

In many countries, for around half a century or more, degree courses have contained elements in which students have been put into work-related situations. Not just so-called 'sandwich' courses, in which students primarily following science and technology courses would spend significant periods of time on placements in industry, but also an increasing range of courses in languages, in fields of professional education (related both to well-established and to newer emerging professions) and other more specifically academic fields (such as anthropology, archaeology and history), call upon their students to experience situations of *practice* of varying kinds. Increasingly, universities are inviting students to embed themselves in activities in the community. Such activities may offer opportunities to students to apply their growing knowledge and understanding (for example, in supporting teachers in local schools).

Action, therefore, is and has been a definite component of undergraduate programmes of study. But action isn't confined to such instances of overt and public engagement; it is also to be found *in situ* in the classroom, the laboratory and the art and design studio. But, equally importantly, it is also evident in the student's engagements at the computer, whether drafting an essay or working on a computer-assisted design. Each discipline or field of knowing has its own practices, which call for skills that the student is expected to develop.

Action, we may therefore observe, is not just a commonplace element of degree courses but is a *necessary* component of them. It is not possible to acquire critical thought and understanding without also acting in some sense. Such action may be overt – as in the performing arts or in the medical and health professions – but it may also be more hidden and more distinctly a purely personal matter, as where the student is acquiring the skills intimately associated with a discipline itself. Even there, however, the more personal character of the student working by herself on a task or assignment in a strictly academic setting can be misleading, for in developing the skills embedded in a form of knowing (computational, argumentative, analytical, and so on) she is also learning how to engage within that form of knowing and to take on the identity of what it is to be a mathematician, a philosopher or a historian. She is acquiring the deep grammar of a discipline and so comes not just to think in such terms (as a mathematician, philosopher or historian) but comes to *be* such a person.

Critical knowing and understanding, therefore, calls not just for action on the part of the student, but action in which the student is engaged. In acting out the practices of a discipline, the student has to become the author of her own actions. Of course, quite often, in order to get started, those actions are modelled on the actions of others that the student sees around her: it may be those of her tutors, the laboratory technician, the expert professional in a clinical situation or even other students. Sooner or later, however, that modelling has to give way to an authentic and first-hand action that bears the student's own stamp. Her arguments, her computer models, her problem solutions, her analyses of compounds or her case histories of patients have to be hers.

'Acting' is a curiously ambiguous term (in the English language) for it not only implies an entering into a persona, an identity, and an engagement with that identity, but also that the identity is not fully taken on. It is *mere* acting; a matter of bad faith. The role – of chemist, mathematician, doctor, historian – can be taken on and put aside at will. But what is surely unquestionable is that the acting out of the role, if it is to be convincing and successful, calls upon the student to impart her own energy and commitment to the role; in short, to engage with it.

It follows that, in the framing of curricula in higher education, knowledge cannot provide a sufficient framework in itself. Space has to be accorded to the students to acquire the practical grammar of the disciplines so that they can take on and act out in a first-hand way their intellectual and professional roles. But it follows, too, that the idea of 'skills' in the framing of curricula needs to be deployed with circumspection, for at least two reasons. First, a focus on skills as such can neglect the personal involvement that should accompany their display. To put it more formally, it is to overlook the point that a proper deployment of skills calls for agency on the part of the individual concerned (Archer 2000). Skills, properly understood and developed, require students to acquire at the same time a sense of appropriateness, of context, of respect for persons, of their own selves, of roles and responsibilities and of rightness. In short, the proper performance of skills is part of acting, and action of a good and right kind (cf. MacIntyre 1985; Dunne 1993).

It may be said, of course, that this is what is intended by talk of 'skills' and by calls for skills to play a fuller part in curricula. But if so, it plays no helpful service in running all such ideas together under the single term 'skills'. One may have developed a skill to the highest level, but a situation may be such that its best expression may lie in its being kept hidden or entirely in check or simply unused (for example, determining not to conduct an operation on a patient with cancer). Correspondingly, an individual may be an expert communicator in one setting and may seek to deploy those skills in another setting, oblivious to the contrasting cultural assumptions at work or to the different roles and responsibilities that might be present. One's tone, one's voice and one's putting points as if one was in a certain position may all be counter-productive. In other words, we need to distinguish between skills and their expression.

If we are labouring these points, it is because we believe that the contemporary drive to urge curricula in higher education more in the direction of skills, while laudable in some senses, is running the risk of falling well short of its target. The result may be a 'performativity' in which skills are shorn of reflection, due care and empathy for the particularity of the situations in which they might be expressed.

Being

We are saying two things. *First,* knowledge and skills are both important building blocks of curricula in higher education, but they are each in danger of being interpreted narrowly: knowledge has properly to be understood as an active 'knowing' and skills have to be understood as having their place within a wider zone of willed action and acting, in which the student has and takes responsibility for the way in which his or her skills are realized. *Second,* important as they are, knowing and acting, even when combined together cannot provide a sufficiently firm set of building blocks for higher education curricula. To these two, a third needs to be added – that of *being.*

We can make our argument most tellingly perhaps by returning to the notion of uncertainty. If we live in a world of uncertainty, a world in which all of one's assumptions are liable to be called into question at any time, a world in which all bets are off (Chapter 3), it follows that neither knowledge nor skills (however generously interpreted) are going to provide students with sufficient wherewithal to enable them to flourish in the world. In such a world, after all, one's knowledge is liable to turn out to be inadequate for a sufficient understanding and one's skills are liable to have no point of application (for the world in which one finds oneself may not offer situations in which those skills have application; the world may have moved on).

We need, therefore, a third set of building blocks and here we resort, unashamedly, to a language that is barely heard in higher education (cf. Mills 2002). It is a language of 'self' and of 'being' and 'becoming'. Other terms such as 'capability', 'self-realization', 'self-confidence', 'self-understanding' and even 'self-reliance' also come into play. It is a language that speaks to a student's developing inner self; a self that has to be developed if students are going to acquire durable capacities for flourishing in a world that is, to a significant degree, unknowable.

There may be several reactions to such a set of propositions. *First,* it may be felt that there is no constituency for such a viewpoint and no evidence that such an orientation in thinking about curricula in higher education is necessary. *Second,* this is far too woolly a language and cluster of ideas to gain any kind of robust understanding and interpretation across academic disciplines.

Accordingly, it is distant from academics' characteristic understanding of what they might be trying to do as lecturers and teachers. *Third*, and by extension, it might also be said to be entirely divorced from academics' understanding of themselves as researchers and scholars, and if they would never use such a vocabulary to depict themselves and their academic activities, how could it ever become a vocabulary that might help to frame the curricula that they are going to put in the way of their students? There is simply, therefore, no constituency for such a language as a way of understanding and taking forward curricula. *Last*, even if there were such a constituency, there is no way of 'operationalizing' such a vocabulary: just what could it mean to inject such thinking about *being* into curriculum design such that it could come to form a third building block (alongside knowing and acting)?.

These are formidable arguments but their character, it will be noticed, lies to a large extent not in their contesting our proposed third building block as such but in pointing to the reactions that the proposal is likely to induce. A language of *being*, a language that attempts to do justice to the inner lives of students, may indeed not find an overwhelmingly positive response, especially among academics in certain disciplines, but that does nothing to dent the idea in itself.

There was one argument of a different kind: the argument to the effect that it is difficult if not impossible to operationalize such a language in the design and bringing off of curricula in higher education. We shall try to show in this book that we disagree with this argument, but it is worth here, perhaps, saying a little about why we disagree. Even if the language is unfamiliar, the dimension of academic life that it is trying to capture is surely not unfamiliar. Many academics, perhaps across all disciplines, are familiar with students – and even their parents – saying on graduation days, or perhaps in a letter some years later, that their higher education experience changed them as 'persons' and even 'transformed' them. Academics, too, can be heard to talk, perhaps in unguarded moments, about their 'love' for their subjects (cf. Rowland forthcoming). Students can be seen in surveys to indicate that high in their evaluative criteria of 'good teachers' is an ability to enthuse them and clear signs that the lecturers themselves are 'enthusiastic' about their own subject. Such reflections are indicative surely that there is at least the makings of common sentiments in the academic community – across both lecturers and their students – that the inner life, the being of individuals, is an important element in the constitution of successful flourishing within higher education.

It may be that such a language has not yet found its way in any significant measure into course handbooks or institutional learning and teaching strategies or national 'benchmarking' statements of the collective aims of different disciplines in higher education, but it by no means follows that the dimension of learning to which this language points is missing from curricula in higher education. Indeed, as we shall see, it is evident in daily curricular practices. It is even present embryonically in the language of many employers who are increasingly talking of the qualities that they are looking for in their graduate recruits (for example, in a term such as '*self*-reliance'). Operationalizing such a vocabulary in curriculum design may, therefore, turn out to be less a matter of inserting an entirely new dimension than in making explicit and developing a dimension of curricula that is already present, if only latently in the tacit values of academic staff.

Conclusion

Arising out of both our reflections in this chapter and in the preceding chapters of Part 1, we offer two propositions. *First*, the academic community at all levels should take seriously the matter of 'curriculum' as such. The total set of experiences with which the student is expected to engage, and the environment that is likely to make those experiences come about, has to be given thought anew. That 'has' is as much descriptive as it is prescriptive: it emerges out of our analyses so far. The world of uncertainty that the twenty-first century presents is one of perpetual challenge, which is present in all manner of dimensions of personal, professional and social life. What it is to offer a well-founded curriculum under those conditions is itself both uncertain and challenging and is a world not yet much in view in curriculum design.

Second, even amid a mass higher education system replete with considerable variety across institutions, courses and students, we suggest that there are three essential and common building blocks of every single curriculum; blocks built around 'knowing', 'acting' and 'being'. As we have urged though, the idea of building blocks has to be understood metaphorically. Knowing, acting and being are building blocks precisely in the sense that no curriculum can be complete without all three being present and subject to separate consideration. But they are not building blocks if by that is meant that the three dimensions have to be separately present to the student. The actual relationships between these three blocks of knowing, acting and being has to be the major issue in front of us in the next part of this book. To what degree might these three dimensions be separate or integrated? If they are separate in some sense, what does that separateness consist of? Is it even perhaps an antagonistic relationship? This is not to say that a total integration of elements, even if that was possible, is desirable. It just may turn out that some degree of separateness and tension is actually conducive to the framing of effective curricula in the contemporary age.

With these two sets of reflections, then – as to the desirability of attending to the framing of curricula and as to the possibility of there being a set of (three) dimensions common to all curricula – we turn to gaining a sense of what interpretations are currently being given to these dimensions in higher education in the UK.

Part 2
Signs of Curriculum Life

5

A schema

Understanding curricula, communicating curricula

We are not by any means the first to attempt to pin down the concept of the curriculum. Indeed, as we saw previously, the field of curriculum studies has been a productive subspecialist area within education for many years. Yet curriculum studies has been more commonly associated with compulsory education and tends to focus on the school curriculum. This may not be too surprising, as the compulsory education system in most countries is part of the basic education system and much more influenced by external demands than post-compulsory education, and as such lends itself to greater outside scrutiny.

The higher education curriculum is altogether different. There have been a few studies of the undergraduate curriculum in UK higher education, perhaps more notable through their scarcity than their influence. Squires (1987) suggested that the limited number of investigations into curricula at this level may in part be due to 'the fissiparous nature of academic institutions' (Squires 1987: 129). The specialization of academic fields of knowledge has resulted in what might be considered to be a lack of communication about curricular matters across the disciplines. So although particular course teams may be able to speak confidently with each other about the content of their curricula, there is little discussion across course teams from different knowledge fields about the aims, purposes and content of curricula. Even within the same institutions – perhaps the same faculties – the curricular issues of one area of academic specialization could be unknown to colleagues from a different area. These reflections seem to suggest that there are few common bonds across curricula, and that academic specialists may not be expected to speak across their specialist areas. If this were to be true, we would be hard-pressed to propose a framework for curricula that transcends disciplinary boundaries.

How then do we understand the curriculum and communicate curricular issues across the knowledge fields? In Chapters 3 and 4 we began to propose a general framework by suggesting three domains which could form the basis of a discussion about curricula. The three domains of knowing, acting and being can provide a frame through which to understand and communicate different patterns of curricula across disciplines, courses and curricula. This framework for curricula that we are proposing recognizes that curricula have distinctive but integrated components, as well as allowing for different weightings of each domain within any one curriculum. We can represent this general framework as shown in Figure 5.1 (in which 'C' stands for curriculum).

The schema we are proposing here may not seem entirely unique; indeed, there are echoes of this framework elsewhere. We shall examine this framework in the light of some of the current work in the general area of curriculum development in UK higher education, but first we would like to develop and elaborate our schema. Our research on changing patterns of curricula will form the basis of these proposals, with examples drawn from the fieldwork we conducted.

Our research focused on five subject areas: history, chemistry, electronic engineering, nursing studies, business studies. These subject areas were studied in six institutions, selected as examples of institutions with diverse missions and because they offered undergraduate degree programmes in four of the five chosen subject areas. Interviews were conducted with academics responsible for or who participated in the design of courses for these programmes and curriculum materials were collected. This schema was developed in order to enable us to begin to understand and identify the main components of contemporary curricula, or the 'curriculum-as-designed', and the different patterns of curricula across subject areas and institutions. In this chapter, we shall use this schema to suggest that distinct patterns of curricula are possible across the general subject areas of the arts and humanities, the sciences and the professional subject areas, drawing on examples of institutional differences where appropriate.

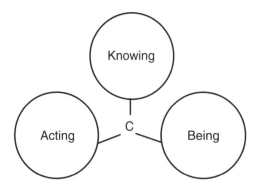

Figure 5.1   General schema

The dynamic curriculum

Given that any diagrammatic representation might lend itself to an inter-pretation of a fixed or static frame of reference, it is important to recall our view that curricular change is dynamic and fluid. Any curriculum will be developed within its particular milieu, or the social, cultural and physical environment in which it is located. There are thus a range of influences on curricula that shape and drive patterns of change, and these influences are embedded across a number of dimensions. We can identify nine *zones of influence* that may be seen to act upon patterns of curricular change (Barnett 2000a):

1 internal and external to the academic community
2 epistemological, practical and ontological
3 criteria of truth and performance
4 managerial, academic and market orientations
5 local, national and global focuses
6 past, present and future orientations
7 context specific and context generic
8 endorsing and critical orientations
9 reflexivity and the promotion of self.

These zones of influence cut across each other, so that curricula represent a mixture of any number of these elements. Furthermore, these influences are not exerting equal pressures. Some elements take on a new significance at different points in time. Past orientations can at certain times become the preoccupation of public debate, influencing curricular design so that it incorporates those elements that have historically been considered import-ant. In times of rapid change, there are often arguments in favour of return-ing to modes of curricula that were valued in the past. Bernstein, for example, has identified the 'nostalgic' curriculum, or the formation of 'retrospective pedagogic identities' (Ball 1995; Edwards 2002) as an attempt to retain or revisit previous orientations. Other zones of influence may come into view in response to particular developments. Concerns with global issues may be foregrounded over local issues when the numbers of international students on a course increases, for example.

These dimensions may also work against each other, thereby creating ten-sions within curricula. The global and local dimension can exemplify this tension, particularly in relation to a key driver of curricular change, namely the student market. When asked about the factors that influence curricular change, it was not uncommon for academics to provide examples of shifting student markets. These could entail a shift towards greater international recruitment, or alternatively, as a nursing studies lecturer told us, towards local student markets. As she said:

> *Recruitment is down, and we are making a play at the moment on recruiting more locally, recruiting more mature women for example, but also men, who have gone through access to higher education courses locally.*

If the market shifts substantially, there may be tensions as to how changes can be incorporated within curricula to respond best to students' expectations. International students, for example, may have quite different perspectives and concerns from students who are recruited locally. The market itself has made a substantial impact on higher education, with concomitant changes in curricula. Consider, for example, the change that institutions experienced when the market dimension was encouraged, as one academic described to us:

> *The place grew from being very small – around 3,000 FTEs [full-time equivalent students] in the early 80s to now probably 12,000 FTEs or 20,000 students . . . somebody described it as 'seismic'. . . . It was left to departments that wanted to grow. It's free market economy stuff, isn't it, really 80s philosophy.*

In just two decades, this university tripled its student intake in a period of rapid expansion that many institutions will have experienced. Curricula across this university will have changed substantially in response, as course programmes strive to meet the demands of its new student markets. Adapting a model from Clark (1983) intended to indicate the relationship between higher education with the state and the market, we would suggest that the market increasingly has influence, as shown in Figure 5.2.

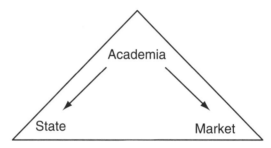

Figure 5.2   Changing curricula: relationships between academia, the state and the market (adapted from Clark 1983)

The second of the nine dimensions identified above – epistemological, ontological and practical – reflects not only a range of implicit pressures on curricula, but also distinguishes between three domains that are fundamental to the schema we are proposing for curricula in higher education. These dimensions echo the domains of knowledge, self and action through which we will now describe possible patterns of curricula across several subject areas. Through the identification of these domains, we can begin to describe and communicate the constituent elements of curricula.

Frameworks for curricula
Arts and humanities

We turn first to curricula in the general subject areas of the arts and humanities. The schema can be represented as shown in Figure 5.3.

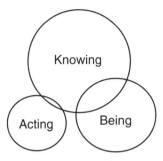

Figure 5.3   Curricula in arts and humanities subjects

In the arts and humanities, as the schema suggests, the knowledge domain forms a dominant component of the curriculum. What can also be seen is that the action domain is, as of yet, a smaller component that tends not to be well integrated with either the knowledge or self domains. The self domain does have a significant role within curricula in these subject areas and is integrated to a certain extent with the knowledge domain. We can illustrate what this schema represents through a few examples from our research.

The knowledge domain usually forms a large and important element of any set of curricula and may be the component most frequently discussed by those who design curricula. By describing it here as a main component of arts and humanities curricula, we are recognizing that curricula in these subject areas are often designed first and foremost by the knowledge content that is deemed necessary to transmit to students. Some lecturers in history, for instance, may offer virtually the same content within a course for many years: in these cases the knowledge of the discipline may remain fairly stable over a period of time. A course surveying Europe during the Renaissance may have been based on much the same reading list for quite some time; or a course on moral philosophy may remain largely unchanged.

Yet this is not to ignore the dynamic nature of the wider epistemological changes that exert pressures and shape the knowledge domain. In the 1970s, for instance, feminist academics began to argue for a re-examination of history in order to uncover women's roles in society at particular points in the past (for example, Scott 1991). This epistemological shift had a significant impact on the curriculum: the knowledge of history deemed to be legitimate began to be reconstructed from a new perspective that incorporated knowledge of women's contributions to society. As De Groot and Maynard (1993) suggest, the knowledge content of curricula changed in response to such interventions as women's history first of all with 'recuperative' actions;

challenging the silencing, stereotyping, marginalization and misrepresenta-
tion of women which was prevalent in academic knowledge. Second, these
changes were reconstructive: feminist scholarship attempted to review and
revise the methods and content of the established disciplines. More generally, the present and past orientations of curricula intersected in order
dynamically to reshape the knowledge domain, as the more recent concerns
of historians specializing in women's history enabled new understandings of
the past to be constructed.

We encountered numerous examples of such changes in the knowledge
component of curricula in different subject areas when speaking with academics. The knowledge fields of the arts and humanities subjects are fluid; a
landscape reflecting the hinterland of shifting epistemologies across academic communities, institutions, professions, the corporate sector, student
markets and state agencies. Yet in spite of these dynamics, the knowledge
content of curricula can often appear overbearing and heavy-handed,
reflected in the concern we often encountered with the 'overcrowded curriculum'. As new knowledge is added to the syllabus, the knowledge content
deemed necessary for students becomes greater.

To return to our previous example, the new epistemologies of women's
history are often added into the curriculum rather than prompting an overall reconstruction of the entire history curriculum. New books by women
historians are included within an ever-expanding list of key history texts. The
knowledge component of curricula is therefore often perceived to be more
stable and unyielding than it perhaps needs to be. The temptation for many
course designers seems to be to continue adding new knowledge to the
curriculum, rather than slimming down or reconstructing curricula.

The self domain is also a dynamic component of the arts and humanities
curricula. Our interviews with historians indicated that history students are
commonly socialized into academic identities or ways of being that have
strong values related to scholarship. Some historians saw this curriculum
identity of historians as a self domain that encompassed notions going beyond
academic rigour and a critical orientation towards notions of citizenship.
Furthermore, these values were seen to be enduring, in that many history
graduates have been expected to undergo the same socialization processes
over several decades. Again, there can be a type of nostalgic perspective that
stabilizes the self domain, as one historian in an old university made clear:

> *I feel I must say that the sort of training we gave students twenty years ago is still
> as valid today as it was then. I can't see what's changed. I may be wrong but . . .
> is it so different today?*

This sentiment is also bound up in perspectives on the action domain, which
in a similar way can be perceived as being stable even during times of great
change. The scholarly rigour and the abilities to evaluate evidence critically
and to construct an argument based on reason: these actions are deemed as
important to history curricula today as they were perhaps 20 years ago.
Today these actions are more likely to be identified as key skills, but there is

arguably a strong nostalgia within the subject of history for valuing the orientations of the past history curriculum in the face of external pressures to change.

Yet external pressures cannot be ignored. The history student who learns to 'do' history in a traditional manner may, for example, be required to perform certain actions such as conducting archival research. This particular action has long been a component of history degrees, yet also has a dynamic aspect as technological advances make different types of historical searches possible. Within the history courses we studied, modules such as 'Computers in History' were being incorporated into some courses. The act of 'doing' history is changing through the wider practical influences of technological advances. Again, this may have an institutional dimension at work in that some history lecturers and their institutions are making available the technologies that enable these innovations to a greater extent than others.

There may also be an institutional dimension in that the cultures of different types of universities either hinder or enable the dynamic relationships between the self and action domains. The traditional academic values described above are under pressure from the wider debates around higher education's relationship to the economy. While in general the self and action domains in history are influenced by debates about transferable skills and preparation for work, in some institutions this is shaping curricula to a particular extent. Some of the newer universities, for example, may have lecturers with more sympathy for the inclusion of transferable skills – however they may be defined – within their curricula. In other institutions, traditional academic values still strongly shape the self and action domains, fixing the notions of what it means to be and act like an historian within curricula.

Sciences and technologies

The sciences and technologies subjects offer a pattern of curricula as shown in Figure 5.4.

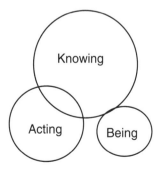

Figure 5.4 Curricula in sciences and technology subjects

This schema illustrates the dominance, once again, of the knowledge domain in curricula. Yet the striking difference between this schema and the proposed arts and humanities schema are the sizes and the extent of integration of the action and self domains. Here we are suggesting that the action domain is a larger component of the curriculum, with a smaller self domain that does not integrate to a great extent with the knowledge domain. We can examine these different patterns through illustrative examples.

The action domain in subjects such as chemistry is a significant component of the curriculum and is continually reshaped to integrate new modes of practice. Chemistry students may spend a large proportion of their studies working in laboratories, for example, and the equipment within these laboratories may change each year depending on the resources of the university. However, the action domain that students encounter within chemistry curricula is widening in response to employment practices external to the university. Industry is a rapidly changing context, not just in terms of advances in technologies – although these are significant – but also through the expectations of employers. Again, there may be an institutional dimension in the extent to which the university engages with industry or is willing to engage, especially in relation to curricular change.

The employment market for graduates in chemistry is a factor worthy of attention here. Our interviews with chemists indicated that the security of research jobs in industry has weakened, and in response the chemistry curriculum has incorporated new skills. Some of the chemistry lecturers we interviewed acknowledged the pressures to inculcate certain types of transferable skills in order to enable chemistry graduates to enter a broader employment market. For example, communication skills may be required through the assessment of student presentations. As one chemist noted:

> *[Skills that] previously students would have picked up by 'extra-mural absorption', such as report writing, information technology and scientific communication, are now intrinsic parts of the curriculum.*

These different forms of action are a response to the wider shifts in the economy that have been reflected in employability concerns in chemistry curricula. The action domain of the curriculum is taking on new modes of practice that may enable students to graduate with a broader range of specified capabilities than before, even if they are not epistemologically related to the field of chemistry as such.

In many of the science fields, changes in the knowledge domain are also rapid and explicit. Advances in technology and industrial research often result in major curricular change. Some of the science lecturers we interviewed spoke about new courses that rapidly became obsolete as scientific advances were made. Changes in the knowledge content of courses, however, may be influenced by factors within the education system. In chemistry, for example, some lecturers described how they began to offer courses in mathematics when their student population arrived at university without the mathematical knowledge that acts as a foundation to chemistry.

The interviews with chemists notably raised concerns about the overcrowded curriculum, as advances in knowledge seemed to some as requiring additions to curricula content. As one chemistry lecturer explained: ·

> *In most chemistry departments, we are so busy pouring things down people's throats that we never consider how long it takes for them to absorb them or whether they need to find out how to apply the facts. It is not only an ongoing debate, the overcrowded curriculum is something that has become a desperate concern. They have been pushing more and more in and taking less and less out. The point about it is that the average chemist would say there is no half measure – you have to know it all – which is nonsense. And furthermore, it is getting to the stage where there is so much to know that there is no possible way of knowing it.*

Here, an over-emphasis on the knowledge domain in chemistry curricula is apparent. There are two questions we might ask about this dependence on the knowledge domain. First, as the lecturer points out, is it necessary or helpful to view the knowledge content of curricula as fixed, to the extent that content can only be added and not removed? Second, does the continual increase in the knowledge domain eventually crowd out the action and self domains? Here we would suggest that our schema could be helpful, first for considering whether it is knowledge as such that the curricula should be imparting, or instead a more active 'knowing'. Furthermore, even beyond an active knowing, the self and action domains could be brought more explicitly into view in the shaping of curriculum. We can pursue these lines of thought in our final example of how a curriculum schema might look in the professional subject areas.

Professional subjects

The professional subject areas may offer the following curriculum pattern, as shown in Figure 5.5.

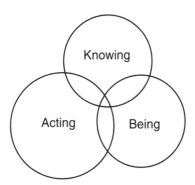

Figure 5.5   Curricula in professional subjects

The knowledge domain in the above schema is given less prominence, as the professional subject areas tend to be externally oriented and their curricula often significantly reflect the professions that they represent, rather than changing concerns within the academic disciplines. Even so, there are similarities in the changes in the knowledge domain with the other subject areas we have discussed. The content of the business studies curriculum may be changed, for example, through new developments in sociology or economics. However, although curricula in the professional subjects are often derived from a range of relevant subject areas, there is also a strong orientation in curricula towards the practical, external demands of the professions.

In the professional subject areas, the action domain is a substantial component of curricula. Business studies students, for example, are increasingly asked to perform the types of action that will be necessary in their employment. They may act out role play scenarios as managers, or work on problems of management through case studies from business. The action domain is also fairly explicit within nursing studies, as students practise the techniques that are required in their profession.

Yet the key factor about curricular patterns in the professional subjects is the integration of the self and action domains. Particularly in nursing studies, one of the subject areas we studied, educational theories on topics such as reflexive practice have been influential. In the nursing studies curriculum, it is common for students to be asked to keep 'learning journals' or diaries, or reflective log books in which they are required to reflect on their learning and professional development. As students advance through their course, their sense of self is shaped by this component of curricula, as they take on new professional identities and begin to reflect upon their practices.

The example of nursing studies in particular offers an insight into the ways in which the self, action and knowledge domains can be integrated in the curriculum. Each domain plays an important role, and yet the domains can also be integrated with each other in the development of new modes of being for the student. This sense of integration is emphasized in the following statement from a nursing studies lecturer:

> *I would say that what makes a graduate practitioner a graduate practitioner is the ability to be able to be critical about what they are doing, to be able to evaluate that and to be able to move on that evaluation. And to be able to do that they have to have the knowledge-base to support it and the skills to do it with.*

The above quote offers a role for each domain: the propositional knowledge that is crucial for the nurse practitioner; the ability to incorporate that knowledge into practice; and the capacity for critical self-reflection and self-development through their knowledge and actions. The close integration of these three domains provides the possibilities for being, acting and knowing that together bring new student subjectivities to the curriculum.

In the examples from our research into the professional subject areas, we found many instances where the students were asked to undertake activities designed to develop their sense of being a professional, with an underlying knowledge base and associated practical skills. Curricula in the professional subject areas offer an insight into how the domains of knowledge, action and self can be reshaped into a curriculum based on being, acting and knowing. However, this is not to suggest that these subject areas have somehow got it right, and that all curricula in higher education should be patterned after the professional subject areas. Rather, we would contend that curricula with a high degree of integration between being, acting and knowing could offer a degree of depth to the purposes of that curricula.

Conclusion

We have proposed a framework for understanding the main components of curricula and we have seen how these may differ between general subject areas. The different patterns of curricula we have identified are shaped by a variety of drivers, some external to the academic community and others that are internal to academic concerns. We have seen, for example, how the market is becoming a powerful driver of curriculum change. Yet we can also identify changes in academic knowledge that are exerting influence on curriculum.

The above schema are not intended to offer a 'snapshot' of curriculum patterns at a particular point in time. They were developed during our research into contemporary changes in curricula, and we continued to refine the schema beyond the life of that project as we wanted to be able to propose a framework that can be employed to communicate and understand the main components of curricula. They are therefore indicative of certain changes that we have seen occurring across curricula generally.

We chose to develop the above schema around differences between three general subject areas – arts and humanities, sciences and technologies, and the professional subjects – as we felt these offered the most potential for indicating where different patterns might be discerned. This is not to negate the importance of other influences on the shape of curricula, such as institutional influences. The cultures of institutions do vary and we will provide examples in the next chapters of how these too can influence patterns of curriculum development. Epistemologies, which are themselves developing (Eraut 1994; Gibbons et al. 1994), remain for now the dominant influence on curricula, but institutions themselves are becoming strong independent variables.

There is one final point to be made about the proposed schema. To state it simply: we need to consider the extent to which curriculum can be separated from pedagogy. The importance of this point is most visible within the examples given above from the professional subject areas, in that the issues raised through the reshaping of curricula into the modes of being, acting and knowing become closely intertwined with teaching strategies. Where does the development of the curriculum end and pedagogical strategies begin? We would suggest that there is a challenge for all curriculum designers in answering this question. We can keep this question in view as we move on to examine further some examples from the contemporary context of curriculum development in higher education.

6

Knowing

Knowledge and the university

Knowledge has the power to transform lives. To acquire knowledge in most societies is to become a full member of that society, and to acquire higher levels of knowledge is to become capable of shaping, changing and even leading society. Especially within a knowledge society, the attainment of knowledge is a significant process. That knowledge is power leads to knowledge being simultaneously coveted, guarded, feared and celebrated. Perhaps it should not be surprising that access to knowledge has historically been restricted, and the regulation of access to specialized knowledge has been a powerful exercise within the ordering of society.

Knowledge has been central to the purposes of university education for as long as universities have existed. To enter university as a student is broadly assumed by many to be a means of acquiring knowledge, often a highly specialized form of knowledge. Although it may at times seem otherwise, universities across the world have been relatively slow to open up their doors unconditionally to all members of society in order to give access to that knowledge.

Universities may be part of society, but they have often been perceived as somehow standing apart from it, casting a critical eye over the outside world or generating forms of knowledge seemingly unrelated to the commonsense knowledge of life. The distinction between academic knowledge and 'real world' knowledge may be familiar, but we can see resistance to it. The production of knowledge unrelated to the concerns of the world outside the universities was a key factor in the traditional autonomy of universities. Without distractions or influences from beyond the confines of the campus, academics and students could be free to pursue knowledge that challenged the *status quo* or provided alternative ways of thinking. However, this academic freedom was the privilege of a select few whose efforts may rarely have benefited anyone not admitted to their ranks. Partly in response to this exclusivity, there has been a gradual loss of autonomy to generate purely academic knowledge as the higher education system increasingly meets demands of accountability and usefulness.

This notion of useful knowledge as distinct from academic knowledge is an important aspect of changes in knowledge production. The general trends in the ways that knowledge production is changing have been identified in terms of performativity (Lyotard 1984) and problem solving *in situ* (Gibbons et al. 1994). Broadly speaking, in the 'knowledge society', knowledge production is no longer confined to the universities. In order to compete with other knowledge producers, the universities must generate knowledge that is useful, practical and immediately applicable to the economy and industry. This is part of the new knowledge economy, in which the economic competitiveness of society is strengthened through continually better means of producing useful knowledge. As Lyotard (1984) suggests, the main criterion of academic knowledge is no longer 'is it true?' but 'what use is it?'

Changing knowledge

As what it means to be in pursuit of academic knowledge is changing, it is worth asking questions about this most fundamental aspect of higher education. Perhaps the disinterested pursuit of reason and knowledge has always existed side by side with the need to produce people who could fill particular roles in society. In other words, the tension between academic knowledge and what might be considered to be more practical professional education – particularly for the elite professions – has a long history. If universities have historically been functioning as producers of useful, practical knowledge, what is different for students today as they embark on a university education? There are several broad generalizations about academic knowledge that we can identify.

Knowledge production has changed with regard to the shifting relationships between the teaching and research functions of universities. An historical legacy is the Humboldtian ideal of the university, often described as one in which research and teaching are intertwined as students and teachers joined in a pursuit of knowledge through a spirit of inquiry. The highest form of scholarship was then the pursuit of knowledge without the imperative to apply this knowledge to practical applications. This ideal form of scholarship is distinct in the suggestion that there is inherent value in the pursuit of knowledge in and of itself. The implicit code of knowledge production here was one of truth and *purity*.

In some of the oldest universities, we can see how this form of scholarship has been highly valued. The tutorial system at Oxford University, for example, was based on meetings between the tutors and one or two of their students for discussions about the topics on the curriculum that week (Palfreyman 2001). This form of engagement with academic knowledge was intimate, ritualized, exclusive and idealized. The tutorials arguably also required a particular form of social and cultural capital if students were to succeed within them. Students had to be self-reliant, articulate and resilient.

Yet in a mass higher education system, and within a changing society, the small and intimate tutorials seem to many to be increasingly untenable. Student numbers are greater, the diversity of students has increased, and their motivations for undertaking higher education are changing. So although there may be aspects of the traditional tutorial system that one might wish to keep – such as an intense engagement in the pursuit of knowledge – there are other aspects of it that are difficult to maintain in a contemporary higher education system.

As academic knowledge becomes more available to wider sections of the population, it becomes more difficult to maintain its exclusivity. The knowledge that is deemed to be legitimate in academic contexts must also become legitimate to more people in order for universities to continue. Although previously the academic communities could decide what would be learned and by whom, there is now a more diverse range of students and stakeholders whose interests must be taken into account. The vast range of subject areas offered for study today would be unrecognizable to an Oxbridge don several decades ago.

A reorientation of the boundaries around academic knowledge is reflected in the responsiveness of knowledge production to the needs of industry, government, students and the economy in general. As one engineer said to us about the applied technology courses offered at his institution:

> *The applied technology programmes are more skills based. The whole programme is built around a very focused skill base. It is back to the niche market. It's what the world out there wants at the moment.*

Providing what the world wants is a new and dramatic reshaping of legitimate academic knowledge. Demands for specialist knowledge and skills emerge, and universities now often respond with new course units, new areas of specialism and even new degree programmes. Academic knowledge must now be seen to be more useful and responsive to external interests.

Furthermore, knowledge is increasingly being produced outside the universities themselves, not only in industry but also in private research companies which some universities have established to increase their revenue. Within a knowledge economy, universities inevitably play a lesser role in producing the knowledge used by society. This expansion in the sites of knowledge production is changing the work of academics, many of whom are challenged to find synergies between their research and teaching roles as a result.

These changes in the production of knowledge are related to another trend. As the curriculum becomes more focused on providing students with the employment-related skills deemed necessary for the economy, a question has been raised as to whether these capacities can be taught in teaching-only institutions. This is a current debate within the UK, as the White Paper on the *Future of Higher Education* (DfES 2003) has led to proposals that some institutions can maintain their teaching functions without conducting related research. In a diverse and mass higher education system, institutions will inevitably have different missions and offer distinct contributions to society. We need to question the foundations on which these diverse missions are based.

These proposals envisage a role for academics that is based on teaching and the transmission of knowledge, and not the pursuit of knowledge through research. The relationship between teaching and research and the benefits of teaching informed by research is a complex matter of debate (Brew 2001; Jenkins et al. 2003). At the heart of this debate is the matter as to whether academic knowledge within a *higher* education system needs to be taught by those who are actively contributing to the production of that knowledge. Yet it is also fundamentally a debate about the acquisition of knowledge in universities, or how students come to know their subjects. Are they to acquire knowledge because it has been deemed useful to them and therefore transmitted to them, or will they be engaged in a spirit of inquiry and pursuit of knowledge themselves?

In summary then, we are noting:

- There are long-standing tensions between academic knowledge as useful, practical and applicable, and the pursuit of academic knowledge as being itself inherently valuable.
- Academic knowledge is increasingly responding to external demands, especially in relation to economic and social concerns.
- As universities are no longer the key sites for the production of knowledge, synergies between teaching and research may become difficult to maintain.
- The expansion of higher education systems also raises questions about institutional missions and the role of teaching-only institutions.

Academic knowledge is being transformed. Boundaries between universities and the rest of society are being weakened, access to academic knowledge is becoming less restrictive, and knowledge is more likely to be transmitted in lecture theatres rather than sought in the pursuit of knowledge in intimate tutorials. All these changes are having an impact on curricula.

Selecting knowledge

It is difficult to conceive of a higher education curriculum that does not feature knowledge. Knowledge remains a fundamental building block within curricula. Knowledge has dominated curricula and has often been the first consideration of any curriculum designer.

If we are asked to consider how the curriculum is related to knowledge, we might be tempted to explain it in simple terms. For example, a chemist might say that a student of chemistry must acquire certain types of knowledge. As one of the chemists we interviewed said: '*The average colleague would feel that unless you knew that copper sulphate was blue and silver nitrate was not a green gas you weren't a chemist.'* Much of this knowledge is transmitted in lectures and available in set texts. The teacher of chemistry selects those books that convey this knowledge, lists them on a syllabus, organizes them according to themes with accompanying titles of lectures and presents this curriculum to the students. The curriculum is a means of selecting the knowledge to be acquired, organizing that knowledge and communicating the result to the students.

Yet there can be nothing neutral or fixed about this task. Each curriculum will consist of selections and representations of knowledge that are the result of choices. Curricula in chemistry, for instance, will differ in many respects. Certainly subjects in the humanities have been charged with more subjectivity and bias than subjects in, say, the sciences. We might consider that even in the 'harder' sciences, where boundaries around subject areas are strong, the curriculum is a product of choices and concerns. The chemistry lecturer who believed that all chemists should know that silver nitrate is blue also explained that the Royal Society of Chemistry often promoted the view that 'there is no such thing as a core syllabus' in chemistry.

There are several aspects to the issue of selectivity in the curriculum in relation to knowledge. There are epistemological differences within subject areas, even quite narrow and specialized subject areas, that open up a range of choices to the curriculum designers. For instance, should a history course on medieval Europe be taught chronologically or through major themes? If taught thematically, which themes should be covered and which can be left out? If chronologically, on what basis other than the progression of time might knowledge be presented?

The choices that individual curriculum designers make are often based on their own personal preferences. Academics spend many years acquiring the specialist knowledge that they teach, and possibly many more years contributing to that field. These areas of specialism may be inhabited by a relatively small number of people who may have only a moderate understanding of what is going on in other specialist areas of their disciplines. Even academics teaching on the same degree programmes may not be fully aware of the curricula of the other modules being taught. The way the curriculum can be individualized became clear to us in discussions with the academics in a history department in one university. A lecturer admitted he had little idea of what subjects his colleagues were teaching:

> We did once have a meeting at which everyone described what they did and it was fascinating and we only got round about half the department. We are a bunch of individuals who usually like each other but we don't have a grand plan except for the core course.

So curricula design with respect to the selection of knowledge can be a matter of personal preference. The curriculum designer may be selecting some of the texts that made an impact on her within her studies; for example, the texts that provoked her, challenged her and maybe even changed her as a person. Perhaps the engagement with certain texts can be so transforming that course designers wish to make these possibilities available to their students. Knowledge in the curriculum can be intimately bound up in the ways we see ourselves and the students. It is not just a fixed body 'out there' waiting to be acquired.

The choices that curricular planners make about knowledge content are complex. They are also choices that are exercised with power, as they influence the students' ideas about which books are important and which authors should be respected for contributing the knowledge that constitutes a subject area. At the same time, the choice of texts and authors conveys ideas about who is *not* deemed to be an important contributor to the knowledge of a subject. Academics may be reluctant to make explicit the power inherent in the selection of 'key' texts and the production of a 'canon'.

Academics creating new subject areas, for example, such as those developed on the margins of legitimate academic knowledge – women's studies, black studies or trade union studies – have both resisted and celebrated the selection of knowledge involved in creating curricula. The selection of core texts for new courses is a pronouncement to the students that these authors represent the emergent knowledge field. Curricula are public documents too and so the pronouncement is made beyond the syllabus and to the wider academic world that these books contain the knowledge of a new academic community. On the one hand, the beginnings of a literary canon can be a celebration of new knowledge; on the other, it is a way of identifying who is 'in' and who is 'out'.

Curricula therefore play a part in the shaping of boundaries around knowledge fields. These boundaries are socially constructed through the identification of legitimate academic knowledge. Yet the 'constructedness' of these boundaries should be kept in mind. Becher and Trowler's work (2001), for example, should remind us of the academic tribes that maintain disciplinary boundaries through dialogue with each other. Knowledge selected for the curriculum is part of this dialogue.

The extent to which identities and communities are formed around narrow concepts of specialization is striking. Even within the same areas of specialism, there may be tribes adhering to different epistemological tenets. Sociologists of the family, for instance, have at times been divided between those who conduct quantitative and longitudinal research and those who produce ethnographical accounts of family life. These academics will represent knowledge of the family from quite different perspectives and even engage in disputes with each other. The curriculum is one means in the whole process of creating order, establishing boundaries and reifying the cultures of different academic disciplines. The knowledge that is transmitted to students is anything but neutral, fixed, static and uncontested.

If knowledge selected for curricula is not neutral or uncontested, then we need to keep questioning the basis on which knowlege becomes part of the curriculum. The key issue here is what role the knowledge domain plays within curricula, and whether we might come to different conceptualizations of curriculum design if we better understand the forces at work in shaping the knowledge domain of curricula.

Curricular packages

There are other choices to be made when designing curricula that are based on concerns that are more practical than epistemological, although the two are interrelated. Curricula are designed in institutional settings and the building blocks of curricula must fit within boundaries of time, space and location. These boundaries have been radically transformed in many institutions, reshaping curricula as structures shift and change. We can see this process most clearly through the introduction of modularization. Modular university programmes require knowledge to be presented within a more tightly prescribed length of time, and they are intended to offer greater choice to students. Yet greater choice can complicate notions of student progression in terms of the acquisition of higher levels of knowledge. Many degree programmes have been restructured into modular courses, raising challenges for the design or redesign of curricula by requiring a negotiation between epistemological concerns and practical problems.

These negotiations can be revealing. The decisions that are made about the ordering of knowledge reveal the ways in which knowledge is not only transmitted through curricula but also actively constructed within curricula. For example, a historian spoke with us about the impact of modularization on the history degrees he taught. He explained that this had had unforeseen consequences:

> We have moved away from a more traditional course structure toward unitariza-
> tion or modularization. It became possible, and not uncommon, for students to
> actually manage to take routes through courses that avoided their dealing with
> some major topics at all. Some time ago, this was recognized as being a hole we
> had created through restructuring.

What had happened with the move to modularization was a structuring of curricula into modular 'packages' to be offered to students for selection. The curriculum planners had to redesign their history degrees: no longer could they offer year-long courses that progressively introduced students to the knowledge of the subject, gradually building on it from one year to the next over the course of three years. The knowledge of the subject now had to be offered in bite-size pieces, which called for a new approach to the design of the curriculum.

Recently, there have been signs that some modularized courses are being dismantled in favour of a return to more traditional degree structures. Yet modularization merits some attention as it demands particular ways of selecting and ordering knowledge, and challenges some of the traditional notions of what it means to acquire disciplinary knowledge. The historians who discovered 'holes' in their history degree were not content to allow only partial knowledge of their discipline to be acquired by students. We were told of other difficulties encountered when moving to modular degrees. Some courses were changed from being based on progressive year-long units to shorter modules of just a few months potentially chosen almost at random by students. The acquisition of disciplinary knowledge in these cases is not the same journey on which the students once embarked.

The move to modularization has been viewed by many academics as an administrative decision rather than one that meets epistemological concerns about the acquisition of knowledge. As one business studies lecturer suggested:

> *The modular thing is just horrendous. The modular structures were being driven not by academics but by administrators. You know, it was convenient to do it, and there is a lack of ownership of modular structures.*

Modularization was initially viewed as an administrative change able to bring efficiency through rationalization, and modules could enable a streamlining of the courses on offer. Modularized programmes were promoted as being able to give students real choice, rather than setting them off passively on a predetermined programme. It could also potentially offer the choice to students to be consumers of their education, as they acquired credits that have an exchange value within a university marketplace. Modularization, in short, can be seen as an example of a performative shift in curricula (cf. Gokulsing 1997), insofar as the drivers of modularization are efficiency and exchange value. Modules become commodities between which the student-consumers make rational choices.

These changes have been resisted in some quarters, particularly in the older, more established disciplines with strong boundaries around know-ledge. In one example, the course designers of a history programme told us how they subverted new modular systems by bending the rules. Traditional year-long units could be maintained if requirements to select certain modules in a particular order were built into the curriculum. This effectively ensured that a year-long unit was repackaged into two or three shorter modules, with the first module a prerequisite of the second, and so on. It was not just the historians who were subversive. In other subject areas too, the reshaping of curricula was said to be a sleight of hand. A chemist, for example, used a revealing choice of words when he admitted:

> *We had to repackage our courses into pseudo-modules as it were . . . It was up to you to make it look modular. It should have been a university-wide scheme, but you could only get another department to teach some module by negotiation and then you had to fit that into your own timetable by moving your own courses around to accommodate that.*

So the practical concerns of curricular design are under managerial pressures, as the curriculum has come to be *managed* (Bocock and Watson 1994). What do these pressures mean in terms of knowledge in the curricula?

What we have identified as a performative shift is an important aspect of curricular change. We can see evidence of the rationalization and commodification of curriculum design: knowledge in curricula becomes part of a package, both in the sense of meeting the interests of the labour market and of the students, and in terms of how administrative concerns for efficiency have resulted in new choices for the consumption of knowledge in curricula.

The performative shift may also indicate the development of a fragmented student experience. Several of our interviewees quoted above point to the fragmentation in curricular design brought about by modularization. Consideration of the student experience is pertinent in this regard. What type of educational experience do students have as they work their way through a variety of modular choices? How do they acquire knowledge, or come to a sense of *knowing* a subject? These are important questions to which we will return.

Technological change

Another aspect of the shifts in knowledge in curricula that we have not yet touched upon is those changes made possible through new technologies. Increasingly, teachers in higher education are exploring new technologies that enable knowledge to be accessed in different ways. Students are also entering higher education with different expectations, many of whom have become accustomed to searching for information on the web and communicating by email and by other electronic media. Information and communication technologies are shaping curricula in new ways.

When lecturers decide to make a syllabus, lecture notes, or other texts available on the web, the ways in which students encounter and access knowledge begins to change. Technologies make possible the accessing of knowledge at a distance, outside of libraries, or in the home. These opportunities may even be changing the relationships that students now have with their universities, as they do not need to be on campus to study or communicate with tutors.

Relationships between teachers and students are being transformed as the ways in which teachers share knowledge with students no longer require lecture theatres, laboratories and libraries. These new possibilities were described to us by some of the lecturers we interviewed as key aspects of curricular change. A nursing studies lecturer, for instance, told us that she now has a new way of communicating with one of her students:

> The business of distance doesn't matter. [The student] did call in to see me a few times, but her reason for dealing with me by email is that she couldn't get the time off duty to come and see me. Her husband has got a new computer so she asked if she could email me. If it works, she may just as well be in Botswana.

How are these new relationships transforming knowledge in the curricula? Often, technologies are viewed as a means of opening up access to academic knowledge to people who previously could not enter higher education. The restrictions to studying at university may have included the inability physically to attend classes and tutorials. These restrictions helped maintain the exclusivity of the higher education system in ways that are now being eroded. Anyone with internet access is technically able to study at a 'distance' where these possibilities are offered, anywhere in the world. The physical campus of the university no longer has the same significance.

Yet there are other transformations underway, particularly in relation to the methods by which curricula are offered at a distance. The number of courses available online may be growing, but so too is the amount of curricula materials available on the web for students both on and off campus. The courses that have been repackaged into modules can now become a commodity on the internet that students can buy or even access for free. One example of the possibilities now available comes from MIT, an elite institution that has made access to its courses free on the internet. What was once the preserve of a select few can now be reached by anyone on the network.

Perhaps potential students may wish to see a preview of the courses on offer at various institutions. The products that universities sell can be advertised on the web simply by being placed there, available for anyone to peruse as though window shopping. Technologies make possible the commodification of knowledge, through curriculum packages, web-based courses and digitized texts. Many of the developments associated with the digital age, the network society and the knowledge economy are transforming academic knowledge through performative shifts, where performativity refers again to efficiency and economic value. Online courses are often seen as a profitable and efficient means of acquiring more and more students: email enables prompt feedback to be sent to students; economies of scale are achieved through a reduction in the amount of paperwork.

Yet what types of changes have technologies brought about in the ways in which students acquire knowledge? It may help to consider how a typical student may now encounter the knowledge offered through her university. This potential student will probably look at university websites, perhaps accessing some of the curricular materials that have been uploaded in order to get a flavour of the course. She may look at the academic staff pages on the web and read about their research interests and, in this way, begin to form ideas about the academic communities she will encounter. She may consider whether these communities offer identities she desires for herself. Once having chosen an institution and a course, she is likely to shop in the catalogue of module choices available to her, deciding which to take through a negotiation of academic and practical concerns. The syllabi might be on the web to download. Later on in the course she can download lecture notes or PowerPoint presentations if she misses a class. The online library catalogue could possibly be accessed from her laptop to find out if the books she needs will be on the shelves. When an essay topic is assigned, the first thing she might do is type in the key words on a popular search engine. As she gains expertise, she will turn to the more specialized bibliographic databases in her subject area.

She might communicate via email with her tutors more than she speaks to them face to face. She will email her draft assignments and coursework as attachments to her tutors, who will email comments back to her. The main resource for her research will be the web, as academic knowledge available online multiplies every day. Almost anything she wants to find out will be accessible on the web. In short, the contemporary student is likely to spend hours and hours in front of a computer: the computer *is* the university.

So academic knowledge is no longer tucked away in university libraries, discussed behind the closed doors of a tutorial, guarded by the gatekeepers and restricted to a select few. Acquiring knowledge in the contemporary university now has different rules and requires a new way of being. What it means to become an expert in a subject is to learn how to use technology in more efficient and sophisticated ways. Academic identities are now partly constructed through digital networks and new modes of communication. Our relationship with knowledge has fundamentally changed.

Access to knowledge may have opened up dramatically during the network age. Yet the ways in which students encounter knowledge, much of it now through online access, denotes a shift in their engagement with knowledge. Even the terminology associated with the digital age – surfing, chatting, messaging – is indicative of a more superficial, efficient and speedier means of finding information and communicating with each other. Deeper levels of engagement with knowledge, through critical thought and analysis developed over time, are challenged by the 'speeded up' era of the network age. The implications for curricula are in the manner in which students are enabled and encouraged to engage with knowledge.

Conclusion

We have been looking at changes in knowledge and its relationship with curricula. This domain, we have argued, does not represent a fixed and static body of knowledge that can unproblematically be inserted into curricula. Instead, it is a contested terrain and its place in curricula is undergoing certain transformations. One change we have identified is a performative shift, but what do we mean by this?

Performativity is a term characterized by some of the changes we have described above: a repackaging of the knowledge domain into more efficient modes of curricular delivery, combined with an emphasis on knowledge with a use value driven by responses to the needs of the labour market. There is a similar performative character to knowledge acquisition through digital technologies, whereby access to knowledge becomes quicker, more convenient and undertaken on a more superficial level. In other words, knowledge becomes a commodity to be accessed and consumed.

Yet there is another sense in which we can identify changes in the knowledge domain, which may offer a more encouraging interpretation: that is to denote a shift from *propositional* knowledge towards an experiential *knowing*; or a moving away from knowledge with underlying truth claims to a means of coming to know through encounters with problem-solving situations, practical tasks or other *in situ* experiences. We might wish to identify this (drawing from Gibbons et al. 1994) as an emerging Mode 2 domain of knowing, as distinct from a Mode 1 domain of propositional knowledge. In other words, we are seeing signs that students are being encouraged to develop knowledge through their own enquiries into 'real-world' problems or working out of case study scenarios. More and more courses, most notably perhaps in the medical sciences, have been transformed through the development of problem-based learning curricula (Savin-Baden 2000).

Admittedly, we did not encounter many signs of this possible shift to a Mode 2 domain of knowing in our own study. But we do know that in other sectors of higher education this type of curricula is emerging. In an MBA in Higher Education Management programme on which we both teach, for example, students spend a large part of the course in syndicate groups, working together to solve practical problems typically encountered in the management of universities. This is to offer a dimension of curricula based on experiential knowing, whereby students come to a sense of knowing about management through becoming professionals or practitioners themselves in the syndicate group tasks. In these forms of curricula, the students are not just acquiring knowledge, but engaging themselves in the act of knowing.

We see here, then, two contrasting forms of knowledge accomplishments opening up in the higher education curriculum. In one, characteristic of both the virtual university and an overforming of specific outcomes, students are coming to acquire *skills of knowing*. This knowing is one that is less concerned with knowledge as such, but more concerned with being able to manipulate knowledge in knowing performances. This performativity is a knowing without knowledge. In the other kind of knowledge accomplishment, we see developing a form of knowing in which formal knowledge is brought to bear and its limitations revealed in the struggle to engage with problems of the world. This is a situation in which knowledges – both formal and informal – are brought together in the session of an enlightened and even ethically grounded set of actions.

In the former situation, we see knowledge shorn of its process of enlightenment and collective transformation. In the latter kind of knowing, we see the prospect of universities living up to one of their modern claims of bringing about a more enlightened world. This knowing is a relationship with knowledge that even transcends 'evidence-based' curricula, for it not only acknowledges but also shows up the limitations of formal knowledge in the messiness of bringing it to bear on the real world.

Thus, the curriculum that sets out to encourage students to *know* a subject may also be intimately bound up with ways of being and acting. A curriculum in which the domains of being and acting are not integrated with knowing offers a fragmented experience, perhaps lending itself to a more performative character rather than a deep engagement with knowledge. The relationship between the dimensions of knowing, acting and being are key to our understandings of changes in curricula, and so we move now to explore further these concerns in the next two chapters.

7

Acting

Action and the university

Whereas the knowledge domain in the previous chapter is an obvious concept to address in the context of the contemporary university, 'action' is not so readily apparent. Academics in many subject areas might be unaccustomed to thinking about a domain of 'action' as a separate element of curricula. Is it possible to understand the types of action that universities might inculcate?

Such matters might be addressed by considering what the term action implies. An immediate response might suggest that action is about doing. Especially when set within the context of the higher education curriculum, the action domain within curricula might be considered as that part of a student's education that requires practical skills and know-how. The concept of an action domain might also connote those aspects of the curriculum that require students to perform some type of specified task.

These connotations are accurate, but they are not the full sense of the action domain that we wish to explore here. There are a number of different ways in which action has recently been developing in curricula as a distinct component of curricula. The action domain might be determined by the demands of a subject area, such as the actions required within clinically based professions. They might be considered to be transferable across subject areas, such as the practical skills involved in the use of computers. Or actions may be considered to be the tasks that students need for employment, such as the specific skills that electronic engineering students must acquire in order to perform their jobs.

Even in making these distinctions between subject area based skills, transferable skills and employment-related skills, however, we run into ambiguities and challenges. The action domain of curricula is not formed through a simple process of identifying skills. Skills are desirable because they are embedded within notions of what competencies graduates of certain subject areas should acquire. But, then, what value do these skills have in preparing students for a broader range of life and employment experiences beyond the boundaries of their subject areas? Should the acquisition of skills be more than an indication of graduate capabilities within subject areas, and if so in what ways?

An even greater challenge becomes apparent when we examine the action domain in relation to the domains of knowledge and self. If subject-based skills are only valuable within the confines of a subject, is the potential for the development of students' self-identities similarly embedded within the context of the subject area? In other words, is it possible that the knowledge, action and self domains can overlap to the extent that graduate capabilities have little significance beyond the particular subject area studied? What are the implications of an action domain that is not integrated with the knowledge domain of curricula? Can skills be developed without corresponding knowledge and self components and, if they can, what would this imply in terms of the capacities of graduates?

These are complex matters. Yet throughout the higher education system, the language of learning outcomes – including terms such as subject-based skills, generic and employment-related skills – seems to be being promoted without a full consideration of the implications of these terms for the types and purposes of education that they foster. We can illustrate these complexities further through some examples from our research.

Action within subject areas

There can be little doubt that skills have become a key component of contemporary curricula. We have already seen how the implementation of quality assurance mechanisms has required the identification of learning outcomes, and how these requirements have encouraged the identification of skills, capacities and competencies as they are developed from within the boundaries of the subject areas. We are seeing, then, a promotion of skills that is both outcomes-based and subject-based.

Of course, academics who design curricula have always had ideas about the types of skills they would like to see their students acquire. These ideas can reveal less explicitly formed notions of action in curricula that do not conform to our more recent expectations of appropriate, subject-based learning outcomes. When we asked lecturers what their expectations of students' capabilities were, the answers sometimes hinted at tacitly held conceptions of skills shaped by the academic cultures of different subject areas. We can illustrate the ways in which quite different academic cultures permeate notions of similar skills through comparing examples from an interview with an historian and a chemist. The history lecturer in an old university exposed an implicit notion of the types of skills that he would like his students to achieve when he said:

It seems to me that even if nothing else is achieved, people who have spent three years here ought to be able to support a decent conversation at dinner. They ought to know at least enough to support a few sentences on most of the major thinkers of the modern world. I think that is an absolute minimum.

This is not a notion of a graduate capability that we would expect to find in an explicit statement of intended learning outcomes for a course; it is a *tacit* conception of the action domain of curricula. The historian admitted as much in this interview. Indeed, his purpose in describing such a skill was to draw attention to the challenges he faces in now making such tacit notions explicit. As such, it reveals insights into how the action domain is conceptualized in curricula and the drivers that are sometimes shaping this domain.

The skill identified here is the ability to conduct 'decent conversations' at dinner. Within the general aims of a history degree, in which debates and discussions about intellectual ideas are important skills to acquire, it is perhaps an understandable desire and even a valuable outcome to identify. It also hints at ideas about the wider purposes of a university education in history, insinuating a desire for a type of intellectual public life where the 'major thinkers of the modern world' are a topic to be discussed amongst friends.

There may be academics in other subjects who might also broadly support this aim, albeit in different terms. In an interview with a chemist, for example, we were informed that discussions at a Chemistry Industrial Association meeting focused on the desirable skills of graduates, which included:

how they communicate with the general public. If you want to find out how badly chemists communicate, go out and ask someone what they think chemistry is! You will get an answer straight away which isn't very good for chemistry.

This is another reference to communication skills, shaped here through the concerns of a different subject area. In the context of a chemistry degree, effective communication is associated with the desire for scientists to be able to relate their work to the general public. The lecturer here is pointing to the value of a chemistry education, in that it should foster the ability of scientists to convey their expertise to a public audience.

The ability to communicate effectively with others is a capacity stated in various terms within the context of many subject-based learning outcomes. In these two examples, they *tacitly* reflect the values and concerns of particular academic cultures, and begin to articulate the wider purposes of a degree in their subject area. Yet if they were stated as *explicit* learning outcomes, we may have difficulties distinguishing between them. A familiar learning outcome such as 'effective communication' can hide a range of tacitly held concerns developed within the contexts of different academic cultures.

These academic concerns may also be shaped by institutional cultures. The desire for decent conversational skills may reflect tacitly held notions of the explicitly stated aims of history degrees, yet on a different level it also reveals how an institutional ethos can imbue notions of appropriate actions. This history lecturer is speaking from within the context of a fairly prestigious institution. The comfortable surroundings of his book-lined office and the small tutorial sessions he described as taking place there suggest a middle-class notion of university life and the attributes of its graduates. The legacy of the Oxbridge tutorial system, perhaps, with its emphasis on intimacy and paternalism, is invoked in this *habitus*.

Supporting 'decent' conversations at dinner is in some senses a metaphor of being 'cultured', or competent within particular discourses and social settings. This is a skill that would not pass muster as an intended learning outcome, a fact of which the history lecturer is well aware. However, he did also recognize that graduates may be required to obtain capacities that have value beyond this social attribute. He admitted:

> *It is true that we take the transferable skills for granted, but in truth with some reason. Our students, in fact, do go out and are quite successful. I think the most common single career is City law firms and for the last ten years our students were very good at getting into them. Clearly, we don't train them to be lawyers, but they've come out being able to do as well or actually better than people who do law degrees. It's about crafting arguments.*

Here we have an attempt to make the tacit more explicit. The crafting of arguments is a more solidly defined notion of the types of capabilities inculcated in students of history. The tutorials in the lecturer's office become a pedagogic strategy designed to develop skills that are valuable for certain types of employment. Students learn to weigh up their arguments, pit them against each other in a reasoned manner, develop their ideas through articulation of them, and in so doing become capable of a specialized form of action.

The preparation for employment in City law firms points again to an institutional influence. The definition of a successful graduate promoted here is one of a career in a prestigious field. Again, we would not expect to see an intended learning outcome identified as a career in a lawyer's office in the City. What his statement reveals are tacit notions of action that only particular institutions can embrace as part of their purpose and ethos. Different types of institutions will foster various ideas about the desirable and successful outcomes of their degree programme. Ideas about action and capabilities are therefore formed by the cultures of disciplines *and* institutions.

Yet there is also a recognition within the above statement that subject-specific skills are not all that is required in statements of action-oriented learning outcomes. The value of the capacities that students of history are expected to gain extends beyond the boundaries of the discipline. We can see how the idea that skills should be transferable to other contexts has gained currency. The above lecturer, in defining subject-based skills as transferable, is acknowledging that there is value in the identification of competencies that can be used in other contexts. However, it is difficult to

imagine a straightforward correlation in which the debating skills he
encourages his students to acquire are valued in and of themselves by
employers in City law firms. In other words, there are other forces at work
here that are harder to identify, such as the institutional prestige and
academic cultures that City law firms are likely to favour.

We have concentrated here on fairly specific examples as they offer
insights into the shaping of skills that can be found across subject areas and
institutions. One key point is that even though subject-based skills are
becoming a predominant framework for the identification of learning outcomes, it should be recognized that tacit notions of skills are embedded
within and shaped by both disciplines and institutions. Part of the process of
identifying learning outcomes is making these tacit notions explicit, but in so
doing we lose sight of how they were originally formulated through the
values and purposes associated with particular academic cultures. We can see
similar forces at work in relation to notions of generic or transferable skills,
or those skills identified as non-specific to subject areas.

Action as generic skills

An interest in personal, transferable skills has been gaining ground. There
are actions associated with such skills: word processing, effective time management, making a presentation, working in a group, and so on. The inclusion of generic skills in curricula may seem, on the surface, to be a sensible
approach. In the UK, the Dearing Report (NCIHE 1997) established a concept of transferable skills that has been widely accepted: that a certain level of
competency in numeracy, literacy and IT should be required of all graduates. In other words, a graduate of the higher education system should have
acquired these competencies to an acceptable standard. To expect anyone
holding an undergraduate degree to be able to function competently in
basic skills, at the very least, must surely be expected.

These expectations are now an explicit aspect of curricula in many universities. Indeed, in some cases the preoccupation with skills can dominate
debates about the curriculum, as was evident in an interview with the
lecturer in chemistry we discussed above:

> The Chemical Industry Association held their annual meeting and had a dis-
> cussion on what they called essential skills. Essentially it is what Dearing called
> key skills, but of course in a chemical industry context. Very interesting meeting.
> We had a meeting that went on for two days and chemistry, actual chemistry,
> hardly got a mention. It was all about how we were going to get these students to
> work in teams, how we were going to get them to talk to people, to communicate
> effectively.

For lecturers in almost any subject area, these references to teamwork and
communication will now be familiar. In the contemporary university, they
have become commonplace such that their inclusion in or addition to the

curriculum is accepted, even though their form and purpose may be debated. We were provided with many examples of how course teams have begun to incorporate the teaching of transferable skills.

How do we distinguish between those skills necessary for a competent outcome within a specific subject area and those which may be transferable across subject areas? Teamwork, for example, is a skill that can be acquired through subject-related activities. The group tasks that students of business studies will undertake may be based on practical examples from the business world and are therefore rooted within the competencies expected of business studies graduates. Yet teamwork has also been identified as a skill that crosses subject area boundaries, so that students who acquire teamwork capabilities are expected to be able to apply those capabilities in other contexts. What has not become clear is exactly how students transfer their capabilities across contexts, or indeed whether the teamwork skills of a business studies exercise has transferability across contexts.

The idea that anyone who achieves a degree should have acquired generic skills is also common in other countries, but in some of these cases the purposes of generic skills have been made more clear. In the USA, for example, many universities require students to complete courses in their first year that provide the fundamental building blocks for competencies that should enable them to proceed through their degrees. One university, to give an example, calls these courses Principles of Undergraduate Learning (PULs), which include such skills as constructing spreadsheets and presentations on computers (Bantu and Hamilton 2002). These courses offer year-long inductions into the skills necessary for another three years of study. They are also intended to be lifelong skills, but their immediate purpose is clearly identified as enabling students to be successful in their degree courses.

Generic skills can become fuzzy in their purpose when they begin to take on associations with personal skills. A lecturer in business studies, for example, explained that her courses now included the identification and assessment of personal skills:

> *One of the key changes that has gone on, not just in this school but in a number of schools, is the development of what we call Personal and Professional Development (PPD), and that takes a lot of staff time but it is absolutely essential for keeping a hold on our students, particularly in the early years . . . I think in general the university has probably always had the idea that we are about developing the individual – not just about knowledge. But that, in a sense, has come out from a tradition of what the university has always been about, and that was about being close to the professions, applying people for the work, and strong links with employers etc etc.*

In this statement, personal skills are viewed as the acquisition of competencies that go beyond the specific subject area outcomes. The notion of action here orients capabilities towards business and industry, and the notion of professional development suggests they will be skills transferable to and appropriate for the world of work. There is still an ambiguity around the purpose and nature of these skills, and a suggestion that institutional values have helped to shape them as an important component of curricula. The expectations of graduates are partly formed by the institutional ethos – strong links with industry – and invested with notions of the role of the university within its community.

The inclusion of transferable or generic skills may yet be seen to lack a clear purpose in some cases: if they are competencies for employment, to which jobs are they best suited? If they are intended to develop capabilities that cross disciplinary boundaries, how do students transfer their skills from one context to the next? Without a well-defined purpose, the identification of transferable skills can become an exercise of making tacit notions explicit. In other words, the activities that have existed within curricula, such as group exercises that include teamwork, can be relabelled as activities that inculcate personal or generic skills. In these cases, where the curriculum has only changed to the extent to which activities are explicitly described, we still need to question what value these skills offer to students.

It could be the case that the emphasis on transferable skills is a result of the subject-based, outcomes approach that is becoming more established in higher education. Course designers are encouraged to identify skills that transcend their subject areas in order to satisfy concerns that graduates should have capabilities that go beyond their specific fields of study. Or to put it another way, a notion of transferable skills cannot exist without a corresponding notion of subject-based skills. As we have seen through the earlier example of communication skills, however, there can be an ambiguity around the distinction between those skills that are subject-based and those that are transferable.

More importantly, the identification of transferable skills arguably satisfies concerns that higher education must have value within the labour market. Transferable and generic skills are most usually identified in relation to skills that employers might want. We will turn next to the notion of employment-related skills as they have developed within the action domain of curricula.

Action for employability

The term 'employability', in the UK at least, has become increasingly prominent over past decades. Although there have been ongoing debates about what the term means in practice, employability can be related to the acquisition of certain types of job-related skills. In some of the examples we have discussed thus far, we have seen how a concern for employment-related skills has been made transparent in different ways within curricula. The 'development of the individual' identified within a business studies curriculum in the last example, for instance, takes on the meaning of capabilities related to professional and work-related contexts. This phrase – 'development of the individual' – distinguishes it from subject-specific skills, but then it can be ambiguous without any further reference points. However, in the interview with the business studies lecturer, the significance of the phrase was clearly being related to employability outcomes, rather than, say, the development of an individual's capacity to function as an effective member of civil society.

The preceding examples illustrated that tacit notions of the action domain could be shaped by the cultures and values of institutions and subject areas. When we examine employment-related skills, we find yet another layer of influences at work on the notion of skills: the demands of industry, the professions and similar external stakeholders. In chemistry, for example, the industries that employ chemistry graduates are making demands on the identification of skills in curricula. As one chemistry lecturer explained:

> *I think industry are realising they are not getting the graduates with the kind of qualifications they want any longer. They tell us what they want is somebody with a good general education in chemistry, a logical thinker, numerate, self-reliant, someone who is adaptable, versatile, so really they are going to take that person and train them for a particular position. The raw material that they require is somebody who is coming out of a degree course with an ability to plan their time, to plan their research, to have the ability to be conversant with the subject, cognisant of their subject, but also have the dexterity, the ability to do practical chemistry.*

These sentiments are becoming a familiar refrain in higher education: that industry expects graduates to have generic competencies that are adaptable to whatever form of employment they provide. In response, course designers are thinking carefully about the action domain of their curricula and the extent to which the skills fostered will enable their graduates to be versatile in the labour market. A successful outcome in this model is the graduate who has acquired competencies that will ultimately enable her to continue acquiring further and more highly specialized employment-related capabilities.

Yet to what extent are these employment-related competencies dependent on the subject area from which they originate? Capabilities such as logical thinking, numeracy and self-reliance are perceived as important outcomes within many subject areas. There are potential tensions for curriculum designers in meeting demands for subject-specific learning outcomes and at the same time responding to the requirements of external stakeholders for generic skills. In the face of such challenges, it is perhaps not surprising that one chemistry lecturer stated that 'chemists do not want to teach people who are not going to become chemists'. He admitted that although in practice chemists must teach students who enter other types of employment, his sentiments point to a loss of the inherent value of skills in chemistry degrees. Value is now determined more through outcomes with a wider, employment-related applicability.

We can see other challenges across the different subject areas. The professional subjects, for instance, usually seek accreditation for their courses through external professional associations. These associations are particularly powerful stakeholders in the curriculum as they seek to uphold high standards within the professions, and with good reason. Many professionals must acquire levels of responsibility of care for others and work within specified codes of conduct. In nursing studies, for example, the importance of particular graduate attributes was illustrated by a lecturer we interviewed:

> *The world has moved on and so has nursing and I don't think that is a bad thing. It had to move. It has had to move to a level that we can operate in an environment where you can make decisions about the care that you are giving, because nurses spend an awful lot of time with their clients in a community setting, and they carry an awful lot of responsibility. You go into somebody's home and there ain't no backup team. Now, you have to give people the wherewithal to do that.*

These statements reflect a desire to instil in students the forms of competencies that enable them to be self-reliant and adaptable to different situations. In some senses, these are similar attributes that the chemistry lecturer described, in that they encourage autonomy and independence. In other words, the action domain in these curricula emphasizes a capability to act independently as a professional in a variety of different professional contexts.

As the above nursing studies lecturer indicates, the professional role of nurses has been changing, and in turn curricula have adapted in order to inculcate the capabilities now required of them. In a statement reflecting this new discourse of graduate capabilities, she goes on to explain:

> *It's not about collecting skills in a bag and I will fight that tooth and nail. The difference here, I think, is teaching people how to learn and equipping them with the skills to continue that learning . . . hopefully we are giving people an awareness of the world they are in. As professionals, you are going to be accountable and responsible for what you do.*

This lecturer suggests that 'collecting skills in a bag' is not enough. In other words, the domain of action should not be a fragmented, non-integrated component of curricula. Moreover, again we see in these comments a desire to develop autonomy, self-reliance and a capability of 'learning how to learn' within the action domain of the curriculum. We have been critical of this now familiar terminology in previous chapters, and here can point to variations between the extent to which they are integrated within curricula in different subject areas. We can compare the nursing studies lecturer's comments with similar statements from a history lecturer who said:

> *There are things I would like to see more strongly represented. Like, for instance, a move towards more independent learning. I think this is more important than I*

thought it was because a recent survey of employers' attitudes stresses the import-ance they have in terms of students knowing how to learn.

On the one hand, then, we have similar terminology being used within chemistry, nursing studies and history in the identification of certain cap-abilities to do with learning how to learn, self-reliance, and so on. In all three cases, the driver for including these capabilities in curricula is the context of graduate employment as it is perceived by these lecturers. On the other hand, the extent to which these capabilities are seen to be integrated with the knowledge base of the subject area varies between them. The chemists in the earlier quote, for example, who discussed skills without chemistry 'getting a mention', might be seen to be leaning towards a more fragmented curriculum in which the domains of acting and knowing are distinct.

Designers of curricula are thus faced with a choice as to whether the capabilities they include are distinct from or integrated within the know-ledge domain. There is another crucial point about the employment-related capabilities being identified – autonomy, self-reliance and knowing how to learn – in that they carry a particular significance in relation to the domain of self or being. We have seen that these 'learning how to learn' capabilities are emerging within curricula as forms of acting that require self-reflection, and so it is to their relationship with the self domain that we now turn.

Acting and being

The forms of action required within the 'learning how to learn' discourse of capabilities may be more or less related to the subject area in which they are acquired, but their relationship with the self domain is also of interest. To take some specific examples, in nursing studies it is now common to require students to keep reflective logs or learning journals of some type. As a part of the action domain within curricula, reflective logs are often written by the students on a continual basis throughout their courses, as they learn to express in writing their actions and evaluations of those actions. A similar activity can be seen in certain electrical engineering courses, where students write records each week in logbooks of the sequences of actions they have taken in the laboratories. These methods of recording and reviewing are, on one level, designed to encourage autonomy, accountability and self-reflection. They are also capabilities with the potential to require students to develop their own conceptions of themselves.

Yet what is the extent to which this self-reflection occurs in practice? If designed as a distinct or non-integrated component of curricula, the action domain takes on a fragmented character. The activities of self-reflection can thus become performative. By this we mean that the independence of the action domain from the knowledge and self domains can result in performances, or an acting out of particular tasks, as students learn that there are skills required of them that are not embedded within the other components of the curriculum. The logbook must be produced, for example, but not necessarily with much thought about subject area knowledge or self-reflection. We might call this a 'self-monitoring performativity', as students learn that the main goal of the exercise is the production of a logbook which may or may not have enabled them to develop either as subject experts or as self-reliant learners.

Self-monitoring performativity suggests activities that are shorn of their relations with other curricular components. They might be considered types of 'meta'-activities, transcending subject area boundaries and easily adapted across a range of curricula. Increasingly, these types of activities are emerging within curricula. Yet are we going too far, perhaps, in describing the production of logbooks and journals as types of self-monitoring performativity? After all, the pedagogic strategies associated with them are often based on valuable goals or learning outcomes such as self-reflexivity and autonomy. In theory, these aims are appropriate for a higher education curricula, although in practice there might be other factors at work.

The use of portfolios in assessment provides a useful example of the potential for a self-monitoring performative activity. Portfolios as a method of assessment are now being used in a number of different disciplines, whereby students gather evidence of the skills they are acquiring and are asked to reflect on their performance. Klenowski (2002: 76) suggests that, within an outcomes-based curricular approach, portfolios can become a meaningless activity if their 'pedagogy is limited because of the demands to prove rather than to improve learning'.

This emphasis on accountability and 'evidence' can override learning outcomes such as self-reflection: quality assessment now often demands the 'proof' that certain activities are taking place in curricula. The logbooks used in electrical engineering courses may intend to encourage students to evaluate their actions, but also seek to provide evidence that certain actions have been conducted. Portfolios, too, emphasize the collection of evidence that verifies students are competent in their performance. Although students may be required to reflect upon that evidence, processes of reflection are in tension with the emphasis on outcomes. Students may record what they consider to be the desired outcomes as evidence, rather than recording their 'true' actions that may not portray them in the best light. The need for students to demonstrate that they are competent is perhaps in conflict with the pedagogic aims of improving their practices.

These criticisms of outcomes-based assessment methods are well known in the field of vocational education in the UK where outcomes-based competence models have become dominant. We are now seeing the same models creeping into higher education (Holmes 1994). The portfolio has been one of the main assessment methods for the General National Vocational Qualification (GNVQ) and is now appearing in higher education curricula in subjects such as teacher education, nursing studies and business and management studies. As higher education lecturers are encouraged to develop innovative methods of assessment, their use will probably continue to grow.

The potential for the self-monitoring performativity of portfolio assessment in higher education should perhaps be attracting some of the same criticisms levelled at their use in vocational education, yet they are now being promoted in higher education rather unproblematically. The use of learning journals, logbooks and portfolios as methods of assessment may encourage the types of activities that are more about the production of evidence than learning. These examples are pointing to an action domain within curricula that is quite separate from the dimensions of knowing and being. It may seem odd to be describing the production of learning journals as action independent from knowledge and self, when it would seem that the aims of learning journals are intended to enhance knowledge about the self. What we are suggesting is that if the outcomes of the activity emphasize evidence or proof, however unwittingly, we may have an action domain that has not been integrated with the knowledge and self domains. If the dimensions of curricula become fragmented in this way, so too surely does the student experience.

Conclusions

We have been identifying an action domain within curricula that requires students to undertake certain activities and develop particular skills. We have distinguished between skills that are based within subject areas, skills that are intended to be transferable and employment-related capabilities. However, these distinctions are not always easily maintained: there may be ambiguities between the different types of skills and their different purposes within curricula. Furthermore, there may be tacitly held assumptions about skills in response to subject area concerns and institutional values. In an outcomes-based curriculum, some of these tacit notions are translated into explicit learning outcomes, and we have raised questions as to whether the value of these skills can be clarified through what is basically a semantic change.

We have also raised questions about the relationship between the domain of action and the dimensions of knowledge and self. Where curricula have been constructed in a fragmented way with little integration between the three dimensions, the action domain can take on a performative character. Students may produce the required tasks, but their products stand more as evidence that the work has been done rather than as a reflection of deeper levels of engagement in the activities taking place. We might be tempted to refer to such actions, shorn of their relationship with other curricular dimensions, as a type of 'acting' in the sense of performance but we want to reserve the term 'acting' for a more positive connotation.

We prefer the term 'acting' for this domain in our schema for the same reasons that we have identified the domains of knowing and being (as distinct from knowledge, self and action). We wish to suggest that curricula including the domains of knowing, acting and being are indicating processes that should, to a certain extent, be developed together and be working together. There cannot be *complete* integration or overlap between these domains, as this format would not enable the student to stand in a critical space outside the subject area. Rather, a certain level of integration is required between the dimensions of knowing, acting and being in order for the students to embark on a fuller level of engagement with curricula involving themselves, their knowledge and the activities they are required to undertake.

Admittedly, these are not easy suggestions for curriculum developers to incorporate in their course designs. However, we hope we have illustrated that curricula are changing in response to a variety of new concerns and demands, and that we are in danger of the emerging curricula taking on unwanted characteristics if we are not clear about the purposes of the different dimensions within curricula. One of the dangers we have highlighted is the potential for fragmentation between the acting and being domains, whereby the student's sense of self is not engaged through the required activities. Yet this is a tricky relationship to pursue, and so we now turn to the dimension of being itself in order to explore more fully its potential function within curricula.

8

Being

Introduction

We have been suggesting that curricula can helpfully be understood as educational projects that work in three dimensions – knowing, acting and being. In one sense, the first two of these are relatively non-controversial: 'knowledge' and 'skills' have long been part of the promptings by which academics have come to understand and even interrogate their curricular practices. In fact, as we have seen, the terms 'knowledge' and 'skills' turn out to be highly problematic. On the one hand, they are complex terms in themselves; on the other, there is evidence – from our own study at least – that the interpretations given to these terms in the micro-practices of curricula may be undergoing significant changes. 'Knowledge' is becoming more a matter of students' capabilities in relation to knowledge; as we put it, knowledge becomes a matter of 'knowing'. At the same time, 'skills' become important in their own right rather than simply being practices associated with and embedded in knowledge. Even so, the idea of *being*, in contrast, is particularly problematic.

First, unlike 'knowledge' and 'skills', 'being' is not a term that is fashionable, nor does it even enjoy a common usage. Perhaps especially in the empiricism of the Anglo-Saxon culture, the term has overtones of metaphysics, of undetectable entities or human qualities and even of lofty ideals that just sit uncomfortably with many. It is even, so it might be said *sotto voce*, a term with its locus in the philosophy of continental Europe, and said in a tone that is intended to close the conversation. Second, 'being' *is* problematic: its meaning is far from clear. Third, the idea of 'being' simply does not fit with the dominant discourses of the age, performative and instrumental as they are. Being does not obviously yield to unambiguous statements of course or module aims and objectives. Performance indicators are not easily derived from the term, at least of a determinate and cashable kind. ('The students failed to complete their course but, at least, their being was enhanced' is hardly a credible construction.) Lastly, with the best will in the world, even if the idea of 'being' secured assent in principle as a helpful concept in the context of higher education, it is far from clear how one would go about deriving curricula and pedagogical strategies that would do some justice to the idea.

Why, then, might we want to claim that the idea of 'being' offers a significant dimension along which contemporary curriculum change in higher education can be understood? After all, if our preliminary observations about the problematic character of 'being' hold water, it follows that it is highly likely that the term is not going to spring out from daily curricular practices. This, indeed, at one level at least, is the case: for example, in our approximately 100 interviews in which we explored with lecturers their understandings of, their approaches to and their constructions of curricula, not once did we encounter the term 'being' whereas we encountered 'knowledge' frequently. On the other hand, the terms 'action' and 'acting' were hardly in much evidence in our interviews, even if 'skills' was often present.

We, therefore, wish to introduce and develop the idea of 'being' on two accounts. First, we believe that an *ontological turn*, as we might term it, urgently awaits curricula in higher education. If curricula are to provide the kinds of experiences that are likely to sponsor the kinds of subjectivities called for by a world of instability, knowledge and practical dimensions are necessary claimants for our attention but they cannot be sufficient. A world of uncertainty poses challenges not just of knowing and of right action but also, and more fundamentally, on us as beings in the world. How do I understand myself? How do I orient myself? How do I stand in relation to the world? These are questions that impose themselves in a world of incessant change and uncertainty and which are characteristic especially of professional life (into which most graduates move). Curricula in higher education, therefore, have this challenge in front of them: how might human being as such be developed so that it is adequate to a changing and uncertain world?

Second, we shall try to show, through some examples, that the concept of 'being' is embryonically already present. It may not be recognized as such, either by course teams in their course descriptions or even by the individual lecturer as she engages in imaginative interactions with a large group of students in a raked lecture hall. But this dimension of being as such is to be observed daily and, perhaps increasingly so, in teaching practices.

Modes of being

We want to suggest that curricula are educational vehicles for developing the student as a person. This may sound uncontroversial but, then, surprisingly, the idea seems hardly anywhere in sight, at least in public debate. Neither is the idea of students as persons evident in the 'subject benchmark' statements issued by the UK's Quality Assurance Agency; nor is it obviously present in the template for the 'programme specifications' that is being drawn up for all programmes of study in higher education in the UK. To be fair to it, the

Report of the UK's National Committee of Inquiry into Higher Education (the Dearing Report) hinted at this idea. For instance, the very first of the 'four main purposes of higher education' as seen by the Committee was:

> to inspire and enable individuals to develop their capabilities to the highest potential levels throughout life, so that they grow intellectually, are well-equipped for work, can contribute effectively to society and achieve personal fulfilment.

> (NCIHE 1997, 5.10: 72; our emphasis)

Here, it is hoped that individuals will 'grow intellectually' and be 'equipped for work' but will also gain '*personal* fulfilment'. In other words, there is an implied sense that the student's development as a 'person' is *additional* to her or his intellectual or work-related development. In short, as well as being centres of knowledge and understanding and of action in the world, students are *persons*. We want to hang on to that idea and press it further.

Students cannot be mere assemblies of competencies or reservoirs of knowledge. Any competencies or knowledge that they may obtain are acquired by a particular *person*. Again, this may sound so straightforward and uncontroversial as not to bear noting. Yet, as we have just observed, this understanding is by and large absent from much thinking and reflection on higher education. It may be said that the point is absent precisely because it is so obvious. Alternatively, it may be remarked that the point isn't customarily made because it is misleading. The thought might be entertained that it cannot or should not be a responsibility of higher education to concern itself with students as persons. It is their higher learning, their higher intellectual qualities or even their higher-order skills towards which universities have a responsibility, and not students as 'persons', whatever that may mean.

We disagree with both points. So far as the first point is concerned, it is far from obvious that students are always regarded as persons. In our project, we saw hints to the contrary. For example:

> [In chemistry,] students do not use libraries . . . what students learn very rapidly is that you go to the lecture, you listen to what is said, you write it down as well as you can, and you reproduce it as well as you can and you get good marks. The danger is that if you go and read a book and it says something which your lecturer has not said and you write it in a report, it is quite likely to be marked wrong.

Here, far from students being recognized as persons, there is the implication that pedagogies – here in chemistry in a pre-1992 university – downvalue students precisely as persons in their own right. The students' capacities for independent thinking and action are not being properly developed by such pedagogies, but neither are such students, we can surmise, likely to enhance their sense of themselves as autonomous agents or to form a positive self-conception or even a sense of themselves at all. Their role is that of faithful reproducers of others' accounts of the world. As a result, their own sense of self as a site of independent consciousness is surely bound to be diminished, if not actually thwarted.

To know is to be

Forms of knowing produce forms of being. This seemingly abstract statement is crucial to our argument and has supremely practical implications. In practising their trade, in getting students on the inside of modes of thought, academics are also inviting them into a way of being, a form of life. They may not interpret their practices as lecturers and tutors in this way, but they are doing it nonetheless. This is *not* to say that lecturers have an interest solely in self-reproduction. It is not to say that teaching acts simply contain the tacit injunction 'be like me'. Whether we are in the presence of academic self-reproduction is a separate matter, even if that is commonly to be found. We want here just to confine ourselves to the point that forms of knowing bring forth forms of being. For example:

> *We used to concentrate on analysis in great detail in you know you construct a mathematical model and you play about with the maths of the model and you construe how the physical thing works from the mathematics . . . and then you go and test it and see if it does that . . . but we don't do that . . . because we find that is not the way that our students either want or are able to look at problems.*

There are various ways of 'reading' this set of observations (from a lecturer in electrical and electronic engineering at a post-1992 university). At one level, it indicates that mathematics as such plays a less significant part in the curriculum in that subject than it used to do. In other words, the passage can be read purely in terms of the balance of knowledge elements in a curriculum; an 'epistemological' story can be told. We don't want to discount such an interpretation but we want to suggest that an additional story is to hand, and one that is slightly more complex. In this observation – the like of which we came across not infrequently among science lecturers, particularly in the new universities – we can glimpse not merely a falling off of mathematics but an awareness of it being linked to certain kinds of disposition on the part of the students: '[working from mathematical models] is not the way that our students either want or are able to look at problems'. The students are able to take on or *unable* to take on certain kinds of knowing, given their dispositions; given the self. The self, the being, makes possible the knowing. But the relationship between the knowing and the being doesn't stop there. The lecturer in question goes on to suggest:

> *And whereas those analytical skills were prized by the IEE [Institute of Electrical Engineers] and professors and the academic hierarchy, I am pretty sure if you go into industry and talk to people . . . really, they are not interested in technical skills they are interested in the broad-brush, problem-solving approaches and we*

find we can justify taking that approach with our students because . . . it is what employers want.

The mathematics, then, is being replaced – it would be appear – by what are referred to here as 'problem-solving approaches'. Just earlier in the interview that lecturer had spoken of the students learning 'by doing lots of examples and they can eventually see the pattern and apply it'. So we see here the possibility that a way of knowing may shape the student's way of being. Again, the story can be told purely in epistemological terms: mathematical modelling gives way to the reproduction of problem solutions and problem solving. We can glimpse here a shift from academic competence to a more operational competence, crudely from knowing that to knowing how. But in that shift of knowledge elements in the curriculum, in that epistemological shift, we can hypothesize that an accompanying shift is likely to take place in the student's mode of becoming – and we explored that shift in earlier chapters. What we may be witnessing here is a shift from a curriculum – and knowledge – that shapes a mode of being of an analytical if not of a contemplative kind to a curriculum that shapes a mode of being that is much more immediately 'in the world'.

In offering this kind of interpretation on these few remarks from one lecturer in one institution, we do not claim any definiteness for this interpretation. All of our comments are deliberately tentative but nevertheless suggest what we believe to be a significant double story: first, that the idea of students as persons, who are more than thinking and acting beings, while always dimly present in the rhetoric of English higher education, has been underplayed of late; second, that there is evidence that a stronger sense of the students as centres of being and consciousness in their own right, as having their own selves, is now beginning to develop in curricula. This evidence is, as yet, mere hints and snippets. For example:

> *[On the examination of projects] there's a first report they have to produce, and then there's a project presentation and there's a final report and then there's a talk they give right at the end, plus the project report, so there are several components of their project.*

Here we see a lecturer in electrical and electronic engineering indicating the range of curricula and assessment elements: the one project gives rise to 'several components'. But we see too that the components in question call for different capacities on the part of the student for they include, as well as the writing of different reports, both a presentation and a talk. The writing, we may surmise, itself calls for a range of forms in which data are presented and analysed, arguments are made and recommendations are couched.

We may be tempted to suggest that these different elements call simply for a range of skills. Whatever the validity of that way of construing the matter, it is surely insufficient, for what is more fundamentally in question is the ways of being in the world that the student is being invited to develop. Being disposed to write in different genres and to present a case in an effective way to an audience and to talk and presumably discuss a significant matter with others call for different forms of engagement with the world. What forms of engagement with the world, what kinds of self-understanding, what kinds of identity is the student taking on? In short, what kind of a person is the student *becoming*? These are not matters that can be caught by crude distinctions such as thought/action, or introversion/extroversion. They call for a sense of nuances, of dispositions and of qualities that the student may be willing, or even unwilling, to extend him- or herself into.

That this same lecturer is enthusiastic about the way in which curricula are now beginning to extend students as persons may just be glimpsed in a critical remark made later in the interview (about curricula as they had become): 'We've got the idea that we've got this body of material which we have to teach.' Here, the lecturer is surely implying that knowledge, if it is to take hold in the student's imagination, cannot be assimilated in itself. Knowledge is not a mere corpus, simply to be assimilated as a task. Rather, knowing – if it has to have educational value and a student is to be taken forward in the process – has to involve the student as a person. The student, we might add, has to be involved from the outset. The knowing, in other words, starts from the being and then returns to the being.

The lecturer is also surely implying a criticism of curricula construed in terms of filling a curriculum space (with knowledge). The logic here is that curriculum design has to be seen not as spaces to be filled but as the imaginative construction of spaces in which students – as adults – are likely to build their own energies and commitments and so come to flourish in worthwhile ways.

Even without necessarily being able to make the matter explicit, therefore, lecturers and tutors in higher education are commonly interweaving knowing and being into their everyday practices. These are not simply 'abstract' or 'academic' considerations but are matters of actual and concrete practice in higher education. What we would wish for is to see lecturers and tutors develop the capacity for reflecting more systematically on their everyday achievements, and on the complexity of what it is that they are bringing off. To do that, of course, requires both a language for engaging in those reflective processes and a collective will do so.

Student voice

In an interview in a national magazine on learning and teaching, an employer was asked to identify 'the most important skills you would like to see fostered in undergraduates by HEIs (higher education institutions)'. He responded in part by stating that 'the main qualities are:

- a passion for excellence
- integrity
- energy and enthusiasm

- leadership combined with an ability to work with the team
- desire and openness to learning and development (including self-awareness)
- energy and enthusiasm' (Miller Smith 2002: 10).

'Energy and enthusiasm', it will be observed, appear twice! That it does probably arises out of an editorial slip but the double appearance of the phrase 'energy and enthusiasm' may also be a sign of the significance of the ideas that the term represents today in the world of work. What is significant, from our point of view here, are two things.

First, talk of knowledge and skills is eschewed by this employer. There was certainly mention of 'knowledge and skills' elsewhere in the interview but, put on the spot, the desirable attributes of graduates for the world of work are here described as 'qualities'. Second, the qualities that are enumerated here look to individuals having their own sources of energy. The term 'energy' appears in the list along with other attributes such as 'passion', 'enthusiasm' and 'desire'. What terms such as these surely betoken are individuals who are not just energized but whose energies are played out in the service of personal aims or beliefs. After all, one has 'passion' or 'enthusiasm' or 'desire' not just abstractly but for some thing. The thing in question may be a value, an interest or even, presumably, an institution (such as a corporation or organization). Such passions or desires are not to be held blindly, however. There can be no possibility of sheer allegiance to a cause, or falling in with the collective mood of the moment, for what is also wanted, so we are told, is 'integrity' and an 'openness to learning'. There has to be a capacity, therefore, for self-critique.

These two dimensions of human being – self-drive and self-critique – surely together represent much of what it is to be a person in a western culture. It would appear that the world of work in an uncertain age is coming to want something akin to a western liberal education. There is a sense here of personal autonomy, of a determinedness not to be boxed in by dogma or fashion but to find a way forward that retains one's 'integrity'. Certainly, so we are informed, the way forward has to be worked out with an eye to 'excellence' and will doubtless involve taking on board others' points of view in working 'with the team', but the double sense of a personal voice and a strong self are surely in evidence here.

To what degree, then, can we see evidence of a concern to develop the student's voice in the shaping of contemporary curricula? To what extent is there a belief that the student experience should help to develop the student's own personal autonomy, his or her own self? Some entertain both a sense of disappointment and an optimism for the future. One of our respondents saw the matter in this way:

> *I think students are coming in with less skills . . . They know how to pass exams and they've been very well taught [in schools] . . . but they really haven't had to stand on their own two feet . . . They expect me to do much more and I'm perhaps my own worst enemy because I do it for them . . . Everyone gives handouts now but*

the handouts are bullet points and it's just like secondary school . . . because they don't seem to be able to do it without that.

[We] have always tried very hard to assess oral presentations so if you looked at one of my third year students who has done a lot of history of art they would be much more confident about speaking in public. They might not be particularly articulate but they are incredibly confident. . . . We are going to have to think less about specific course content and more about an approach to learning.

There are surely two striking features of these comments. First, both pessimism and optimism are present at the same time. 'It's just like secondary school' is, we may take it, not meant as a form of praise. On the other hand, the same person considers that the students in question 'are incredibly confident'. Second, 'voice' is present here not metaphorically (the student expressing herself boldly and independently in an essay, say) but literally: their voice is heard directly. They might 'not [be] . . . particularly articulate but [they are] . . . incredibly confident'.

This lecturer's students take on the world and inject themselves into it with vigour and enthusiasm and they do so, we might surmise, through having a positive self-regard. The world might be an uncertain and even chaotic place but these students are not 'fazed' by it. As we might put it, their being is not outside the world, reflecting on it and even hiding from it, but is actively in the world. Their ontologies are supremely practical in nature in the sense that their practices in the world fire them up, excite them and energize them.

All manner of questions arise here for curricula in higher education. Are we witnessing a change in ontologies? Are young people today, for example, especially practical in their hold on the world? If so, how might more reflective dimensions – of the kind that universities might encourage – be brought into their lives? What would it look like if curricula were designed to develop even more of a positive self-regard among students, such that they felt able to engage in the world with confidence? What kinds of curricula are necessary in order that students might feel that they have an effective hold on the world? Lastly, how might curricula be so fashioned to nurture the student voice, to give students powers of human expression in appropriate and telling ways in different contexts with different listeners?

Authenticity

For over 20 years, a running theme in the literature on students' learning has been that of 'meaning'. Researchers have been interested in students' approaches to learning and have identified contrasting orientations towards their studies which students take. A 'meaning' orientation is implicitly endorsed in these studies. The student who possesses such an orientation is characteristically portrayed as making connections across the various elements of her or his experience and as someone whose learning is more likely to be more secure and even more effective. In contrast, learning orientations on the part of students that are 'atomistic', 'surface' or 'strategic' in nature are implicitly downvalued.

A number of questions could be raised against this research 'paradigm'. For example, does it not privilege a 'meaning' orientation over a more strategic orientation? Is there empirical evidence to the effect that meaning orientations lead to a higher likelihood of success and to better degree grades? The questions have point but here we want to set them aside. That the research paradigm does load the dice in favour of meaning over a surface approach to learning itself indicates how integral to the western idea of higher education is the personal involvement of the student him- or herself to the perceived quality of that learning. The research paradigm is itself testimony to a set of values embedded in cultural assumptions about the nature of the university.

Ideas of meaning and depth point to a felt sense of the significance of authentic learning. In the end, learning of any value has to be the students' own learning. It arises out of their own motivations and, in the process, they inject themselves into it. On this conception, students *have* to will their own learning. This is not an empirical point but a logical point about how learning of any significance is construed within the university. With this willingness, this injection of self, emerges a learning that is authentic in that there is an identity between the student and his or her learning. It is not imposed, not alien, but arises from within. There is a willing assent to the learning.

We are not suggesting that conversations along these lines are frequently or, indeed, ever to be found among course teams or between lecturers, but we can glimpse such sentiments in the way they describe and construe their perceptions of their students. For example:

> *After five weeks, one day we turned up about half an hour later than them and they were doing exactly what they would have been doing with us. They were organizing a discussion and of course they were adults, they didn't need us for that. We became more the resource.*

> *Things change in industry and obviously employers want students to know how to be self-motivated in terms of learning and to have an open mind and that sort of stuff.*

In both examples, drawn respectively from a professional area (nursing studies) and one of the humanities (history), each lecturer indicates an endorsement of self-propelled learning. In one example (nursing studies), the students got on under their own steam, unprompted by the lecturer. In the other there is an acknowledgement that the external world values such self-motivation on the part of graduates and that the curriculum might be reviewed and developed to drive up such qualities among students.

The concluding clause, 'to have an open mind and that sort of stuff', is not without significance. 'An open mind' may be felt to be valuable in the world of work, where organizations and companies are finding themselves beset by continuous change and also by challenges of unexpected kinds (not just of finances, resources or markets but also of stakeholder values, of counter-claims, of shaky foundational systems). There is an assent here to the idea of an open mind; an assent that is hardly surprising for the idea of an open mind is embedded in the deep structure of the western university and speaks again of authenticity. An openness of mind, after all, implies an individual person, someone who is not easily swayed by her experiences but yet pre-pared to engage with new ones. This is a mind whose learning is likely to be authentic for it will be formed by the person's own judgement.

So the open mind that our lecturer endorses looks in turn to a curriculum that sponsors openness, authenticity and personal judgement. Our lecturer is also aware, if only somewhat hazily, that with such concepts go yet other ideas of educational aim and curriculum development; at least that surely is the hint in the throwaway ending 'and all that stuff'. As with asking 'how many children had Lady Macbeth?', conjecture here is untoward. We cannot even guess as to what our lecturer might have preferred, if pressed. But openness, breadth, authenticity, personhood, self-propulsion and judge-ment are not a small set of ideas with which to develop curricula for the uncertain world that the twenty-first century is opening up.

Engagement

Engagement is a further idea that speaks to matters of the student self, of the student as a human being and even of the student's *being* and it is a term to be heard in the contemporary public debate about higher education. 'Engagement' here, in relation to curricula and the student 'being engaged', works surely at two levels. First, there is the matter of what it is *for* the student to be engaged. Second, there is the question of how, in general terms, cur-ricula are to be so shaped that there is a likelihood that engagement on the part of the student will come about. In other words, what is it actually to engage students?

So far as the curriculum is concerned, how might we understand the logical priority of these two matters? Is it that we sort out what forms of student engagement might be striven for and then engineer the curriculum to produce those capabilities, or is it that we attend in the first place simply to bringing about a level of engagement among students in, say, the seminar room, trusting that the student's wider powers of engagement will fall into place? This phrasing of those plausible alternative curriculum strategies, of course, gives the game away. The language of 'engineering the curriculum' to 'produce' capabilities on the one hand, and of simply 'trusting' that it will come out all right in the end on the other is tendentious. *Both* curriculum ploys, however immediately attractive, are to be resisted. As in all curriculum challenges, educational processes and intended achievements on the part of the student have to go hand in hand. We cannot hope to bring about certain kinds of engagement within students unless those very processes are intimately reflected in the shaping of the curriculum. Nor does it make sense to think of curricula, however well designed, as producing, say, 'engagement' simply as a set of outcomes; means–ends models have to be eschewed.

With 'engagement' we have yet another term that may not be actually much used by lecturers in higher education, but yet the concept (of engagement) is in evidence. Admittedly, its presence may not hit one in the face but it can surely be detected. Take the following quotation, from a lecturer in business studies:

> *The students that came here when I came here were no brighter in terms of A Level scores than they are now, but they knew why they were here . . . I think now there is a higher proportion of students who go to university because that is what school leavers do or whatever, so we have to work more with their aspirations.*

'So now we have to work more with their aspirations': is not another way that this might well have been put that of saying 'so now we have to work more so as to retain their engagement'? The reflection that the students' aspirations have to be developed suggests that those aspirations are deficient in some way; they are not all that they could be. In short, those aspirations need to be *engaged*. But to say this is precisely to invoke the double meaning to which we have just alluded: in order for the students' aspirations to be engaged, we as their teachers have to work directly on engaging with those aspirations. 'Engagement' engages both student and lecturer. Taken seriously, the idea of engagement invokes a pedagogical entailment. It is not something that will come about spontaneously within the student or even as a mechanical outcome of a learning process, but calls for the lecturer to engage him- or herself with the student. To put it more formally, the development of the *being* of the student calls for the insertion of the *being* of the lecturer. We can see this idea of engagement embedded in the thinking of lecturers more generally. Here, we may return to two quotations that we have looked at earlier (in Chapter 7):

> *Nurses spend an awful lot of time with their clients in a community setting, and they carry an awful lot of responsibility. You go into somebody's home and there ain't no backup team. Now, you have to give people the wherewithal to do that.*

> *If we go back to Dearing, what struck me is that he is saying really that we've got to educate people who are going to earn a living. And they won't earn their living because they know how to produce a particular molecule in a particular way, that's not the way people earn their living these days.*

In the first quotation, we see a lecturer in nursing studies reflecting on the pedagogical challenges of developing the human qualities required in nursing: 'you have to give people the wherewithal to do [what is required of them]'. The 'wherewithal' in question is not a form of knowing but a form of *being*. Here, it is the *being* that comes with the acceptance of responsibility. But it is clear from the passage cited that responsibility is not simply accepted but is enacted: 'they carry an awful lot of responsibility'. They carry it; they engage with it.

The second quotation has a particular significance for our thesis in this book. Here, a chemistry lecturer reflects that chemistry graduates won't be earning their living by '[knowing how] to produce a molecule in a certain way'. Both knowing and acting are inadequate for prospering in the modern world; something else is required. The emphasis here is on 'earning' a living. In other words, the graduate is going to have to invest something of her- or himself in order to gain that living. The logic surely would run, such an investment of the graduate's self – beyond knowing and acting – comes about through a personal engagement with the work situations that present themselves.

The term 'engagement' may not yet be part of the common vocabulary of lecturers in UK higher education but the idea of engagement is surely present, if only embryonically, in both the thinking and practices of lecturers and teachers. It is an idea that has point where not just the *knowing* or *acting* but also the *being* of the students becomes of interest and concern in curricular practices. It is a dimension that now has an anchor in curricula and is growing in the weight that attaches to it; and that weight will assuredly continue to increase.

Conclusion

Curricula do not stay still. Even if non-consciously, they move in their shape, their positioning and their implicit hopes for students' development. Our more specific and immediate view has three strands to it.

First, in the context of the increasing integration of higher education with the wider world, it is likely that messages (subtle and unspoken as they may be) will come suggesting that knowledge competencies, however widely drawn, will offer an insufficient framing of the curriculum.

Second, our own value position is that in principle we herald any such encouragements. For too long, curricula in higher education have been drawn overly narrowly as projects of knowledge. It is time to open up curricula to other forms of human development. Third, we can see signs of such opening up of curricula. Evidently, we can see indications that students are being encouraged towards forms of practical achievements. The curriculum has already become – even if unevenly across the disciplines – a site of *acting* alongside *knowing*. Less evidently, but emerging, is the curriculum manifestly as a site of *being*.

Tacitly, of course, this has always been the case. One cannot acquire the cultural accomplishments of being a chemist or a philosopher unless one is brought to a particular form of *being* as such. Now, however, as we have seen in this chapter, there are glimmerings that indicate that curricula are being shaped through a project of *being* in a conscious manner. More than that, the forms of being now being released and encouraged are much more those of being-in-the-world rather than forms of being-in-knowledge. Increasingly, it is the students' capacity to fend for themselves in the wider world that is coming into view, their capacities to sustain themselves, to engage with the wider world, to be resilient and to prosper – not just economically – in it. We are witnessing the emergence, surely, of a curriculum for life.

Part 3

Prospects for Engagement

9

Engaging the curriculum

Introduction

In this chapter, we want to pull together the strands of our argument and to do so by developing an idea that we have touched on from time to time – the idea of engagement. This idea has recently entered the debate about higher education (Bjarnason and Coldstream 2003) and we find it potentially fruitful. However, it also holds some traps for the unwary.

Two metaphors of engagement

'Engagement' is a term that offers to do different kinds of metaphorical work. One potential metaphor is that of cogs meshing – *engaging* – with each other. In its trail come further connotations of efficiency, power, work and outcomes. A second metaphor possibly implicit in the term 'engagement' is of a much more personal character, where individuals engage – and may even on occasions be 'engaged' – with each other such that there is a mutuality and long-term interconnectedness of an emotional character.

The two metaphors – mechanical and transactional – are strikingly different in at least one respect. In the mechanical metaphor, energy is dissipated in the engagement: the energy that results from the cogs meshing has to be less than the energy supplied to get them going in the first place. With transactional engagement, on the other hand, energy can be multiplied: new forms of motivation can arise that supply new energy.

This, then, is one of the challenges for a curriculum for engagement: does it simply assume, as it were, a fixed amount of intellectual and personal energy and seek to direct it in particular directions with as little energy loss as possible (but being obliged to recognize in the evidence of decreasing retention rates that the energy losses are continuing to mount)? *Or* is it so framed that it seeks to encourage students to generate new sources of energy in themselves, thus adding to their involvement in their courses and their attachment to their studies? Accordingly, a curriculum *for* engagement positively sets out to heighten the energy within a course and to add to students' engagement with it.

On our schema of knowing, acting and being, the possibility opens for students to engage, while on their courses, in three dimensions – those of knowledge, action in the world and the self. The terms 'knowing', 'acting' and 'being' point to different *forms* of engagement on the part of the student and, therefore, different forms of potential energy from the student. For instance, knowledge is not external to the student but has been incorporated into committed knowing acts; the student comes to make claims of her own, however tentatively, however half formed. They are *this* student's own claims to know, not another student's. Further, the student is put into situations, whether in the classroom, studio, laboratory, or even outside the campus, where she is obliged to act, to intervene in the world in some way and to take personal responsibility for that action. The student is *acting* a role and is taking the part of student, certainly, but she is required to do it in her own way and invest herself in it, for there are no precise scripts to follow. The student becomes increasingly able to articulate her experience as a student and even be self-critical. As such, the student comes into herself in new ways: she comes more fully into her own *being*, becoming both more daring and more deliberate all at once.

We have seen signs in earlier chapters of each of these three forms of engagement opening up in curricula in the UK, but we have also seen signs that such a curriculum for engagement is in some jeopardy. We have witnessed examples of lecturers observing the closing off of the space for intellectual engagement, often with the best of motives, as they seek to ensure that all the members of a heterogeneous class of students have certain kinds of basic problem-solving skills. We have also glimpsed signs of staff wanting to keep tight control of the student experience – of the 'pedagogical frames' – such that the students' opportunities for coming to know themselves and to have a wider and more incisive sense of self are put at risk. Much of this is understandable as a set of responses to the situations of rising student: staff ratios and increased demands being placed on tutors who are working ever-rising numbers of hours per week. But in any event, noting responses of this kind by no means tells the full story.

We have seen, after all, examples of positive tendencies. We have seen curricula where the knowledges that students are encountering are widening and where they are being challenged to take up active stances in their knowing acts. We have noticed curricula where students are being placed in an increasing variety of situations and where they are being encouraged to develop their dispositions for acting purposefully. We have glimpsed curricula where students are expected to develop their powers of self-reflection and so heighten their sense of self as emotional as well as intellectual beings.

What is significant about these positive ways of eliciting wide-ranging forms of engagement from the student is that these curricula accord *curriculum space* to the student. The student is not continually boxed in but is given space in which to develop herself, to come into herself and to feel a proper ownership of what she thinks and does. Sometimes the space accorded to students is happenstance. Recall, for instance, the example in which adult students unexpectedly found themselves alone in a timetabled session. In that non-intended space, things happened that were of positive educational worth: the students organized themselves and their task and proceeded productively together.

A curriculum for engagement, accordingly, cannot be a curriculum where the student is regimented against her will, whether in the laboratory, in the acquisition of factual knowledge, or in the lecture hall and seminar room. In a curriculum for engagement, a student comes to develop and impart her own energies and for that to occur she has to be accorded space that she can call her own.

An ambiguity

'Engagement', then, turns out to be a nice metaphor for describing the basic triple-fold schema that lies at the heart of our story, but which contains an ambiguity that we noted earlier. That ambiguity deserves a little development.

As we have just seen, a curriculum for engagement can be viewed in a mechanical way, as the ordering of curriculum elements so as to produce the greatest output possible as economically as possible. Under this conception of a curriculum for engagement, much thought will be given to making explicit learning outcomes and to ensuring that they are brought off with as little student 'wastage' as possible. At the same time, students will be seen to take on definite skills, especially those that will have high value in the labour market. Efficiency and economy will be maximized and even, it may be said, effectiveness as well. The curriculum is 'producing' precisely those outputs intended to be produced at minimum cost. 'Engagement' comes into play here in more ways than one. The curriculum is engaged with the immediate needs of the economy and the world of work; it is engaged with the very real needs for institutions of higher education to run efficiently; it is engaged with national debates as to good practice in curriculum design; and the students themselves could be said to be engaged as they take up the opportunities for skills acquisition and development opened up to them in their learning environment.

In itself, this reading of a curriculum for engagement is not invalid. But a curriculum for engagement that was developed only in this way – and many of the promptings in contemporary debate and development inspire such an approach – would fall far short of the actual possibilities that are present in our schema, which we see signs of day in and day out across the disciplines in higher education. The further possibilities for engagement that are implicit in our schema are those of personal engagement on the part of the student.

By 'personal engagement' we mean acts on the part of the student –

whether in knowing, acting or self-understanding – that point to the student's *self*-becoming and even self-transformation. In this engagement, the student's will comes crucially into play: she is energized to will herself forward, even at the price of emotional risk. The student lays out her vulnerabilities in voyaging her *self*. She does it when she goes beyond her immediate data or experience, her chosen texts and scholars and their offerings, to venture a claim or a suggestion herself. She wills herself forward in becoming involved in a group task rather than being a voyeur of the group. She tackles her apprehensions about strange situations by placing herself in them and acting out her own part in a committed way, interpreting it and colouring it as best as she can. And she comes to a more insightful understanding of her own strengths and weaknesses as when, for instance, she reflects on a critical incident that may have occurred in a clinical setting in which she was intimately involved.

Another way of expressing this point lies in the idea of voice. In our view, a curriculum is not only a vehicle for giving students a space in which to express their voice, but also for providing them with a space in which they can find and develop their voice. 'Voice' is again a metaphorical term for it can be expressed in each of our three domains. A student can find a voice of her own in her knowledge claims (an epistemological voice), in her actions (a practical voice) and in her own self, in her very being (an ontological voice).

A curriculum therefore has to be understood as an educational project that not only engages the student but also enables and indeed encourages the student to engage herself. Spaces have to be inserted into the curriculum not for the student to take time out but which require her to become engaged on her own terms. Such a curriculum is necessarily imaginative (Jackson 2002) and its design calls for an empathy-in-advance with the student's situation and the innovative creation of spaces that call for involvement and action on the part of the student. An engaged curriculum is necessarily a *curriculum-in-action*.

Counter-views

For many, our triple-fold schema – of knowing, acting and self-understanding – through which we might understand and try to bring off a curriculum will be problematic. There are at least three sceptical positions:

1 *It does not begin to do justice to the many curriculum challenges that have opened up and been placed upon lecturers and others involved in teaching and managing curricula, especially in the UK. After all, the whole battery of 'outcomes', 'competencies', 'skills' and their many variants ('core skills', 'transferable skills', 'domain-specific skills') and 'modes of assessment' have made only sporadic appearances in our discussion.*

2 *It does not do justice to the many and varied curriculum objectives that lecturers*

and others are forming, day in and day out, in developing and bringing off success-
fully curricula with which they are associated. Curriculum objectives, caught in
terms such as 'apply', 'analyse', 'organize', 'create', 'solve', 'formulate' and 'evalu-
ate', have not been much apparent in our discussion either.

3   *It does not do justice to the developing academic literature on the curriculum. For*
example, to take one idea that has contemporary currency, the concept of 'construct-
ive alignment' has made only a fleeting appearance in our analysis.

All three charges can be taken together for collectively they amount to the challenge that our discussion has failed to go as far as it might in laying out the design of curricula. The argument might be that we could and should have been much more precise. The components of curriculum design could have been specified in much more detail such that the relationships between those components could have been better defined and its outcomes more assured. We disagree. Indeed, part of what we are about here is to contend against the developing curricular images of our day, which are heavily mech-anistic in character. For our part, we have tried to depict the curriculum such that it is invested with human being. The key terms – knowing, acting, being – imply actions and states of being that are saturated with human meaning. If this is understood as a feature of curriculum design, then there are going to be considerable limits to what can be said or even designed in advance in any particular situation.

Understood in this way, a curriculum cannot primarily be a matter of so arranging matters that a definite outcome will result. It cannot be a matter simply of putting students *in situ*ations where they are obliged to exhibit certain kinds of behaviours (such as analysing, solving, synthesizing, judg-ing, and so on). Nor can it even just be a matter of 'aligning' the constitu-ents of the curriculum with the original intentions behind it and ensuring a congruence across those various components. Two kinds of instrumentalism are at work here. On the one hand, there is an assumption that the sheer acquisition and exhibition of skills itself leads to, as it might be termed, capability. The assumption ignores the point that skills in themselves are bankrupt without a will to put them to use (quite apart from good judge-ment to use them in due measure and with some degree of sensitivity to context). On the other hand, there may be an assumption that the sheer alignment of curricular components will lead to the formation of a higher learning. This is a mechanistic conception of curricula construction, but out of mechanistic conceptions of curricula can come little more than machines.

It might be said that our approach to curricula involves putting the student first; but that *would* be a crude description. At one level, all we are doing is identifying and heralding certain of the practices to be seen on a daily basis in our universities. These are practices that are intended to develop the range and level of students' skills but they are much more besides. The practices we have been underscoring are those in which there is a concern to allow students to come to their own knowing acts such that those acts are invested with personal meaning by the students. In such curricula, while much may be done to lead students on, to encourage them and to affirm them, in the end and even in the beginning students have to will their own interventions – of knowing, of acting and of self-understanding – for and by themselves.

Pedagogies for engagement

Curricula that engage are full of personal and collective energy, of authentic effort and, indeed, of engagement. It follows that *curricula for engagement entail pedagogies for engagement.* Indeed, in a sense, there can be no curricula for engagement as such: curricula only become curricula that engage *through* their pedagogies. If curricula are the intentional imagining and ordering of educational experiences, it is through pedagogies – through the teaching approaches and the pedagogical relationships between lecturer and student and even student and student – that the curriculum is realized, if at all. A curriculum for engagement, built around the promotion of knowing, acting and being, can only be brought off consistently, can only engage the students *en generale,* if engagement is present in the pedagogical relationship.

Admittedly, these are large claims. We could say that they are borne by our own immediate personal experience as university teachers. We could also say that they are reflected in student evaluations of teaching: students, by and large, tend to respond positively – if not uniformly – to teaching effort expended to heighten their interest in the experiences put before them. But the main point is more a priori in character: a personal engagement in their experiences cannot be assumed to be already present. That indeed is one of the aims of teaching and therefore of curricula in a university – to bring about that personal involvement in their own *acts of learning* on the part of the students. Such personal engagement has to be brought about as part of the pedagogical process.

But having said that, there are two matters yet deserving further elucidation. With what is it that the student is engaging? What does it mean to be engaged? Answers to the first question are readily to hand: the student, on our schema, is engaged in her acts of knowing, acting and self-direction. Where a curriculum for engagement is working well, in each of the three domains there is a firsthandedness, an immediacy, in those acts on the part of the student. This is not to say that things always go smoothly or are full of 'truth', but it means that the student is investing herself in whatever it is that she is doing. There is a personal commitment to the task in hand such that it is not just a task that has been set – within the framing of the curriculum, to achieve certain outcomes – but a task that has been internalized, in the student's interior space. Engagement, then, is a relational concept: it indicates an identity, to a significant degree, between the student and the act of learning.

Curriculum-in-action

We are proposing, then, that the idea of curriculum design as an educational project which can be accomplished as an office exercise has to be abandoned. A curriculum is always, in part, a *curriculum-in-action*. It is always being realized *in situ*. However, this simple point has various implications. As we have just seen, curriculum design has to open spaces so that the student can develop in different ways and in her own style. A curriculum has to become like so many ultra-modern buildings, full of light and open spaces, different textures, shapes and relationships and arrangements for serendipitous encounters.

Indeed, like many modern university libraries, a curriculum is a set of spaces in which a student can move as she wishes to find herself, to discover her own interests and develop her own capabilities in her own way. Essays, laboratory and studio work, learning in the workplace, problem-based learning: all these instances can be regarded as spaces in which the student can develop, has to develop, by herself. But these are structured spaces and it is the interplay between its spaces and the structure that makes for an imaginative curriculum. The student is encouraged to find ways of catching and engaging her attention and her own imagination. It is the spaces, as much as if not more than the structure, that engender the student's energies and her own engagement.

But then there is a related process of engagement at work so far as the tutor is concerned. For the tutor himself has also to be engaged in the experiences being put before the student. The tutor has to open the spaces in front of the student and this injunction calls in turn for the tutor's engagement *in situ*. This engagement takes place both horizontally and vertically. *Horizontally*, the tutor has to have a personal stake in the student's becoming, in the three domains of knowing, acting and being. By this we mean that the tutor has to be personally involved, to some degree, in the field of knowledge being extended to the student.

This is not a plea to the effect that the tutor has herself to be 'research active', although that may help, but the tutor's identity has to be in part structured by the knowledge field in question. It means too that the tutor has to identify with the field of knowledge *in action*.

The tutor's possible identifications with the field in action may in principle be infinite in scope, so what is required here is a sympathy extended to the value of the field in action. Its exemplifications will be probed, with students being put into different situations, whether in the laboratory, simulator, studio, or with different societal settings, professional dilemmas and texts. It means also that the lecturer has an empathy with the student's being as such. Of course, with large classes characteristic of a mass higher education system, it may be difficult or impossible to know each student even at a superficial level. But the lecturer can extend an empathy to the student nevertheless. Therefore, in a curriculum-in-action there is a necessary three-fold symmetry between the ways in which the student engages and the tutor engages.

If the three domains of knowing, acting and being offer an opportunity for the lecturer to be engaged with the student experience *horizontally* (in the student's knowing, acting and being), there remains a sense in which that lecturer's engagement with the student experience can also be accomplished *vertically*. The vertical engagement is captured by the student who remarks, in a module evaluation, that the lecturer in question was 'inspirational'; or at the graduation ceremony or even some years later, that the course in question 'changed my life' or simply that 'the course gave me a new sense of self-confidence'.

How can we make sense of remarks such as these? We may do so through a sense of *vertical engagement* on the part of a lecturer or even on the part of a course team. In vertical engagement, the curriculum is so orchestrated that the lecturers play with it. The metaphor of play is triply apposite here. There is a sense of play as such: the lecturers so do justice to their educational role that a spirit of play is never far from the surface and may even break through from time to time: a curriculum can hardly be working effectively if it never yields smiles and even laughter.

Second, there is here a sense of play in a disinclination to take oneself too seriously. After all, students can hardly be expected to acquire the capacity for self-critical thought and action if they cannot also acquire a sense of self-irony. And such a sense of self-irony will in turn hardly develop unless their teachers also display such a capacity. Lastly, the lecturer as an accomplished educationalist will exhibit his or her expertise by being able at any moment to call upon a repertoire of possible actions, behaviours, thinking and communicative styles. He or she will be able to play with that repertoire of capabilities so as to produce the maximum effect in the exigencies of a moment.

Why term such capacities for play on the part of the lecturer as teacher forms of 'vertical engagement'? The explanation is that in such playfulness there is a quality of *depth* in the effects on the student's being. More accurately, the teacher so plays with the curriculum moment by moment that the student is induced to opening herself to the experiences to which she is exposed. Not every student will open herself in this way, that is true. However much the dedicated teacher strives to orchestrate the curriculum so as to stir his/her students into a stance of engagement, some will remain unmoved; and perhaps for good reasons as they perceive matters. But the effective teachers are precisely those who can move the majority of students into such an engaged receptivity.

One way of describing such educational effectiveness would be to say that, here, we are in the presence of an engaged curriculum becoming also an engaged pedagogy. Or, even more accurately, a curriculum becomes a project of educational engagement only insofar as it is taken up and given energy, interpretation, colour and even joy through pedagogies of play. A difficulty, of course, in putting things in this way in our culture is that talk of pedagogies of play may sound as if they are lacking in seriousness: play and seriousness are set off from each other and never the twain shall meet. But such a polarization of pedagogical dispositions has to be repudiated. The kinds of human qualities that an age of uncertainty calls for – fortitude *and* self-irony, resilience *and* capacity to let go, openness *and* determination – will only be developed in our universities if seriousness and play interweave in a liquid curriculum, at once fluid yet purposeful.

The engaged curriculum, therefore, reaches down into students, but only provided they open themselves and engage with it. The curriculum engages through pedagogical engagements that gain their effect by being ontologic-ally engaging. In short, the students are hooked but hook themselves, as it were, just as much as the curriculum and the chosen pedagogies hook the students. The engaged curriculum is a place of mutual engagements.

Two versions of curriculum design

We can now return to the idea of curriculum design which we looked at earlier in Chapter 4. There, we distinguished four senses of curriculum design, but here we want to refocus on just two of those senses, which hinge around the matter of timing. The first and most obvious sense of curriculum design lies in the process prior to its enactment, prior that is to the associated teaching and learning. Here, the task is that of producing a specification of the curriculum that sits in course proposals. This is an important stage of curriculum design, but it can only be a proto-curriculum, a sketch of the curriculum. The curriculum has *subsequently* to take shape, complete with its open spaces, *in situ.*

Imagination and daring are called for at both stages, but the imaginative challenges differ between the two stages of curriculum. The first stage is literally two-dimensional: it can be caught in paper form (and be subjected to the scrutiny of a course validation committee). The second stage of cur-riculum design is fully three dimensional. (There is here, we may note, a parallel in the distinction made by Michael Gibbons and his colleagues between Mode 1 knowledge and Mode 2 knowledge. Mode 1 knowledge is formal and propositional, the kind that can be caught in textual form; Mode 2 knowledge is problem solving *in situ.*) Crudely, we can depict *curriculum-design-in-action* and its relationship with *curriculum-design-in-advance* in the form shown in Figure 9.1 (see page 132).

In the triangle, we see *curriculum-design-in-advance* standing in a dynamic relationship with pedagogy and learning. To put it formally, learning is in part a function of both the curriculum-as-designed and the pedagogy, and all three can be said to constitute the *curriculum-design-in-action.* Clearly, it fol-lows that curriculum-design-in-action is a larger term than curriculum-design-in-advance since the former includes the latter but much more besides. It is in curriculum-design-in-action that the really large challenges lie (for the course team as well as the student).

We can derive, from this triangle, two further points. *First, curriculum-design-in-action is inescapably a relational matter.* It is curriculum-as-designed, pedagogy, the pedagogical relationship, the student experience, the assessment

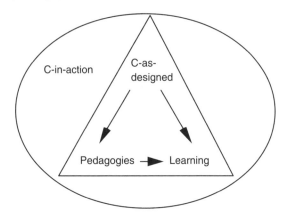

Figure 9.1   The curriculum-in-action

process and the student's learning all coming together, or not as the case may sometimes be. Where they do not come together in some kind of satisfactory way, there lies student dissatisfaction, even disenchantment and possibly failure to complete the course. This is not to say that all the elements have to sit harmoniously or have to be completely aligned with each other. Educational development may be heightened by some degree of managed 'disjunction' between the elements of curriculum (Jarvis 1992).

Second, the reasons for general confusion about the meaning of 'curriculum' are surely evident from this triangle and its distinction between curriculum-as-designed and curriculum-in-action. 'Curriculum' is inherently and doubly ambiguous. Not only is there an ambiguity between the sense of curriculum being designed *ab initio* on a blank sheet of paper and its being played out imaginatively *in situ* in classroom settings, but there is also an ambiguity as to the components that could be said to constitute the curriculum-in-action. Might it include the student's failure to complete the course as well as his counterpart's success? Our hope is that by recognizing that curriculum-in-action has many components that stand in complex relationships to each other that have to be worked at day in and day out, non-completion may be significantly reduced, even though it cannot altogether be avoided.

Curriculum ecologies and prospering within them

The curriculum is a site of varied *curriculum ecologies*, as we may term them. Curriculum-as-designed, pedagogies, pedagogical relationships, students' experiences, student–student relationships, students' development, student assessment and the institutional infrastructure: all these stand as so many *curriculum forces* in various relationships, pulling and pushing each other. At the same time, the three fundamental curricular dimensions of knowing, acting and being stand at the centre of this curriculum ecology, in turn supported and buffeted by those many curriculum forces. And behind these dimensions of knowing, acting and being stand disciplines, professions and cultural values. In this maelstrom of forces, spaces are closed off to students but others open at the same time. It follows that the working out of a curriculum is unpredictable to a significant degree, however much effort is expended on curriculum-as-intended, for the curriculum-as-intended is but one element in the total curriculum ecology.

Placed against this concept of curriculum ecologies, it is readily apparent that our fundamental schema – of knowing, acting and being – runs against the idea of curricula as a vehicle for producing behavioural changes of the kind reflected in lists of verbs, as 'can-do' statements. But it is perhaps less clear that our schema parts company too with the conventional triple schema of knowledge, skills and attitudes. Prima facie, after all, this latter schema represents a more sophisticated conception of curricula than a checklist of behavioural outcomes. It recognizes that there are minds at work (which are going to acquire 'knowledge') and even persons (the development of whose 'attitudes' can be a suitable project for higher education).

Our difficulty with the conventional triple schema of knowledge, skills and attitudes is that it simply doesn't go far enough in repudiating a checklist of behaviours as the basis for curriculum design. As it stands, a curriculum built on knowledge, skills and attitudes is liable to be inert. It fails to acknowledge the intricate and dynamic sets of relationships embedded in a curriculum-in-action, sets of relationships that we refer to as a curriculum ecology.

Let us assume that such a curriculum built around 'knowledge, skills and attitudes' is completely successful. In that case, all a course of study at best would have succeeded in achieving is precisely the acquisition of knowledge, skills and attitudes. Certain kinds of knowledge have been acquired, certain skills have been taken on and even certain attitudes have been taken up. But then a whole series of considerable questions remain: What understanding of the knowledge acquired does the student possess? To what extent is she able to stand back, be critical of it and have a sense of its limitations? Is the student able to determine in which settings her newly acquired skills should be put to use, or not at all? Is the student able critically to interrogate her attitudes, to place them and go on widening those attitudes to take on others and even discard earlier ones?

Our triple schema offers answers of a kind to all these questions. First, the domains are interacting – albeit in varying relationships – and so can critically inform each other. *Knowing* can be brought to bear on being and on acting: *being* can inform acting and even knowing: *acting* can act as a test for knowing and for being. Second, the three sites are themselves dynamic: the '*ing*' ending indicates that each site is a dynamic, problematic, testing domain. For the curriculum to be designed so as to invite the student to enter into such a dynamic domain is to have regard to the unfolding being of the student. It is to recognize that the knowing, the acting and being are life forces; they are sites of potential energy that can be encouraged by appropriate curricula, or extinguished by them.

Thirdly, in our schema of the three dimensions we place the student's *being* first: it is the student's being that gives strength, courage, colour, imagination and indeed energy to the other two domains of knowing and acting. Without a fully infused being or at least a being that has its own centre, its own unfoldingness, the domains of knowing and acting are going to be flat, thin, impoverished sites of the student's becoming. At the heart of a curriculum ecology lies not just a student's knowing, acting and being, but more especially her being. It is her unfolding being that will determine whether the intentions of the curriculum will be realized.

Of course, the student bears a significant responsibility for that unfolding, but to return to a point that we made at the outset of this book, the major responsibility lies with her tutors and the course team collectively. It is they who wield the major power and responsibility for the well-being of the curriculum-in-action.

Certainly, the idea of a curriculum ecology implies that no course team can exercise total control of a curriculum. Indeed, it is part of the character of a curriculum at the level of higher education that the course team cede significant control to the students, offering them spaces to develop their capabilities in regard to knowledge and action as well as their own inner selves. These curriculum spaces, though, have to be structured spaces, or at least spaces with elements of structure written into them. Students become irritated if they are set tasks whose objectives are unclear, and rightly so. To suggest, then, that a curriculum is a kind of educational ecology in which many forces and influences are acting on each other is not to deny a continuing responsibility on a course team in the playing out of those elements.

Principles for an engaging curriculum

Can generalizations be offered that hold across all courses, all disciplines, all institutions and all kinds of students? We think that they can. If curricula in higher education are to be designed and carried off in such a way as to engage the three domains of knowing, acting and being, and likely to enable the student to engage fully and effectively in the world, then:

1 The student has to be brought forward and brought to a state of willing compulsion so that she enters into new states of knowing, acting and being.
2 Knowledge, for example, is understood to be not an inert corpus but an open perspective on the world in which students can not only invest themselves but even come to make their own claims on it in acts of personal knowing.
3 Knowing, in turn, will be even more alive and meaningful where it is

experienced in different settings, where it becomes a resource for different forms of action. Such action itself has meaning where the student has room for her own interpretations, her own manner of acting out.

4 Knowing and acting call for personal space to be accorded to the student so that her own being can develop. To the extent that the time of students is constrained in advance – whether cognitively or experientially – so the space for that being to flourish will be diminished.

5 For these personal energies to emerge, *curriculum design* has to be understood as the design of *educational spaces*:

- *epistemological space* in which students can acquire a deep understanding of knowledge and take up informed and critical stances in relation to it
- *practical space* so that students can develop the capacities for purposive but critically judged actions, which may be both logically tied to their forms of knowledge or professional fields or more life oriented (such as action in the community)
- *ontological space* for the development of the student's own being has to be a central consideration in the design of a curriculum for higher learning.

6 The idea of curriculum space here is not that of an empty space but of a *structured space*. For instance, students may be invited to wrestle with value dilemmas in relation to their own field of study (a student taking pharmaceutical chemistry may be asked to address the issue as to the level of risk that might be associated with a new drug being accepted for general use). More prosaically, work in a laboratory or studio, or on an essay are forms of structured spaces.

7 A challenge in front of all curriculum designers, therefore, is the balance to be struck between the space to be accorded to students and the control of those spaces, or in other words the *agency–structure* problem of the curriculum. This is not a matter of how much time is devoted to lectures and other pedagogic devices, for 'lectures' come in all manner of forms. Indeed, interactive lectures can accord students uncomfortable amounts of space.

Conclusion

At the heart of any curriculum that is going to be adequate for the twenty-first century lie three projects readily identifiable by characteristic questions:

1 How can students come to make legitimate claims in a world of uncertainty? How can they gain the courage to make their own claims, knowing that those claims are always going to be susceptible to challenge? (*The project of knowing*.)

2 How can students come to act in the world, to engage effectively with

others, to be able to live out in the world their dispositions for knowing with all the limitations and challenges of so engaging? (*The project of acting.*)

3 How can students come to have a firm sense of *themselves* in a world which is open, fluid and full of contestation even as it is full of opportunity? How can they come to be capable of monitoring themselves, so that they may guide themselves towards right action and courageous knowledge acts? (*The project of being.*)

These three projects are not separate: if integrated human beings are going to be brought forward there will need to be *some* measure of integration. The three domains have to engage with each other, within the design and the enacting of the curriculum. Separateness leads towards performativity in which action and knowing are separate and, in turn, a fragmentation of experience. On the other hand, complete overlap of projects – even if it were possible – would be a *total curriculum* without spaces and would lead to uniformity and compliance. Curricula are gradually widening out, not only to embrace the project of being but also to recognize that knowledge and action are inert unless they become domains of engagement by each student, turning them into places of knowing and acting.

Curriculum change is moving in the right direction but it is going too slowly. It is lacking a due measure of informed steerage and there are pitfalls close by, especially of an imbalance across the three domains. In particular, a traditional over-emphasis on the knowledge domain may be overturned such that curricula come to over-emphasize the action domain. There too action may be seen as the acquisition of pre-selected skills. Just at the moment when so much is possible, when higher education reform is creating spaces for imaginative curricula that can at once do justice to the challenges of the three curriculum projects, spaces and options could be closed off.

A major difficulty turns on the notion of curriculum design itself. At a time when curriculum matters in higher education are being taken seriously and the different educational challenges are being identified, there is an understandable temptation to think of design as finding imaginative ways of *filling* curriculum spaces. Our view is entirely the opposite. In an age of complexity, effective curriculum design lies in the imaginative creation of *structured educational spaces* in which the student's own energies are likely to be prompted. It follows that curriculum design has to pay explicit attention to the matter of engaging students and it is to that which we now turn.

10
Engaging students

Introduction

Unless curricula are in some way engaging the students for whom they are intended, nothing much will happen so far as the students' development is concerned. Students are not automatons, responding mechanically to their surroundings; curricula cannot be realized as technical projects in which things are done *to* students. Students have to be personally involved in and committed to their own development. Successful curricula have to win over their students. To return to our starting point, curricula fall short of their potential unless they engage students.

That students need to be engaged also emerges naturally from the argument that we have been advancing in this book. If higher education curricula are going to help students develop the kinds of human qualities and dispositions that the twenty-first century calls for, we have suggested then students need to be understood as human beings with their own unfolding 'takes' on the world. If students as human beings are not just to survive but add to the world and be exemplars of human *being* as such (which presumably are desirable aims for a higher learning), then they will have to be able to engage with the world and put in something of themselves. But they are hardly going to be able to develop the will, the energy, the courage and the resilience to engage with a changing and challenging world unless they are also engaged in suitable ways in their curricula.

Accordingly, curricula should be taking account of the challenges of the twenty-first century much more than they are, and in the process they should be imagined as projects of engaging students. Our triple schema – of knowing, acting and being – is no less than a typification of three challenges of engagement: students will need to engage in firsthand ways with the knowledges that they encounter, with opportunities for action, and with possibilities to become more fully themselves. Spelling out these challenges – of a curriculum that engages students as knowers, as actors and as human beings – is itself a challenge, but one that cannot be shirked if an argument about curriculum is to hold substance.

Space for engagements

We have already noted (in the previous chapter) that the idea that students should be engaged by curricula is ambiguous. The point, though, bears some further development. The proposal equivocates between, on the one hand, a curriculum in which students are engaged in activities *and*, on the other, a curriculum in which students come to be engaged in their activities. The distinction may seem elusive but we believe it to be important.

On the one hand, a curriculum may seek to get students involved in, say, their own projects, group tasks, problem solving (in chemistry or business studies), researching a topic (in history), or a computational exercise. In all these ways, we can say that the student is engaged; the curriculum engages the student, perhaps even with other students. The student simply cannot complete the set task with any degree of success unless she engages in the activity. This is a kind of *operational engagement*, in which the student engages in the activity in question.

This is a crucial part of a curriculum that engages students. It is crucial not least because until recently the range of experiences offered to students in higher education curricula were relatively limited. The opportunities for them to become engaged were narrow in scope. As we have seen, that has changed and continues to change. The ways in which students can engage – in cognitive and practical activities and with themselves – are continually widening. As a result, students are widening as persons: they can engage with the world in ever wider ways, in acts of knowing, of doing, and of understanding themselves. (We have also seen how such widening may also be accompanied by narrowing, as skills may be acquired without critical reflection and as knowledge may be acquired without much understanding.)

On the other hand, however, there is an important sense of engagement that is more hidden. This is the level of engagement that reflects the student's inner and personal involvement in her acts of learning. Here, the student to a greater or lesser extent *commits* herself to the situations in which she finds herself involved. Opportunities, experiences and possibilities that the curriculum makes available are readily seized upon by this student. She may even try to extend the boundaries of the curriculum, seeing what possibilities are available in terms of the assessment regulations, or in terms – via the course evaluation procedures – of further development of the course itself.

In this *ontological engagement* she does not simply engage as a willing response, however energetically, with the experience put before her. She engages with the task in hand – with the other students, with the problem, with the particular practical challenge – because she aligns herself to it wholeheartedly. She wills herself *into* the task. She tackles it with enthusiasm, with élan, with imagination. She gives of herself to it and in so doing comes into it. She and the task – in this moment – are one. It is *her* task. There is, in such an instance, a unity in being and learning.

This, then, is the *double challenge of engaging the student*: first, to array before her a wide range of experiences that can draw her out in understanding, in practical involvement and in the emotional and experiential range that she has to offer; second, to allow her space to enter into herself such that she engages herself fully and willingly. Both forms of engagement are important: a curriculum for the twenty-first century won't succeed unless it engages in both directions. The student needs to be extended in a variety of ways. Otherwise she will not develop the personal resources to sustain her through the myriad experiences that will confront her in a complex world. The student also needs to be given the curriculum space to be brought into herself, such that she wills herself into new challenges.

The trouble is that curriculum innovation is too readily understood in just the first of these dimensions of engagement (as *operational engagement*), with the result that the curriculum is packed with all manner of well-meant experiences that are usually worthwhile in themselves but which, taken together, can diminish the space available to the student to come into herself (and so fail to engage in our second – and *ontological* – sense). As a result, curricular innovation can be counter-productive; it becomes a matter of giving students more experiences, more ways of knowing and more things to do (cf, Silver and Silver 1997).

There are both push and pull elements to this infilling of curriculum time. On the one hand, the academics are joined by professional bodies, employers and state agencies in identifying topics, skills and issues that should be represented in the curriculum and so curriculum time is rapidly exhausted. On the other hand, the students busy themselves, prompted enormously by the multi-textual resources of the internet with its seductive quality. In turn, curricula become as it were *embodied*, filled up with students being busy and, as a means of coping with their busyness, being strategic in all that they do; trying to accomplish the many tasks put their way (not to mention meeting the many challenges of managing their commitments alongside their studies). The logic at work here is quite straightforward: a lack of curriculum space invites a strategic approach on the part of the student in relation to the experiences that confront her.

Attitudinal space

Unless the curriculum is designed to accord students space and time to come into a positive relationship with their experiences, the necessary commitment and engagement just will not occur. But how might a curriculum evoke for the students 'a positive relationship with their experiences'? We consider that there are *three dimensions* to this educational aspiration.

First, the students have to feel that their learning is worthwhile in the sense that they are engaged in a worthwhile programme of study. Coming into play, therefore, are perceptions as to the character and worth not only of the course but also of the institution offering the course. How are the course and the institution regarded? The relative importance that a student accords to her course and institution will doubtless vary. For some students, it may not matter very much if their institution has a poor public image provided that the course experience is sound and the course is well regarded, but it is difficult to see how the two aspects can be kept entirely separate.

Second, the student has to form a positive view about her learning. She will want to feel that she is likely at least to pass and may even want to pass at a high level. She will want to have a sense that her learning and development are proceeding at a pace and direction such that she is likely to meet the aspirations she has for herself. She is likely to want to be able to have a positive regard for her assignments; she has invested much time and effort into them, after all. They are hers. She is likely to want to feel positively about them and to have that sense reinforced by her lecturers and tutors. She will hardly be wanting to claim an ownership of her learning, her work, her tasks and her assignments if others do not accord them some positive recognition.

Lastly, the student will want to feel positively towards herself. Unless the student has a positive self-regard, it is difficult to see how her learning can proceed. We may term these three forms of a hoped-for positivity as (i) orientational; (ii) curricular/pedagogical; (iii) ontological. We suggest that (i) and (iii) are logically prior to (ii). Unless a student has a positive orientation towards her course (i) and has a positive self-regard (iii), she is unlikely to form a positive regard towards her own learning. She is unlikely to invest time and effort in her learning unless those two other conditions have been met.

It follows that each curriculum has to be framed and brought off in such a way that students will come to have a positive regard for the course. Here, institutional factors come into play, such as the quality of the teaching rooms or the library services. Indeed, the total infrastructure – the course handbook, the environment, the balance of the different units, and so forth – has to be in place and be of obviously sound character. But it also follows that the pedagogical relationships have to be such that they encourage the students to come to form a positive view of themselves. The pedagogical relationship is not just a matter of those instances where there is direct interaction between tutors and students. It also includes those moments of space accorded to the students where they are able to work on their tasks, whether individually or in groups, their projects and their assignments.

These three dimensions – in which students can develop positive or negative dispositions – we can term the *attitudinal space* in which a course is situated. The student will take up attitudes to her course, to her learning and to herself. Such attitudes are developed over time and sustained over time. Perhaps the signal most important role that lecturers and tutors can play is that of nurturing a positive self-regard among their students. Students are hardly going to sustain their studies over time and develop the courage to form their own views unless they have a positive self-regard. Sustaining and developing that positive self-regard, therefore, is a task that is never complete. It has to be worked at continuously throughout the time that students are registered on courses.

Collective space

Engagement implies not just a coming together but an interaction. The student may be changed through the curriculum, but if the lecturers and the students are wise both they and the curriculum might also be changed by the student(s). The curriculum becomes co-created *in situ* by the students, their tutors and lecturers in concert. Such a process, of course, requires that the lecturers and tutors are themselves correspondingly yielding, malleable and ready to allow unforeseen things to happen. If they are, then the curriculum becomes a relational and dialogic site in which all listen to and respond to each other.

This *togetherness* quality of a curriculum is crucial. That tutors feel reluctant to run a course for a handful of students has little if anything to do with the dean's insistence on courses and modules having minimum numbers to generate a suitable income. It is effectiveness, not efficiency, that is in question here. A tiny number of students will not be able to generate the collective *esprit de corps* that is vital if a course is to take off and thrive educationally. Even though, in our conception, the test of an effective curriculum is the educational development of individual students, it by no means follows that a curriculum is purely a transaction between a course team and individual students. On the contrary, a necessary – though not sufficient – condition of an effective curriculum is that it encourages the students forward collectively.

Our own experience is precisely this: that a curriculum gains a liveliness, indeed comes to life, when the students are engaging well together. There are three points here. *First*, in working well together, students generate their own *collective space*, which in turn offers collective safety in an otherwise potentially vulnerable situation. Collective learning reduces personal risk. *Second*, the students becoming a 'learning community' (Lave and Wenger 1999), acts as a stimulus for educational creativity. To have, say, a large class of students working positively together in groups multiplies the opportunities for newness in each of our three key dimensions – knowing, acting and being. Students can become other than they are. Curricula can become animated. *Third*, a curriculum-in-action is a kind of theatre in which the students have their parts to play within the spectacle; and different students will tend to play different roles. These parts have to be extemporized. That is the wonder of an exciting curriculum-in-action: it is a forum in which everyone is engaged, is playing their part and is being creative, caught up in the complexity of the myriad interactions among many intelligent and committed individuals.

It follows too in such a hurly-burly that the tutors cede some of their power in providing space for the students collectively to flourish. This is necessarily so, for the collective flourishing produces innovation, the unforeseen, the exciting. One consequence, therefore, is that the curriculum – as we envisage it – becomes imbued with *collective power*. It is a site of educational happenings that would not occur under other circumstances. But note too that the tutor's responsibilities in this curriculum are not diminished but are positively heightened. Keeping the show on the road when the students have such collective space of their own and are engaging together is a demanding and complex matter.

Time in curriculum

Characteristically, courses in higher education are some years in length, even if they are composed of shorter units (such as modules or semesters). A curriculum therefore calls for a commitment on the part of students through time. This aspect of time, this presence of time, is not often remarked upon but it is a crucial aspect of curricula in higher education (though see Hassan 2003). The personal changes – in understanding, in capability, in human qualities, in self-belief – cannot be rushed or accomplished in a short space of time.

This consideration about time reaches deeply into the framing of the curriculum. For any curriculum aim, what duration of time is required to bring it off – three months, a year, three years? How much time should be accorded to *different* tasks? How much time should be accorded to tutorials? How much time should be granted to individual students? What proportion of the curriculum should take the form of tasks in which students work together? To what extent should such tasks be open-ended in the sense of either permitting a variety of ways of tackling them or a near infinite range of responses or 'solutions'? Curriculum decisions are, in a sense, simply decisions about time and its shaping and its playing out.

Change in human beings, then, has a time horizon. It will vary for different students. It may also be uneven. Little of the sought-for changes may be apparent in a student and then, quite suddenly or in a very short space of time, she will be seen to have moved on considerably: she has acquired a new self-belief; she smiles; she engages in the group tasks; she shows not just that she has an understanding of key concepts but is on the inside of them, able to play with them to communicate with effect; she now writes with authority. But all of those changes, which may even happen simultaneously, will often be the 'result' of considerable work and patience on the part of her tutors and lecturers.

The curriculum, therefore, is like an ocean, moving through time, often without much apparent dynamic or force, but hiding within it considerable energy. It may take some time for those energies to have an impact. Indeed, their force may build over time in and through the student. The step change that can be seen in students has to be given time to come, to emerge. At last, something suddenly breaks; the student comes into a new position, having given herself and having placed herself in the hands of her lecturers. Delighted, dazzled and even confused and made anxious, the confusion and anxiety may not be utterly resolved but can now be lived with and lived through with some cheerfulness.

The energies that are latent in a curriculum are not finite. On the contrary, as we have seen, in a curriculum that is working well energy levels can be raised. Students can come to enthuse and motivate each other. They can even come to motivate their lecturers and tutors. The energy levels within the curriculum can continue to rise. Things can take off. But such a phenomenon does not and cannot happen immediately. It takes time for individuals to come to know and understand each other such that they can trust each other, look for support from each other and infuse each other. This can happen in any curriculum situation (in the laboratory, the studio, the seminar, the group task, and even sometimes in the bar). *Human being* develops through human being*s*. It cannot be brought off mechanically or quickly but can be worked for painstakingly over time.

A curriculum, then, has to have time in which to work. It has to have time to give students space to come into themselves. It has to have time for the students in a class or cohort to come to know each other and to develop relationships of trust. It has to have time for convivial pedagogical relationships to break away from the formal relationships of power and judgement that are often present (Illich 1973). It has to have time in which the student can form new understandings, new capabilities and a new sense of self. Time has to do its work. The curriculum is necessarily a set of educational projects that endures *through* and *in* time.

In well-founded curricula, time and space work together. Time – well used – creates space, and spaces may, in a sense, produce time. For spaces may generate new energies which in turn impart additional effort, which is a form of time. The students do more than they otherwise would have done; they take time to take care because they are energized to do so.

Time for being in the world

The other sense in which personal change through a curriculum is enduring lies in the continuing effects that a curriculum may have. These effects, or rather the most significant among them, are not always immediately apparent, at least to the students themselves. It may be several years after graduation that former students are able to identify the most important aspects of the personal legacy of their course of study. How are we to understand what is going on here?

Curricula in higher education, aided and abetted by pedagogies, can change students forever. They do so by latching onto the dimension of *being* that we have identified within our triple schema. *Being* trumps both *knowing* and *acting*. Students can only venture a bold argument or undertake a challenging procedure in the laboratory or engage on an imaginative course of action if they have a strong and abiding self within themselves. The personal qualities of courage and the resilience required if knowing and acting are to be brought off successfully are just that: such qualities are *required*. They are required as a kind of personal – or *ontological* – substrate for bold knowing and imaginative action simply to get off the ground. The student's being, her *self*, therefore, has to come first. Unless and until this is in place, first-hand knowing and acting of any substance cannot and will not be forthcoming.

Academics who take teaching seriously know this. They may not have worked it out in any explicit way to themselves but they know that they have to reach into students as human beings if the transformations that they are looking for are to come about. The tone of the curriculum in its pedagogical encounters – in the lecture hall, the laboratory or the seminar – is all-important. Students reveal this in evaluations, where there may be comments about humour but also, more fundamentally, about respect. In a marketized age students may or may not want to be stretched cognitively and personally, but they will not develop in significant ways if the atmosphere is one of indifference, disrespect, undue gravity or excessive emotional risk. If curricula are to achieve the promise and possibility of the transformations associated with higher learning, human dimensions have to be secure. These human dimensions have to be apparent *in the first place*. Students cannot yield themselves, give themselves up to a long-term project designed largely by others, unless the human dimensions are significantly present.

As we say, academics who take their teaching seriously simply attend to such matters as part of their own personal approach to teaching. For them, getting the students to feel good about themselves, about being in the company of each other and about the experiences that they have, are paramount. They will spend time in getting to know each student by his or her name, and helping the students to come to know each other. On part-time courses, there may be a dossier compiled in which students tell each other something about themselves. Pedagogical encounters will be opportunities for smiles and perhaps even some laughter. Care will be taken over feedback to students, in the actual words used, and there will be a sensitivity to students' cultures and individual dispositions. Of course, mass higher education, with its student:staff ratios of 40+:1 pose considerable challenges to all of this. But the quest for injecting personal and human dimensions into the learning experiences are not abandoned on that account.

The point of drawing out these observations here is that unless attention is paid to building up the student's self over time, all the other educational projects inherent in a higher education curriculum will be vitiated. The student's courage to make bold claims and to act in imaginative ways, or even the fortitude and determination to go on managing her time and coming to an understanding of huge numbers of new concepts or even – in the sciences – fundamental 'facts': all this will be placed in jeopardy. Yet in ways that perhaps nobody understands, many of these qualities – the foundations of which can especially be laid in higher education – may not come fully to fruition nor show themselves for several years after graduation. It follows, then, that if space is denied to the students – a space that students themselves are helping to close off – so too is the likelihood that the curriculum will fail to realize its potential for long-term personal transformation.

Being is what matters. The student has to open herself to possibilities for deep-reaching personal change. Seeing the world in new ways, living with confidence amid cognitive turbulence, developing research capacities (that will often involve engagement with unknown others in the give and take of *interviews*) and being willing to venture into new situations (as with student expeditions in, say, geology, geography or anthropology) may call for new ways of living: these are changes in the student's capacities for *knowing* and *acting* that may persist through life. But these are changes in capacities: they will not be taken up by the individual concerned and will not come to structure her – 'transform' her – as a new human being unless the student's will and being have been transformed at the same time.

Curricula therefore have the potential literally to change students for life. They do so by changing students as persons. Students can come to look at the world differently and act in it differently, and come to be willing to have a go cognitively and experientially because they have acquired inner qualities of self-belief, assuredness, resilience and sheer will. Once laid down, these inner qualities are more or less permanent, or at least they have a durability over time. This is so because in the process of their formation the student's own being is developed; the student is changed as such. Her hold on the world and her relationship to the world is changed, for her self-understanding is changed as a result of the student changing *herself*. During this process, new forms of will, energy and motivation are developed within the student. These formations reach deeply into the student. She is changed utterly. There can be no going back.

Significant being

To say that the domain of the self, of being, is paramount is to express the point as a principle for curriculum design and practices. It says nothing about individual students. Historically, it may be considered, lecturers and tutors in higher education have not needed to give consideration to students as centres of being for, in elite systems of higher education, the students presented with a strong sense of themselves, with a firm inner being. Their social capital having grown through their lifetimes, they already possessed the capacities to take on whatever came at them in their student experience. Consequently, lecturers and tutors could focus their attention on their own epistemological interests. Curricula were significantly epistemic projects, although room still needed to be found for students' more personal and interpersonal qualities and even, on some courses, their practical competencies.

As a result, there was a nice symmetry at work. Lecturers and tutors could concentrate on curricula largely as epistemological projects. Attention to the more personal and interpersonal qualities could be explicitly separated from the curricula – and labelled thereby as not all that serious – in extra-curricula spaces (the debating society, sports field, university newspaper, a 'sandwich year' unincorporated in the course). In turn, such social and personal strengths as the students possessed enabled them to withstand lopsided curricula and pedagogies that lacked human dimensions. In a sense, these students did not require their curricula to take on wider educational projects for their social and economic capital gave them resources that would compensate for their impoverished curricula.

The phenomenon of students presenting with considerable social and economic capital can be seen today in another guise, that of mid-career professional development. Many courses, particularly at postgraduate level, are intended to attract individuals who are well advanced in their careers. Their curricula are such that professional experience and professional capital on the part of individuals are key resources on which they have to draw if they are to be able to take advantage of the course itself. (The emergence of 'professional doctorates' is a particularly recent example.) Such individuals often have not just some years of experience but have held positions in different companies, now hold a position of some responsibility (often having responsibility for others in their company), enjoy a commensurate status and may even earn more than their lecturers and tutors. These are often individuals with a firm sense of themselves, with a strong self and a core being of some unshakeability.

On a personal level, then, individuals may present with a relatively strong personal being: for such a person at the outset of the course, the circle depicting the domain of being would be larger than the others and the knowing domain could be considerably diminished. The dominant curriculum challenge here, therefore, would be to bring the three domains into balance for the individual concerned. Unless that can be achieved, the domain of being may actually prevent the student making progress in the domains of knowing and even of action that she otherwise could make. Her strong sense of herself might be such that she would be unwilling to yield to the demands of fields of knowledge and of right thinking and communication in a discipline or even to give herself up to engaging with courses of professional action that embodied strange and even counter-intuitive concepts or principles.

Curriculum spaces revisited

We have noted that the challenge of engaging students is twofold: first, to array before the students a wide range of experiences that draw them out in their understanding (their active knowing), in practical involvements (their acting) and in the emotional and experiential range that they have to offer (their being); second, to give them space in those experiences so that they can engage themselves fully and willingly. The hope must be then of any curriculum that it generates enthusiasm, optimism, self-belief, energy, forti-tude, resilience (for when the going gets tough) and enduring commitment. But for such self-development to occur, spaces have to be provided into which a student's energies can flow.

All this may be achieved in myriad ways, depending on the discipline, the interdisciplinary possibilities, the sheer resources that are available (not just immediate physical resources but on the accessibility to opportunities that the institution's local, regional or international positioning make possible) and on the imagination of the staff concerned. There can be no blueprint for a successful curriculum: all manner of possibilities are open today. There are real challenges that many course teams face, whether in terms of student numbers, the heterogeneity of the intake, or indeed the limited resources available.

Engaging the students, therefore, is a heady mix of educational tasks. On the one hand, a curriculum has to be designed, nurtured and drawn out in the company of the students such that it is likely to engage them. On the other hand, the individual student has to engage herself. No one can do that engaging for her. So there is a peculiar and subtle set of interacting processes of engagement taking place. Subtle adjustments will be made to the curricu-lum – perhaps to the design of a project or problem-solving tasks – as the students' responses, or lack of them, are monitored. Positive developments in the students' knowing, acting and being all need to be evident. Students working collectively together can help considerably in bringing off this triple set of educational challenges, in developing each other's understandings, in collaborating in an activity (whether in the field or in the university) and in self-affirmation.

It follows that a key question for tutors – both separately and as members of a course team – is that of determining not just the extent but the char-acter of any moves that they make in bringing off a curriculum. *Each move on the part of the tutors should be seen as an intervention in spaces that are the students'*; this is not to say that unsettling is to be avoided: a certain degree of ontological discomfort can be educationally worthwhile, provided it is contained within a climate of mutual respect. The horseshoe configur-ation in which the desks are arranged generates a space that is the students', but the tutor – with care – can transgress its boundaries to good effect. Moving into the students' space may be unsettling for some, but it may also be educationally stimulating as students are voyaged out of their comfort zone.

In all such interventions by tutors, eyes will be focused not only on the body language but also on all other forms of language. The scribbled note in the margin of an essay can either lift or deflate. One instance of a tutor expressing the view in writing on a student's essay that 'this has been written very quickly' can lose in a moment the student's self-belief that has just begun to form and be apparent. The self can quickly be lost to view and in the process will disappear any hope of the student coming to engage – with confidence and fortitude – the experiences that are being put her way.

A curriculum for engagement, therefore, calls for a teaching that is likely to engage, to connect, to lift, to enthuse and even to inspire. A curriculum for engagement, in other words, calls for a *pedagogy for engagement*. It is a pedagogy of deep and abiding respect for each student, of generosity and of space and time. It is a pedagogy in which the students are enabled to develop a strong voice, but a voice that is responsive to others and the challenges and standards inherent in the experiences opened up. It is a pedagogy that understands that ontological engagement precedes intellectual and even practical engagement. The self has to be granted the central place and to be given space in which it can flourish.

As the tutors make their interventions in the spaces extended to the students, therefore, it is the students as individuals that have to be uppermost in their minds. Only in this way can the higher education curriculum, in an uncertain world, live out its promise of *critical engagement* on the part of the student (Barnett 1997). Critical engagement calls for courage to take a stand, to declare oneself, to be clear about one's point of view, one's argument, one's position. A curriculum cannot bring all this about unless, therefore, it is endorsed by a pedagogy that provides spaces for the development of such personal strengths – courage to be clear, courage to take on authorities. A curriculum for engagement cannot rest with just being concerned with standards; it has to *create* spaces for affirmation and development. The self has continually to be nurtured through curriculum design as a creative but continuing process. The self is a long time in the making and a very short time in the dissolving.

Conclusions

What then, given our basic schema, would it mean to design a curriculum that is likely to fully engage students? Six principles suggest themselves:

1 Ideally, the three domains – our three circles – of knowing, acting and being should be more or less of equal weight. (The circles should more or less be of equal size.) Each domain should be playing a significant part.
2 The circles should overlap to some extent but should not coincide. A position of total overlap, of identity, would imply that the student's self and capacities for action are framed almost entirely by the rules of the discipline. The student just becomes a chemist or historian locked into the contemporary norms of the discipline, unable to step outside and critique them, for there is no position outside. A position of total separateness, on the other hand, implies a fragmentation of being, a divided self, where neither thought nor action are brought under critical control, nor tied into the individual's being as such. She or he simply 'performs': it

is a particularly strident form of performativity and one conducive to a state of totalitarianism.

3 The weightings and relationships between the domains do and properly will vary. Different courses will perhaps particularly emphasize one domain, whether the cognitive, practical or emotional/ experiential. (The third domain will be especially important in certain areas, for example, courses on counselling, drama or human-oriented professions such as those allied to medicine.) Nevertheless, our first and second principles still hold: all three domains have to be significantly present and in a proper relationship with each other.

4 The domain of self, of being, is paramount in that without it being given attention the others can never get off the ground.

5 The self will be energized where it is given the space to be energized. Lectures will continue to have their point both because they can open epistemological spaces and so intellectually energize the student. (It might be noted that they do not always quite live up to this billing.) They can also provide the student with some of the cognitive resources that she can bring to bear in the spaces that the curriculum otherwise extends to her.

6 Where a curriculum extends collective space to the students, such that they are prompted to engage with each other, it is likely that students will be energized and develop in the three key dimensions (of knowing, acting and being). Epistemological space, practical space and ontological space may all be enhanced through collective engagement among the students, for through collective engagement students gain educational *power*.

The making of a curriculum is nothing other than the making of the student self. The disciplines and relevant professional practices have certainly to be engaged, but they will not be found to be engaging unless the student is herself engaged. Since the self is never exhausted, engaging the students is a curriculum and pedagogical project that is itself never exhausted.

11

Engaging academics

Introduction

Our basic argument has been a simple one: the idea of curriculum is not one that is *explicitly* seen to be much in evidence in higher education and deserves, even needs, to come much more into view. With rare and evident exceptions, this is the case in all kinds of spheres in public debate about higher education, in the thinking in key national agencies, in the projects concerned with learning and teaching underway in institutions, and in course teams. This void is apparent, we have noted, in the academic literature: even those who concern themselves with thinking about and researching into teaching and learning matters in higher education have shrunk from attending to the curriculum as such.

There is, therefore, a large set of challenges in engaging academics over the curriculum. Thinking about the curriculum, discussing it, coming forward with imaginative ideas for conceptualizing it, designing research projects that examine aspects of the curriculum, actually developing and putting in place new kinds of curricula with an explicit associated rationale and developing momentum in favour of the curriculum as such: there could hardly be a larger project ahead of the higher education sector. It is a project that could and should take off at different levels: at course level, at departmental level, at institutional level and at national level (Becher and Kogan 1992). It is a project that has implications for structures, for values and for individuals. It is a project that would have both research and developmental dimensions. It is a project that could be taken up not only within the academic community itself but in the wider community, including the press and other public media.

The invisibility of curricula

Identifying possibilities for such a project at the different levels in higher education is far from straightforward, involving as it does structures, values and individuals. But in addition is a further challenge that we have not quite brought out in our book so far. Why is it that, in the UK at least, there are now hundreds of projects in the higher education sector being conducted on aspects of teaching and learning, but little explicit attention being given to the curriculum? A number of reasons could be ventured, some of which we have implied in our discussion at the outset of this inquiry. An absence of 'curriculum' among teaching and learning projects can be understood, in part, as the outcome of a confluence of interests precisely in *not* wanting to see the matter of 'curriculum' being given overt attention. To raise up 'curriculum' for public debate would be likely to press on sensitivities that we exposed earlier, which are associated with values and interests of the different stakeholders: the academics for whom teaching is characteristically a set of processes that hinge, in the first place, around their epistemological interests; and the state and employers as consumers for whom higher education is more a matter of marketable skills.

But there is another reason for the invisibility of the idea of curriculum, even in projects that are focused on learning and teaching matters. This is that there is an invisibility about the curriculum itself. One can go into a classroom and, however misguidedly, believe that one is observing both teaching and learning. In fact, at best one is observing a rather limited portion of the activities covered by the concept of 'teaching' and one is barely observing learning as such at all. Indeed, it is not at all clear that one could ever observe learning: that learning is taking or has taken place can only be a matter of judgement over time, an inference drawn from evidence accumulated over time. But at least one could be forgiven for thinking that in going into a classroom one is observing teaching and learning: in front of one are activities in which, characteristically, at least one teacher and several or many students are involved, activities that are intended to induce learning.

In contrast, curricula are much less obvious candidates as objects of perception. It is rather like seeing a train on the move down a railway track and imagining that such a spectacle can tell one much about a railway system. Indeed, 'curriculum' is an even more problematic concept than 'railway system' for it is something in which teachers, students and others are implicated in a way that engines are not involved in railway systems. Curricula live in and are subject to the interpretations and intentions of those conducting the activities that in part constitute a curriculum. Curricula live in hearts and minds, it might be said; more formally speaking, in intentions. But curricula also live in educational structures (courses, programmes, and the like), in educational concepts and in institutional and disciplinary cultures.

All of these features of curricula are self-evidently elusive stuff. Being elusive does not make them flimsy, however. On the contrary, educational structures and concepts, and institutional and disciplinary cultures are robust. They supply boundaries and demarcation lines and even student identities (as Bernstein and Bourdieu, in their different ways, spelt out). But they possess, nonetheless, an invisibility that teaching and learning do not share in quite the same way.

Rather than an invisibility, perhaps it would be better to speak of the elusiveness of curricula. A feature, surely, of this elusiveness is the many different conceptions of curricula that we noted in the earlier part of our book. On the one hand, there are the largely tacit conceptions of curricula, whether it be that a curriculum is an initiation into the mysteries of a discipline, a vehicle for personal transformation, or a means of affirming or even denying a level of pre-existing social capital. On the other hand, there are the more analytic and even educational interpretations of curriculum, especially evident in a *curriculum-as-designed* and a *curriculum-in-action.*

All these interpretations of 'curriculum', whether they be presuppositions held by practitioners or more analytic accounts proffered in scholarly mode, underwrite the elusiveness of curriculum. 'Now you see it . . .' Curriculum, in any of these interpretations, has a will-o-the-wisp quality. It is a bit like gravity or a set of sub-atomic particles: we infer their presence by certain kinds of happenings. So with curricula: we infer we are in the presence of curricula when we see documents, reasonably orderly behaviour and transactions in particular settings and examination pass sheets.

There is too an instrumentality and an operational quality that attach to teaching and learning that does not so easily attach to curricula. Academics who teach and who are concerned about their teaching sooner or later have to start asking themselves questions about 'teaching' and 'learning'. Correspondingly, it is understandable if the state, in wanting to improve the effectiveness of higher education – in the context, say, of rising non-completion rates – focuses attention on teaching and learning. It is, so the reasoning could easily go, in the student's learning experience that her propensity to complete or to withdraw from a course is determined. There is an immediacy in the link that is being formed in that thinking, between completion (or non-completion) and the learning experience. The concept of the curriculum would not so readily come into the bureaucratic mind intent on improving institutional performance – as marked out by the metrics of progression and completion rates. It is too ephemeral a concept and even – whisper it *sotto voce* – too much an educational concept for it to gain firm purchase in instrumental thinking.

The idea of curriculum, therefore, is a shadowy concept. Glimpses are caught, occasionally, but its substance hardly, if ever, is manifest: on the one hand, only tacitly held within the activities and presuppositions of busy practitioners; on the other, a concept of the educationalists. There is little here in the way of a broad constituency that would propel 'curriculum' forward as an idea for higher education in the twenty-first century. To return to our starting point in this book, it is hardly surprising that there is no public debate over curriculum as such.

There may just have been odd periods when 'curriculum' was more than a discomforting term. The birth, in the UK, of a clutch of universities in the 1960s brought with it much thought – even at vice-chancellor level – over curriculum matters. But times move on. Now we are into a more pragmatic age in which certain agendas impress their weight. On the analysis offered so far, it seems that not only is there no debate about curriculum as such but there never could be; there is simply no room for it nowadays. That would be an unduly pessimistic and premature conclusion.

Moving on?

We have been urging that a serious debate over curriculum is badly needed. But this conjoined elusiveness and invisibility of curricula that we have been noting poses certain challenges to any such debate getting off the ground.

In the first place, such a debate has to create space for itself. As we have seen, almost all the discourses in and around higher education act so as to forbid talk of curriculum, or at least to give it a frosty countenance. Mention of 'curriculum' is liable to receive a veritable cold shoulder. A wide debate about curriculum matters, therefore, is not easily going to be brought about. This is a matter on which academics and others have no wish to be engaged. The sheer establishment of such a debate calls for political adroitness of the highest order. Hearts and minds have to be won over not so much to any particular curriculum idea or model but rather to the very prospect of a general discussion about curriculum itself.

The second challenge that attaches to the task of establishing a debate about curriculum matters arises from its elusive and invisible character. As if the frisson that is liable to break out among pretty well most of the parties present at the sheer mention of 'curriculum' was not enough, its elusiveness and invisibility add further challenges to the would-be debater. Its elusiveness could easily suggest to the faint-hearted that time spent on debating curriculum matters would be time ill-spent. Much better, surely, simply to press on with teaching, research, administration, generating additional income and all the other tasks facing the hard-pressed academic these days. Since the curriculum has an elusive quality, talk about it is at best frivolous and at worst represents a financial cost. Curriculum is distinctly difficult to pin down so why waste time trying to? Just when it seems to come into view – as we box it in through descriptions of course units, aims and objectives – so it flits off again into the even more shadowy form of 'curriculum-in-action'.

And then the elusiveness of curriculum becomes an invisibility. The more we peer at curriculum, the more it seems to recede from our reach. The more we talk about it, the more we examine it, the more mysterious it seems to be. It disappears before us, even as we may think it is coming into view. So, our would-be debater is in for a difficult time, or so it would seem. The discussion would undermine itself for it would reveal the essential trickiness of the concept of curriculum. It is a kind of naturalistic fallacy: what may seem to be potentially within reach and self-evidently in front of one turns out to owe more to the eye of the beholder. A curriculum is not the kind of entity that exists straightforwardly in the world. Like the unicorn or the yeti, it is not so much that no one has ever seen a curriculum in full flight; it is more that it is the kind of entity that never could be immediately witnessed.

Given this dual character of a curriculum, then – its elusiveness and invisibility – it would be hardly surprising if those who are centrally engaged in bringing off a curriculum develop a jaundiced look at the mention of the curriculum. If their interest may be kindled initially, again it would hardly be surprising if that interest was quickly to evaporate as the apparently nebulous quality of 'curriculum' revealed itself. So the task of engaging academics and others in curriculum matters is fraught with difficulties. If engaging academics in discussion about unicorns and yetis is liable to run into scepticism, how much more so with curriculum? In other words, just at the point that one might want to move on, it is far from clear what moving on would mean.

Making space

Developing a debate means in the first place making space within which such a discussion can be held. Space has to be found, from the evidence we have presented here, at all the different levels in the system, from the course level through the institutional level to the national level. This is particularly the case with 'curriculum', even as compared with 'teaching' and 'learning' for, as we have seen, curriculum turns out to be an especially tricky concept. It has an abstractness to it that teaching and learning do not quite possess. Curriculum is, as it were, a particularly *conceptual* idea.

Two ideas, both Greek, may be of help here: *agora* and *ethos*. The first term – *agora* – has been given much air time of late, notably in a book by Helen Nowotny, Peter Scott and Michael Gibbons (2001). The idea of *agora* refers both to a meeting-place and to an actual meeting, and conjures a sense of the significance of public gatherings in Greek society. The *agora* was essentially an open space, both literally and metaphorically. In principle, anyone could go and join the meeting. In practice, as is well known, things didn't work like that and many were excluded even from an open public space. But one of its key features was that conversations were more open than the (Roman) Senate. The *agora* was public in a way that the Senate was not and, in turn, it had fewer rules than the Senate. The Senate was a relatively orderly affair in comparison to the *agora*: the *agora* had much less in the way of public comportment, of a sense of turn-taking and of rhetorical rules.

It is the relative openness of the *agora* that has opened the way for the recent spin put on it by Nowotny et al. For them, the mode of the production of scientific knowledge, especially in its so-called Mode 2 variant, is rather relaxed. It is not lawless, certainly, but it does not obey the formal rules and regulations, so to speak, of Mode 1 knowledge, which has to follow the rules, even though tacit, of the journal editors. Mode 2 knowledge lives in the real world in all its messiness. Its meeting places are much less rule-bound than those of formal and for some archaic Mode 1 knowledge. It solves problems *in situ*, as they arise; and very often these are practical problems to do with getting on or even just getting by in the world.

But a relative lack of rules does not mean that things are easy or that anything goes; neither is true. Things are not easy in the real world of the *agora*: all kinds of voices present themselves and all kinds of practical problems loom into view. The working out of this complex of voices and problems has to take place in a particular context: the *agora* of one town is not the same as that of another. So, it follows, anything most definitely does not go. It may be that there is an infinity of ways of resolving the melée of voices and problems, but at the same time this context forbids certain kinds of solution. The *agora* may not have the formal and easily detectable rules of the Senate, but there are rules, boundaries and even standards. To be heard, to be taken seriously in the *agora*, requires a certain way of conducting oneself.

Is this comparison between the *agora* and the Senate not suggestive for our present inquiry? When we say that there is need for a discussion to be instituted about curriculum matters and for a space to open, is it not more the discussion and the space of the *agora* rather than the Senate that is required? In a matter so elusive as 'curriculum', academics are hardly going to be engaged if the discursive space being offered to them is Senate-like. After all, how many academics these days would willingly and spontaneously attend the meetings of the senate of their own university? The rules preclude a spontaneous discussion; they present a space liable to be filled only by rhetorical flourishes, not for real engagement with the issues. Surely *agora*-like spaces are called for if curriculum matters are to attract serious attention and authentic engagement.

This may sound rather abstract stuff with all this talk of *agoras*, senates and discursive spaces. In fact, we suggest that it is at the heart of the matter before us, which is a supremely practical matter. If there is both a lack of debate in and around the academic community in relation to 'curriculum' and if part of the source of the problem lies in the elusiveness of the very idea of curriculum, then the character of the space that might be opened up for discussion is of the essence. What, indeed, might the chief executive of the UK's new Higher Education Academy or a university vice-chancellor do on the proverbial Monday morning if such a person wishes to help to open a debate on curriculum matters? Our reflections here are surely suggesting that such a debate will never get off the ground if the attempt to fashion it is a highly structured exercise. Anything that unduly frames this discursive space will simply freeze the debate before it ever gets going. What is surely required is an *agora* where individuals will feel welcome to engage and to have their say in their own way.

What would an *agora* look like in practice? What would it mean to create an *agora* in which curriculum matters could and would be likely to be discussed? This question is easily asked – a crucial question of our times for those who care about higher education – and yet it is possibly the most difficult question to answer (in higher education).

What an *agora* would look like in a course team, in a department and in a university would, of course, differ in those different settings. It would differ across disciplines and across institutions. As we have seen in this inquiry, disciplines and institutions shape in subtle ways (and sometimes not so subtle ways) how curricula are understood and practised. So the spaces in which academics can engage over curriculum matters are going to exhibit large variations. More than that, the establishment of such space calls for imagination, which in turn calls for academic leadership, and at the various levels of the sectors from course team to national level.

As we have seen, a national Learning and Teaching Support Network has been established in the UK, formed around individual disciplines, together with a Generic Centre. Therefore, at both discipline and national level there exists a national infrastructure to open up interactive spaces for discussion about curriculum matters. (See Appendix for some examples of such initiatives.) In particular, the new communication technologies present all sorts of possibilities for new interactive spaces, which in turn create issues over the character of such discussions. To what extent are such discussions to be controlled? To what extent are they to be managed, with deadlines, say, for a discussion to come to a temporary end? In what ways might some particular outcome be anticipated from such discussions? How would such an outcome be orchestrated?

In addition to such operational challenges associated with the management of the discussion, there is a further challenge. Suppose no one looked at the websites? In our present context, this is far from being a facetious question. After all, it was part of our earlier analysis that, while it may plausibly be said that every course team and even all university academics possess ideas about the curriculum, these ideas are held largely tacitly. Indeed, the term 'curriculum' is hardly ever used in the higher education community. So establishing websites that carry the word 'curriculum' in their titles is liable to be met with an electronic silence, if not downright antipathy.

Stratagems and strategies

The implications of these reflections are twofold: first, there is the apparently straightforward observation that leadership matters; second, that stratagems are called for every bit as much as strategies. Both of these points are worth spelling out.

If individuals do not have an explicit concept of the curriculum, if the idea of curriculum is itself open-ended, if we do not yet have an academic culture that is collectively concerning itself with curriculum matters, then simply opening up spaces for discussion is not enough. The discussion has to be engendered, and engendered perhaps without using the term 'curriculum' for its sheer use is liable to be counter-productive. On the other hand, the use of the term 'curriculum' may itself help to bring about a receptivity towards curriculum matters. If nothing else were to flow from this book, it might be a cardinal sign of its having an appropriate impact if every institution's *Learning and Teaching Strategy* was to be retitled *Curriculum, Learning and Teaching Strategy*.

But the point goes further than stratagems about terminology. What is at issue here is the preparedness of the academic community collectively to be involved in curriculum matters at some level of reflection.

Curriculum projects and curriculum initiatives (funded at institutional or national level) might be 'badged' as 'learning and teaching' projects and initiatives and much worthwhile and innovatory work might be conducted in that way. But ultimately, if curricula are substantially to develop and we are to have radical new thinking about the curriculum in higher education, sooner or later academics who teach are also going to have to address the matter head-on. Operational and discursive stratagems are important here: they can help get things going within a department, within a faculty, across an institution or across a discipline. Small sums of money can go a long way in curriculum innovation. But if we are to see change in curricula of the required order, the stratagems have to be accompanied by carefully worked out medium- to long-term strategies.

Actually, 'strategies' is too secure a term for what is needed here, even if 'strategies' is itself a flexible concept. A fundamental problem is this: How do we get off the ground a serious debate over curriculum matters if the concept of curriculum is not widely held? But this problem has near clones in more operational settings, for instance: How can we expect academic leaders to inaugurate a debate about curriculum matters if, dare we say, their own concept of curriculum is somewhat thin or desultory? How might a learning community in relation to curriculum matters be established when there is no one signing up for (as it were) courses on curriculum? In other words, 'strategies' – at all the different levels throughout the system – has to be understood generously here to include the fostering of a heightened understanding of and sensitivity towards curriculum matters. Such an understanding has to be fostered at all levels, including the relevant national bodies and the pro-vice-chancellors responsible for teaching and learning.

Engaging academics on curriculum matters calls for imagination in several directions. The course leader, the pro-vice-chancellor, senior officers in the relevant national bodies, heads of department, and learning and teaching coordinators: individuals in roles such as these are well placed to open up the kinds of spaces for action and debate. Pragmatically, the action and debate will probably be found to be mutually supportive of each other. Discussions on curricular matters will begin to have point, even legitimacy, if they are anchored in projects or other activities. But this is not to suggest that the individuals in the key positions have themselves to be 'champions' of curricular development. In their own settings – course, department, faculty, institution, discipline, or the sector as a whole – there will often be someone who either has or could quickly acquire a particular interest in the matter and who can impart energy to such a project.

Drawing on this discussion, then, a series of challenges are suggesting themselves in developing curricular strategies and in engaging academics:

1 *Challenges of language*: finding terminology that is going to resonate with the recipients' interests and situations, disciplinary and otherwise.
2 *Challenges of time and energy*: these two dimensions are separate but they also influence each other. With more energy, more time can be found.
3 *Challenges of resources*: as with learning and teaching projects in general, curriculum projects form a site where a little can go a long way.
4 *Challenges of legitimacy*: in higher education, to say that one is interested in or, more problematic still, responsible for curriculum matters is liable to lead to raised eyebrows or furrowed looks. Therefore, affirmation at the most senior levels in the system is crucial.
5 *Challenges of text*: the academic culture remains supremely literate. Sooner or later, if fast-moving streams of curriculum innovation and curriculum ideas are to be forthcoming, texts of some kind have to be produced. They have to include accessible and open texts, not just relatively closed texts such as academic journals. Texts of the *agora* and texts of the Senate are both needed. Each discipline and each university should be looking to produce lively and attractive magazines that embrace curriculum matters.
6 *The challenge of communication*: how interactive are the communication flows? Who is to initiate the conversation? In what mode or style? Who can join in? Surely, in such a moment of embryonic formation of curriculum debate, it is the open and democratic style of the *agora* rather than that of the Senate that should inform answers to these questions.
7 *The challenge of value*: there is little point in a senior lecturer spending part of her sabbatical leave in studying and thinking about a radical new form of curriculum if such efforts count for nothing in her subsequent application for a professorship. Or rather, there still remains point to the activity but it is unlikely to occur in such circumstances. Therefore, curriculum matters have to be valued and seen to be valued at all levels of the sector.
8 *The challenge of identity*: even if all kinds of reward and incentive structures are in place – both tangible and symbolic – engaging seriously with curricula ultimately is a matter of one's professional identity. It involves engaging with one's ultimate educational values and revealing them in the company of others. Engaging academics in curricular matters is therefore a risk-laden enterprise.
9 *The challenge of diversity*: as is well recognized and as we have seen in these pages, in having contrasting relationships to practice and epistemologies, different subjects will approach curricula in different ways. Efforts to engage academics within, say, a multifaculty university have to be sensitive to the diverse range of inner conceptions of curriculum that are naturally present at hand.

It will be evident in offering these reflections on strategy in curriculum matters that we have not resorted to the idea of 'managing the curriculum' (Bocock and Watson 1994) and we hope it will be clear why this is the case.

For us, perhaps above any other domain of university life, the curriculum presents such a wide range of near-intractable challenges that it is 'leadership' that is required before 'management'. This is a matter, above all, of hearts and minds. The systems certainly need to be organized and properly monitored and evaluated, but long before we get there we need bold imaginative new thinking about curricula. For that to happen on anything like a wide scale, academic *leadership* is required (cf. Ramsden 1998; Knight and Trowler 2001).

The scholarship of curriculum

Lurking behind considerations of the kind we are offering is a yet further matter, which we might term 'the scholarship of the curriculum'. We should like to offer a few thoughts on this phrase but do so by also picking up the idea of *ethos* that we flagged earlier on in this chapter. In effect, this book has been an extended plea that 'curriculum' should be taken seriously in the academic community. We have advanced the prospect of the academic community itself becoming, in effect, an extended 'learning community' in relation to curriculum matters. This is to say two things.

First, it is to say that the academic community, alongside developing a scholarship of its own towards learning and teaching, should also develop a scholarship of curriculum. Engaging in curriculum projects, being part of internet discussion groups and even designing new curricula are fine in themselves, but ultimately that kind of busy-ness, worthwhile as it is, has to be accompanied by more reflective modes of being in relation to curriculum matters. So we arrive at 'the scholarship of the curriculum'. Actually, we are somewhat uneasy with the term: it suggests closure and tight rule-keeping in forms of communication when what is called for is a rather more relaxed approach. But there can be no side-stepping engagement in deliberate, incisive and collective reflection on curriculum matters if well-founded but imaginative offerings are to be forthcoming. Here, something more of the ethos of the Senate is in order. Indeed, the establishment of a journal that was specifically focused on curriculum matters in higher education might be an important early step in this direction.

Second, it is to say explicitly that what is entailed in all of this is nothing short of an *ethos* in which the asking of questions about curriculum and the effort that is involved in imagining into being of an entirely new kind of curriculum are felt to be *natural*. That is, they attract no special attention because they are not special; or at least they are not felt to be special in the sense of being strange. They would remain special, however, because they would be important academic activities and recognized as such. Space would have been carved out by a pro-vice-chancellor for an open workshop, an institutional magazine would have been created to allow members of staff to share their curriculum ideas with each other, a member of staff would have been permitted by her head of department or dean to take a sabbatical (part of which would be devoted to working up a paper or two on aspects of the curriculum), or from time to time departmental awaydays would be devoted to the curriculum.

At one level there is nothing new in any of this. It is what many universities around the world have been doing for some years in relation to learning and teaching. To conjure the phrase 'the scholarship of the curriculum' and to try to install it as a collective *ethos* can be seen, as we have implied, simply as an extension of 'the scholarship of teaching'. Beckoning here is an academic culture in which there is a collective care about curriculum. But there are differences between a scholarship of the curriculum and a scholarship of teaching. 'Curriculum' is, as we have noted, a particularly conceptual idea. Its sheer use invites and even requires care, thought, ideas, imagination. It calls for vision, for hopes of the future and for a positive attitude to the effect that things can go forward in an adventurous spirit. Precisely because it cannot be straightforwardly observed, the term 'curriculum' calls for deep reflection. It is a practical concept – in the end curriculum ideas have to be cashed out and put into action to become curricula-in-action – but it is also an ideational concept. The *ideas* are put into action.

Taking curricula seriously is necessarily a scholarly matter, at least of a kind. The curriculum lives in the mind and it is a proper subject, therefore, for scholarship. It is surely clear too that 'scholarship' here has to be understood generously, to include reflection of many kinds. Indeed, it is important not to legislate too severely here. We require a scholarship of the *agora* as much as of the Senate: the rules of this reflection should not be binding. What is needed is something of the hurly-burly of the *agora* coupled with something of the decorum and space of the Senate.

There is another difference as between the scholarship of curriculum and the scholarship of teaching: the former is characteristically a collective enterprise and markedly so more than the scholarship of teaching. Whereas a starting point for establishing a scholarship of teaching can sensibly be that of individual teachers and their own teaching practices, that individualistic approach makes much less sense in relation to the curriculum. Curricula these days are much more developed as a collective exercise, or at least managed as a collective exercise. But more than that, as we have seen, ideas about curricula are held collectively, even if tacitly. It is therefore the collective assumptions about curricula that need to be brought out into the open and examined, collectively.

An unintended consequence, therefore, of establishing a culture in which there is a positive ethos in favour of a scholarship of the curriculum is that the academic community may help to regenerate itself. Collective and systematic reflection on the curriculum can only help with a university's research activities, for such reflection may well lead to research projects and publications. More to the point here, a scholarship of the curriculum can form a theme in which academics find that they have a common interest in curriculum matters. Engaging the academics in curriculum matters may well turn out to be a way for the university to engage with itself. A scholarship of the curriculum becomes a vehicle for *collective flourishing*.

Concluding reflection

This is a suitable moment to come clean about a problem that we have had, as authors, throughout the writing of this book. The problem can be expressed in a series of questions. Should we talk of 'the curriculum' or 'a curriculum'? Is 'curriculum' more of an adjective than a noun? That is to say, should we talk more, say, of curricular intentions or hopes rather than implying that curriculum is an entity in the world? Is 'curriculum' necessarily singular (always 'a curriculum') or can we talk as if there was a kind of generic curriculum, in the Platonic educational stratosphere? Is it 'curriculum matters' or 'curricula matters' or even 'curricula*r* matters'? This matter of the language of curriculum has bedevilled the writing of this book. However, we mention it at this late juncture because we have felt the problem in a particularly acute form in this chapter.

Why should this problem be felt with such acuity in this chapter and why is it worth mentioning the point now as we move towards the end of our book? The two questions can be met with a single answer. Our difficulty over language takes on an urgent character precisely in the context of engaging academics, or rather trying to engage academics, over curriculum matters. This matter of language is directly related to key planks of our argument and it is directly related to the politics of curriculum leadership.

Our difficulties over language are testimony to the ineffable character of curriculum and to the considerable difficulties in engaging academics over matters to do with it. If the language of curriculum is itself problematic, the task of engaging academics over curriculum matters is thwart with difficulty. In one of our starting points we noted that the absence of the term 'curriculum' does not mean that we are not in the presence of the concept of curriculum: a course team may have and indeed will have some concept of curriculum, even if it does not use the term. Therefore, it may be that academics are best engaged in curriculum matters if the term 'curriculum' is not actually to be heard. Out of sight or out of hearing need not mean out of mind.

Engaging academics over curriculum matters, therefore, calls for academic leadership of the highest order, requiring as it does a nuanced approach that is prepared to play the long game. It has been said that 'if management is the art of the possible, leadership is the art of the impossible' (Barnett 2003). Here though, it might be more to the point to say that if management is the art of the possible, leadership is the art of the imagination. For the task and achievement of leadership here, as has surely emerged, is nothing less than a triple challenge of imagination – imagination of conception (of curriculum), imagination of communication (in finding a language of curriculum in which to develop a conversational space), and imagination of engagement (such that individuals are likely to engage with each other and to develop their own energy in doing so).

Engaging academics in curriculum matters, accordingly, turns out to be nothing short of engaging the university itself.

Summary and reflections

Summary

The key points of our argument have been as follows:

1 There is little in the way of a serious debate about the curriculum in higher education.
2 The near-absence of attention to curriculum in the context of higher education is explicable in the sense that 'curriculum' is here an elusive term (and even a contested concept). We may distinguish four senses of the term:

- thinking, explicit or implicit, about curricula in a discipline – the 'subject'
- a curriculum-as-designed, of the kind put into course validation procedures prior to the start of the course in question
- the curriculum-in-action, which is the interplay of all those involved
- the curriculum consisting of those rules and expectations that accompany disciplinary and professional inquiry: such rules are usually not made explicit and constitute a kind of 'hidden curriculum'.

Failures to distinguish these different understandings of the term add to the impoverishment of such debate as there is.

3 Despite the near-absence of formal debate, at least in the UK, curricula are undergoing major transformations. We are witnessing curriculum change by stealth.
4 The changes taking place are having the potentially beneficial effect of widening curricula but the route being taken, that of a relatively uncritical inclusion of 'transferable skills', is liable to produce fragmented curricula in which knowledge and action are separated off from each other. This is a recipe not just for curricular fragmentation but curricular performativity.
5 We are faced with relatively thin conceptions of curricula and one of the

problems with such thin conceptions of curricula is that they are not going to be adequate to the challenges of the twenty-first century. Indeed, the changes are unlikely even to do justice to the (neo-liberal) repositioning of higher education to play its part in the global economy.

6 The twenty-first century is especially one of rapid and even instantaneous change, and of cognitive and experiential challenge. It is a world of 'supercomplexity' in which all bets are off. The very frameworks for understanding the world are in dispute. A higher education curriculum, if it is in any way to sponsor the kinds of human qualities and dispositions appropriate to such an age, is necessarily one that fosters human beings that are able to flourish amid uncertainty and incessant challenge.

7 Such a curriculum calls for the three dimensions of knowing, acting and being to be developed. There are signs that curricula are *embryonically* doing this.

8 Knowing, acting and being can properly have different relative weights, but every single curriculum should give due attention to each domain and do so in such ways that there are worthwhile connections made across the domains.

9 This does not mean that every element in every curriculum has to be completely in harmony with every other element: complete coherence between the three domains would deny the student space in which fully to develop her critical powers. Some degree of disjunction may be beneficial to the student.

10 Being is the most significant of the three dimensions in that without it the others cannot take off. A student cannot be expected to try to get on the inside of a discipline (with the arduousness that that entails) and engage in challenging practical tasks unless the student has a firm self (a 'self-confidence'); curricula, properly framed, can assist the development of a firm self.

11 Each of the three dimensions – knowing, acting and being – call for the student's active engagement with her experiences, such that she is fully committed to the tasks that she undertakes. The tasks have to become *her* tasks.

12 Such engagement on the part of the student can only develop if the students are deliberately accorded space. By 'space' is meant here opportunities for the student to come into her own experience and will herself into them.

13 Space is of three kinds that parallel the three curriculum dimensions: *epistemological space* (the student widening her understanding of matters, seeing situations through a variety of frameworks); *practical space* (the student being enabled to accomplish actions in academic and non-academic domains); *ontological space* (where the student develops her own self-awareness, self-confidence and capacities for self-critique and self-direction).

14 Curriculum space can be opened to students in many ways. It does not require large amounts of time free from the tutors' voices, although that

may help. Nor does it require significant amounts of time given over to projects or to experience in the world of work or the community, although again that may help. A lecture can open different and even competing frameworks, so widening the students' cognitive frames and it can be interactive with the students, so offering them ontological and even possibly practical space.

15 It follows that, to a significant extent, the design of curricula in higher education is a matter of the imaginative design of spaces that are likely to sponsor the students' flourishing in the three educational domains. Such an architectural metaphor – the design of spaces – invites a vocabulary of textures, of light and shading, of flows, of situations where serendipitous happenings can occur, of different media and of different kinds of conversations.

16 A challenge in the design of such curriculum spaces is that of energy: an effective curriculum is one in which energy is heightened rather than dissipated. The idea of *curriculum ecologies*, therefore, may be felt to be particularly apposite: curriculum energies are not to be squandered but harnessed such that they are self-sustaining.

17 Both the heightening of energy and the maximizing of space can be achieved through the students working together. Through engaging with each other, students can acquire curriculum *power*. They can add to the sense of *curriculum as theatre*.

18 In a word, the test of an effective curriculum is 'engagement': Are the students individually engaged? Are they collectively engaged? If the answers to these two questions is yes, the curriculum is likely to be successful in that it is helping its students to flourish. Indeed, it may well be exceeding the hopes invested in it.

Responses

We can envisage three particular responses to our argument. One response might run as follows:

'Your line of argument is not living in the real world, at least the world of higher education as it has developed over the past 15 years or so. It fails to offer clear guidance to hard-pressed staff faced with the challenge of curriculum design, it fails to engage seriously with issues such as student assessment, it fails to show how one formulates robust aims and objectives and ensures their fulfilment and it fails to demonstrate how precisely the elements of a curriculum might be identified and put together. Even more than that, your thesis fails on its own terms. You have argued that the student's self should be taken on board and the development of her being should be placed at the centre of curriculum design but you have failed to show what this would look like. Your argument, in short, is out of its time and simply won't produce results in today's higher education.'

A second response we can envisage runs entirely in the opposite direction. It might be said:

'Evidently, you want to see your argument as reaching out to a radically different kind of curriculum from that implicit in contemporary thinking and practices. You may even want to see your thesis as revolutionary and as offering us a great leap forward. But the trouble is that your thesis isn't radical enough. It has not broken free of the very instrumentalism and performativity that it is warning against. The diagrams themselves – circles, triangles and squares – all point to a rigidity of thinking that is just inadequate to a complex and challenging world. The very complexity of the world order to which you point requires an altogether different kind of thinking, one that is hardly containable in the A4 pages of a formal course outline. A curriculum for the twenty-first century needs itself to be one that is completely fluid, open and even chaotic.'

A third response is of a yet different order. It takes the following form:

'You wish to see yourselves as offering a vision of the curriculum that reconnects with large ideas of the university and earlier debates. But hardly anywhere have we seen those large ideas come into view. Issues of liberal education, of 'breadth', of connections between the disciplines, of education for citizenship, of higher education as a personally formative process of the kind captured in the idea of 'Bildung': ideas such as these, while occasionally present, have been rather thin on the ground. The book, in other words, has been something of a missed opportunity.'

We can readily understand that each of these responses may be forthcoming and have some sympathy with each of them. That our book has taken the form it has, however, reflects our reservations about each of those counter-positions and we would briefly counter them in the following way.

On the first response, that our text offers too little in the way of practical advice and guidance, we would reiterate our points that, in a diverse mass higher education system and in a changing world, the fashioning of a curriculum has to be taken up afresh on each occasion. But more than that, our text has explicitly inveighed against the precision of templates and the means–end thinking implicit in delineating precise objectives in advance of a curriculum being developed in action. We have deliberately sought to offer an alternative way of thinking. On the other hand, at several points we have offered sets of principles that we believe curriculum designers should heed, even amid the disputatiousness and uncertainty of the twenty-first century.

On the second response (the reverse of the first) that our book has been insufficiently radical, that the very offering of principles runs against the implications of an age of uncertainty, we are happy to leave our argument to speak for itself. We have tried to tread a line between, in effect, saying that 'it is a messy world and every course team must sort things out for themselves' and developing some general guidance that we think will bear some weight.

The promotion of *being* and allowing space for that educational development to be invested with the student's own energies – two of our key ideas – may not readily lead to definite curriculum objectives, particularly assessable objectives (and will doubtless thereby be unsatisfactory to our critics in the first camp). Nevertheless, we believe that it is possible to identify over-arching principles that derive from this way of thinking, even if in doing so we run the risk of dissatisfying our second camp of (postmodern) critics.

On the third response, that we have insufficiently taken up this opportunity to engage with the great curriculum debates of the past and that historic voices (such as Leavis in the UK and Hutchins in the USA) have not been present, our view is simple. It is that we are in new times and that a curriculum language and sets of ideas which can yield a feasible curriculum project have to be uncovered anew. We believe that many resonances could be found between our language and key ideas and, indeed, our general motivation (of wanting higher education to be a fully educational process) and several of those earlier debates and principal authors. But we are now in a different century and a different world and we are writing for new kinds of audience. We like to think that we have kept the faith with those earlier voices and the largeness of their ideas, even if neither have been taken up explicitly.

Spaces for new times

A particular challenge of the twenty-first century is that time has become filled up. Our time is not our own. Partly, this phenomenon is due to the information technology revolution that has brought with it 'chronoscopic time' (Hassan 2003) in which the human brain becomes, as it were, an extension of the computer and is continually bombarded with information which has to be processed instantaneously. But the tyranny of the email is also a metaphor for the way in which time has become super-saturated in modern life. Especially in the public services, which states have found themselves unable fully to fund, professional life has become congested with tasks and with demonstrating that one is performing effectively. Time has been taken away from many if not most in modern life. As a result, optionality has been closed off; or at least there is a pervasive sense that space for determining one's use of time is less than it was.

The higher education curriculum is doubly implicated in this situation. On the one hand, this complex and speeded up world is one in which individuals are having to survive and to do so with some assuredness. After all, it might be hoped that graduates can offer something to the world, some 'value added', rather than simply having added capacities to analyse the world and so become an expert voyeur of it. On the other hand, the curriculum itself is not immune from the chronological congestion of which we have been speaking. The compression of time and the determination to extract every possible value from every moment is working, if care is not taken, to rob students of space for their own development and thinking. Unless the situation is addressed, this technological regime is acting to reduce the space that is needed in which students' minds and being can flourish.

The students, as we have remarked, are often complicit in this development. Keyed up by the possibilities of the internet, they may not simply acquiesce but actually collude in shutting off space – cognitive and practical – for their own development.

In this milieu, we have suggested that curriculum design has to be thought anew. Rather than filling up time with tasks intended to achieve stated objectives, the curriculum challenge has to be inverted to be understood as one of the imaginative design of spaces. That imaginative design of curriculum spaces will allow new things to happen, new networks to form, new ideas to emerge, new activities to be entered into and new values to be formed. The means–end thinking in so much of contemporary curriculum design and its verb-laden statements of objectives that students have to fulfil has to be jettisoned (or if that is impossible subverted). For means–end thinking will result in occluding curricula, in shutting out light and in robbing them of their vitality and creativity. Of curriculum objectives, there will be no end. There is no way out down that path. Instead, the metaphor of curriculum space awaits – for all kinds of creative interpretations. In the process, curricula may emerge that just do some justice to the press of the contemporary age.

As we have seen, curriculum space may be constructed with different textures, offering a variety of curriculum encounters. Epistemological space, practical space and ontological space – for students to be and become not just themselves but new selves: these three forms of space suggest themselves and are embryonically present already in many curricula. But the working out of any curriculum design brings in its wake fresh creative possibilities: curriculum-in-action offers opportunities that cannot be anticipated during curriculum-as-design. To a significant extent, a curriculum is its pedagogy and its interpersonal spaces.

The curriculum can become an extraordinary interhuman setting where different and even contending hopes can be brought into fruitful relationships with each other. The curriculum becomes sets of conversations going on all at once. The tutors, their disciplines, the students and the wider hinterland of 'stakeholders', not to mention the host institution itself: all these can engage with each other through the curriculum as engagements in seminars, lectures, laboratories and studios take on their own character. There are conversations within the conversations; engagements behind and to the side of the engagements. It is a theatre in which, no matter how well the lines are scripted in advance, the players – given sufficient space and encouragement – can improvise and so impart unforeseen vitality to the enactment. It is a play in which there is much, if not all, to play *for*.

Appendix

Selected UK curriculum development projects

History

Directors	Project title	Institutional base	Details from
Neil Strevett Eileen O'Sullivan	Teaching Learning Skills to First Years	University of Glasgow	LTSN History, Classics & Archaeology
Christopher Marsh	Songs of the 17th C: Integrating Popular Music into History Teaching	Queen's University, Belfast	LTSN History, Classics & Archaeology
Nathan Abrams	Discovery Learning	University of Greenwich	LTSN History, Classics & Archaeology
Bruce Campbell	Essay Marking Exercise	Queen's University, Belfast	LTSN History, Classics & Archaeology

Engineering

Directors	Project title	Institutional base	Details from
	Project Based Learning in Engineering		FDTL3 (NCT TQEF)
	Evaluative and Advisory Support to Encourage Innovative Teaching in Engineering		TLTP Phase 3 (NCT TQEF)
Bob Harris	Assessment of Individuals in Teams	Sheffield Hallam University	LTSN Engineering
Warren Houghton	Systematic Learning Guidance for Engineering Students	University of Exeter	LTSN Engineering Mini-Project
Ifiok Otung	Minimal-Mathematics Introduction to Engineering	University of Glamorgan	LTSN Engineering Mini-Project
Daphne O'Doherty	Working as Part of a Balanced Team	Cardiff University	LTSN Engineering Mini-Project
Marion Hersh	The Accessible Electronics Lab	University of Glasgow	LTSN Engineering Mini-Project
Kate Williams	'Day Projects': Intensive Skills Training for Engineering Students	University of Hertfordshire	LTSN Engineering Mini-Project
Rubin Rodriguez	Transferable Skills in Engineering and their Dissemination (TRANSEND)	University of Surrey	LTSN Engineering Mini-Project
Terence Karran	Extended Learning Environment Network (ELEN) (to disseminate a VLE into mainstream courses with learning materials on generic and study skills)	University of Loughborough	LTSN Engineering
Peter Levin Ivan Kent	Marketing Graduates' Skills Project (generic teamwork skills; www.teamwork.ac.uk)	London School of Economics	HEFCE Innovations

Nursing studies

Directors	Project title	Institutional base	Details from
Frances Reynolds	Collaborative Teamwork Skills: How are they developed through interprofessional education and are they applicable in the practice setting?	Brunel University	LTSN Health Science and Practice Mini-Project
Susan Smith	A Qualitative Investigation to Explore the Development of Team Working Skills in Undergrad Physiotherapy Students in a Small Group Setting	Leeds Metropolitan University	LTSN Health Science and Practice Mini-Project
Hugh Barr	Interprofessional Education: Today, Yesterday and Tomorrow	UK Centre for the Advancement of Inter-professional Education	LTSN Health Sciences and Practice
Jenny Phillips	Online Assessment and Feedback (OLAAF) (development of guidelines for computer-based assessment with feedback)	Birkbeck College	HEFCE FDTL4
David Caning	Case study material for teaching and learning (flexible, web-based approach for delivering interactive case material)	City University	HEFCE FDTL4
Carolyn Gibbon	Students Online in Nursing Integrated Curricula (SONIC) (web resources for PBL)	University of Central Lancashire	HEFCE FDTL4
Keith Ward	Creating the Balance in the Nursing Curriculum (case study materials that integrate theory and practice)	University of Huddersfield	HEFCE FDTL4

Directors	Project title	Institutional base	Details from
Mary Chapple	Promoting Key Skills Development through the Use of Portfolios (development of nurses' key skills through electronic portfolios)	University of Nottingham	HEFCE FDTL4
Marion Helme Pawel Miklaszewicz	Interprofessional Education Project (Triple) (Commissioned the Hugh Barr review, above; also mapping IPE practices and developing an interactive database on the web)	King's College, London	LTSN Health Sciences and Practice; LTSN Medicine, Dentristry and Vet. Science; LTSN Social Work and Social Policy
Mark Newman	The Effectiveness of Problem-Based Learning in Promoting Evidence-Based Practice (argues that PBL assists students to achieve specific competencies and is suitable for adult learning; this project will examine the effectiveness of PBL)	Middlesex University	ESRC TLRP 1
Helen Harwood	Universities Collaboration in eLearning (UCEL) (series of national workshops on reusable learning objects or RLOs – sophisticated web packages tailored to each course, so sharing and re-using is 'flexible and extremely cost-effective')	Association of Learning Technologies	UCEL (four major UK universities) and ALT
Catherine Bennett	Supporting Small Group Teaching and Group Work with C&IT	University of York	ESRC TLTP 3
Jenny Brook	Information for Nursing and Health in a Learning Environment (INHALE) (interactive learning materials in a VLE)	University of Huddersfield	JISC DNER Programme

Chemistry

Directors	Project title	Institutional base	Details from
Michael Cole	Enhancing the Appeal of Online-Learning (strategies to maximize the benefits of online learning)	Manchester Metropolitan University	LTSN Physical Sciences Development Project
Jane Tomlinson Andrew Horn	The Development of Exploring Errors Software (software for first-year Chemistry students that addresses misconceptions about experimental errors)	University of York	LTSN Physical Sciences Development Project
Hugh Cartwright	Creating a Central Role for on-line Experiments in the Undergraduate Science Course (flexible access to practical experiments on the internet)	Oxford University	LTSN Physical Sciences Development Project
	New Web-based Learning Tools for Maths in Physical Chemistry (interactive web-based software to stimulate learning of maths)	DeMontfort University and Lough-borough University	LTSN Physical Sciences Development Project
Steve Walker	Software Resources for Remedial Physics Teaching in UK University Chemistry Departments (software to address the problem of lack of physics knowledge)	University of Liverpool	LTSN Physical Sciences Development Project
John Holman et al.	Thermodynamics in Context (resources to support thermodynamics courses for first-year chemistry students)	University of York and University of Leeds	LTSN Physical Sciences Development Project

Directors	Project title	Institutional base	Details from
Keith Adams et al.	Computer Assisted Assessment (banks of introductory chemistry exam questions made available on the web)	University of Ulster	LTSN Physical Sciences Development Project
George Olivier	Development of a Generic Computer-based System for the Assessment of Practical Work in Chemistry (a flexible intranet system for assessment of practicals)	University of Brighton	LTSN Physical Sciences Development Project
Stuart W. Bennett	What do Examinations Really Test? (chemistry exam papers were evaluated to ascertain what they 'really' tested, and a matrix was developed to help other assessment designers do the same with their own exams)	Open University	LTSN Physical Sciences Development Project

Bibliography

This is an indicative bibliography that includes suggestions for further reading.

Abbas, A. and McLean, M. (2003) Communicative competence and the improvement of university teaching: insights from the field, *British Journal of Sociology of Education*, 24(1): 69–81.

Ainley, P. (1998) The end of expansion and the consolidation of differentiation in English higher education, *Teaching in Higher Education*, 3(2): 143–56.

Alverno College (2000) *Alverno College Ability-Based Learning Program*. Milwaukee, WI: Alverno College.

Archer, M. S. (2000) *Being Human: The Problem of Agency*. Cambridge: Cambridge University Press.

Arendt, H. (1977) *The Life of the Mind*. New York: Harcourt Brace Jovanovich.

Argyris, C. and Schön, D. A. (1974) *Theory in Practice: Increasing Professional Effectiveness*. San Francisco: Jossey-Bass.

Assister, A. (ed.) (1995) *Transferable Skills in Higher Education*. London: Kogan Page.

Association of Commonwealth Universities (ACU) (2001) *Engagement as a Core Value for the University: A Consultation Document*. London: ACU.

Association of Graduate Recruiters (AGR) (1995) *Skills for Graduates in the Twenty-first Century*. Cambridge: AGR.

Atkins, M. J. (1999) Oven-ready and self-basting: taking stock of employability skills. *Teaching in Higher Education*, 4(2): 267–80.

Bakhtin, M. M. (1981) *The Dialogic Imagination: Four Essays*. Austin: University of Texas Press.

Ball, S. (1995) Culture, crisis and morality, in P. Atkinson, B. Davies and S. Delamont (eds) *Discourse and Reproduction: Essays in Honour of Basil Bernstein*. Cresskill, NJ: Hampton Press.

Bantu, T. and Hamilton, S. (2002) Barking at straw dogma, in P. Schwarz and G. Webb (eds) *Assessment: Case Studies, Experience and Practice from Higher Education*. London: Kogan Page.

Barnett, R. (1997) *Higher Education: A Critical Business*. Buckingham: SRHE and Open University Press.

Barnett, R. (2000a) Supercomplexity and the curriculum, *Studies in Higher Education*, 25(3): 255–65.

Barnett, R. (2000b) *Realizing the University in an Age of Supercomplexity*. Buckingham: SRHE and Open University Press.

Barnett, R. (2003) *Beyond All Reason: Living with Ideology in the University*. Maidenhead: McGraw-Hill.

Barnett, R. and Griffin, A. (eds) (1997) *The End of Knowledge in Higher Education*. London: Cassell.

Bauman, Z. (2000) *Liquid Modernity*. Cambridge: Polity Press.

Becher, T. (1989) *Tribes and Territories*. Milton Keynes: Open University Press.

Becher, T. (1994a) The state and university curriculum in Britain, *European Journal of Education*, 29(3): 231–45.

Becher, T. (1994b) The significance of disciplinary differences, *Studies in Higher Education*, 19(2): 151–61.

Becher, T. and Kogan, M. (1992) *Process and Structure in Higher Education*. London: Routledge.

Becher, T. and Trowler, P. (2001) *Academic Tribes and Territories: Intellectual Enquiry and the Cultures of Disciplines*. Buckingham: SRHE and Open University Press.

Beck, U. (1999) *World Risk Society*. Cambridge: Polity Press.

Bennett, N., Dunne, E. and Carré, C. (2000) *Skills Development in Higher Education*. Buckingham: SRHE and Open University Press.

Bernstein, B. (1971) On the classification and framing of educational knowledge, in M. F. D. Young (ed.) *Knowledge and Control*, Vol. 3. London: Routledge and Kegan Paul.

Bernstein, B. (1990) *The Structuring of Pedagogic Discourse*, Vol 4: *Class, Codes and Control*. London: Routledge.

Bernstein, B. (1996) *Pedagogy, Symbolic Control and Identity: Theory, Research, Critique*. London: Taylor and Francis.

Biesta, G. (2002) *Bildung* and modernity: the future of *Bildung* in a world of difference, *Studies in Philosophy and Education*, 21(4–5): 343–51.

Biggs, J. (2003) *Teaching for Quality Learning at University*, 2nd edn. Buckingham: SRHE and Open University Press.

Bjarnason, S. and Coldstream, P. (eds) (2003) *The Idea of Engagement: Universities in Society*. London: Policy and Research Unit, Association of Commonwealth Universities.

Blake, N., Smith, R. and Standish, P. (1998) *The Universities We Need: Higher Education after Dearing*. London: Cassell.

Bleakley, A. (2001) From lifelong learning to lifelong teaching: teaching as a call to style, *Teaching in Higher Education*, 6(1): 113–18.

Bloom, A. (1987) *The Closing of the American Mind*. London: Penguin.

Blunkett, D. (2000) *Modernising Higher Education: Facing the Global Challenge*. London: DfEE.

Bocock, J. and Watson, D. (eds) (1994) *Managing the University Curriculum: Making Common Cause*. Buckingham: SRHE and Open University Press.

Booth, A. and Hyland, P. (eds) (2000) *The Practice of University History Teaching*. Manchester: Manchester University Press.

Bourdieu, P. (1984) *Homo Academicus*, trans Peter Collier. Cambridge: Polity Press.

Bourdieu, P. (1990) *The Logic of Practice*. Cambridge: Polity Press.

Bourdieu, P. (1998) *Practical Reason*. Cambridge: Polity Press.

Bowles, S. and Gintis, H. (1976) *Schooling in Capitalist America*. London: Routledge and Kegan Paul.

Boyer, E. L. (1987) *College: The Undergraduate Experience in America*. New York: Harper & Row.

Boyer Commission (1998) *Reinventing Undergraduate Education: A Blueprint for America's Research Universities.* New York: Boyer Commission on Educating Undergraduates in the Research University.

Boys, C., Brennan, J. et al. (1988) *Higher Education and the Preparation for Work.* London: Jessica Kingsley.

Breier, M. (ed.) (2001) *Curriculum Restructuring in Higher Education in Post-Apartheid South Africa.* Pretoria: CSD.

Brew, A. (2001) *The Nature of Research: Inquiry in Academic Contexts.* London: RoutledgeFalmer.

Bridges, D. (2000) Back to the future: the higher education curriculum in the 21st century, *Cambridge Journal of Education*, 30(1): 37–55.

Briggs (1964) Drawing a new map of knowledge. In D. Daiches (ed.) *The Idea of a New University: An Experiment in Sussex.* London: Deutsch.

Byers, W. (2002) Promoting active learning through small group laboratory classes, *University Chemistry Education*, 6: 28.

Castells, M. (2000) *The Rise of the Network Society*, 2nd edn. Oxford: Blackwell.

Certau, de M. (1984) *The Practice of Everyday Life.* Berkeley: University of California Press.

Chambers, E. (ed.) (2001) *Themes in Humanities Higher Education.* London: Kluwer Academic Press.

Clark, B. R. (1983) *The Higher Education System: Academic Organisation in a Cross National Perspective.* Berkeley: University of California Press.

Clark, B. R. (1995) *Places of Inquiry: Research and Advanced Education in Modern Universities.* Berkeley: University of California Press.

Clark, B. R. (1998) *Creating Entrepreneurial Universities: Organizational Pathways of Transformation.* Oxford: Pergamon.

Clarkeburn, H., Roger Downie, J. and Matthew, B. (2002) Impact of an ethics programme in a life sciences curriculum, *Teaching in Higher Education*, 7(1): 65–80.

Coffield, F. and Williamson, B. (eds) (1997) *Repositioning Higher Education.* Buckingham: University Press.

Cottrell, S. A. and Jones, E. A. (2003) Researching the scholarship of teaching and learning: an analysis of current curriculum practices, *Innovative Higher Education*, 27(3): 169–81.

Coulby, D. (2000) *Beyond the National Curriculum: Curricular Centralism and Cultural Diversity in Europe and the USA.* London: Routledge-Falmer.

Curzon-Hobson, A. (2002) A pedagogy of trust in higher learning, *Teaching in Higher Education*, 7(3): 265–76.

De Groot, J. and Maynard, M. (1993) Doing things differently: a context of women's studies in the next decade, in J. de Groot and M. Maynard (eds) *Women's Studies in the 1990s: Doings Things Differently.* London: Macmillan.

Delanty, G. (2001) *Challenging Knowledge: The University in the Knowledge Society.* Buckingham: SRHE and Open University Press.

DfES (2003) *The Future of Higher Education* (White Paper). London: Department for Education and Skills.

Drew, S. (1998) Students' perceptions of their learning outcomes, *Teaching in Higher Education*, 3(2): 197–210.

Drummond, I., Alderson, K., Nixon, I. and Wiltshire, J. (1999) *Managing Curriculum Change in Higher Education: Realising Good Practice in Key Skills Development.* Sheffield: UCoSDA.

Dunne, J. (1993) *Back to Rough Ground: 'Phronesis' and 'Techne' in Modern Philosophy and Aristotle*. Notre Dame, IN: University of Notre Dame Press.

Dyhouse, C. (1995) *No Distinction of Sex? Women in British Universities 1870–1939*. London: UCL Press.

Edwards, T. (2002) A remarkable sociological imagination, *British Journal of Sociology of Education*, 23(4): 527–35.

Ellsworth, E. (1989) Why doesn't this feel empowering? Working through the repressive myths of critical pedagogy, *Harvard Educational Review*, 59(3): 297–324.

Elton, L. (2000) Turning academics into teachers: a discourse on love, *Teaching in Higher Education*, 5(2): 257–61.

Eraut, M. (1994) *Developing Professional Knowledge and Competence*. London: Falmer Press.

Evans, G. R. (2002) *Academics and the Real World*. Buckingham: SRHE and Open University Press.

Fiol-Matta, L. and Chamberlain, M. K. (eds) (1994) *Women of Color and the MultiCultural Curriculum*. New York: Feminist Press.

Freire, P. (1970) *Pedagogy of the Oppressed*. New York: Seabury Press.

Gallie, W. B. (1960) *A New University: A.D. Lindsay and the Keele Experiment*. London: Chatto and Windus.

Gellert, C. (ed.) (1999) *Innovation and Adaptation in Higher Education*. London: Jessica Kingsley.

Gibbons, M. et al. (1994) *The New Production of Knowledge*. London: Sage.

Gibbs, G. (2001) *Analysis of Strategies for Learning and Teaching* (HEFCE 01/37 July Report). Bristol: HEFCE.

Gibbs, G. (2004) *Implementing Learning and Teaching Strategies*. TQEF National Coordination Team. Milton Keynes: Open University.

Giroux, H. and McLaren, P. (eds) (1994) *Border Crossings: Cultural Workers and the Politics of Education*. New York and London: Routledge.

GMC (2003) *Tomorrow's Doctors: Recommendations on undergraduate medical education*. London: Medical Council.

Gokulsing, K. (1997) University education in England and the principle of performativity, in K. M. Gokulsing and C. DaCosta (eds) *Usable Knowledges as the Goal of University Education*. Lewiston: Edwin Mellen Press.

Goodlad, S. (1984) *Education for the Professions: Quis Custodiet?* Guildford: Society for Research into Higher Education and NFER-Nelson.

Goodlad, S. (1988) Four forms of heresy in higher education: aspects of academic freedom in education for the professions, in M. Tight (ed.) *Academic Freedom and Responsibility*. Guildford: Society for Research into Higher Education and Open University Press.

Goodlad, S. (1997) *The Quest for Quality: Sixteen Forms of Heresy in Higher Education*. Buckingham: Open University Press.

Goodlad, S. (2000) The search for synthesis: constraints on the development of the humanities in liberal science-based education, *Studies in Higher Education*, 25(1): 7–23.

Gore, J. (1993) *The Struggle for Pedagogies: Critical and Feminist Discourses as Regimes of Truth*. London: Routledge.

Gosling, D. (2000) 'Communicative action' within two postgraduate courses, *Research and Innovation in Learning and Teaching*, 1(1): 106–18.

Green, M. F. (1995) Transforming British higher education: a view from across the Atlantic, *Higher Education*, 29: 225–39.

Gumport, P. J. (1988) Curricula as signposts of cultural change, *Review of Higher Education*, 12(1): 49–61.

Gumport, P. (2000) Academic restructuring: organizational chance and institutional imperatives, *Higher Education*, 39: 67–91.

Harvard Committee (1945) *General Education in a Free Society*. Cambridge, MA: Harvard University Press.

Harvey, L. (2001) Defining and measuring employability, *Quality in Higher Education*, 7(2): 97–113.

Harvey, L. and Knight, P. T. (1996) *Transforming Higher Education*. Buckingham: Open University Press.

Haslum, M. (1994) A course leader's perspective, in J. Bocock and D. Watson (eds) *Managing the Curriculum: Making Common Cause*. Buckingham: SRHE and Open University Press.

Hassan, R. (2003) *The Chronoscopic Society: Globalization, Time and Knowledge in the Network Economy*. Oxford: Peter Lang.

Henkel, M. and Kogan, M. (1999) Changes in curriculum and institutional structures: responses to outside influences in higher education institutions, in C. Gellert (ed.) *Innovation and Adaptation in Higher Education: The Changing Conditions of Advanced Teaching and Learning in Europe*. London: Jessica Kingsley.

Hermerschmidt, M. (1999) Foregrounding background in academic learning, in C. Jones, J. Turner and B. Street (eds) *Students Writing in the University: Cultural and Epistemological Issues*. Amsterdam/Philadelphia: John Benjamins, pp. 5–16.

Higher Education Funding Council for England (HEFCE) (1999a) *Teaching Quality Enhancement Fund: Funding Arrangements* (HEFCE 99/48). Bristol: HEFCE.

Higher Education Funding Council for England (HEFCE) (1999b) *Institutional Learning and Teaching Strategies: A Guide to Good Practice* (HEFCE 99/55). Bristol: HEFCE and Centre for Higher Education Practice, Open University.

Higher Education Funding Council for England (HEFCE) (2001) *Strategies for Learning and Teaching in Higher Education: A Guide to Good Practice* (HEFCE 01/37). Bristol: HEFCE.

Hill, Y., Dewar, D. et al. (1996) Orientation to higher education: the challenges and rewards, *Nurse Education Today*, 16: 389–96.

Hirsch, E. D. (1987) *Cultural Literacy: What Every American Needs to Know*. Boston: Houghton Mifflin.

Holmes, L. (1994) Competence, qualifications and transferability: beyond the limits of functional analysis, in D. Bridges (ed.) *Transferable Skills in Higher Education*. Norwich: University of East Anglia.

Holmes, L. (2001) Reconsidering graduate employability: the 'graduate identity' approach, *Quality in Higher Education*, 7(2): 111–19.

Houghton, W. (2002) Using QAA subject benchmark information: an academic teacher's perspective, *Quality Assurance in Education*, 10(3): 139–54.

Howard, C. G. (1991) *Theories of General Education: A Critical Approach*. Basingstoke: MacMillan.

Huber, L. (1990) Disciplinary cultures and social reproduction, *European Journal of Education*, 25(3): 241–61.

Illich, I. (1973) *Tools for Conviviality*. London: Calder and Boyers.

Jackson, N. (2002) Growing knowledge about QAA subject benchmarking, *Quality Assurance in Education*, 10(3): 139–54.

Jackson, N. (2004) *Using Complexity Theory to Make Sense of the Curriculum*. www.itsn.ac.uk/genericcentre/index.asp?id=16893 (accessed 20 May 2004).

Jansen, J. and Christie, P. (eds) (1999) *Changing Curriculum: Studies on Outcomes-based Education in South Africa.* Cape Town: Juta.

Jarvis, P. (1986) Nurse education and adult education: a question of the person, *Journal of Advanced Nursing*, 11: 465–9.

Jarvis, P. (1992) *Paradoxes of Learning: On Becoming an Individual in Society.* San Francisco: Jossey-Bass.

Jarvis, P., Holford, J. and Griffin, C. (1998) *The Theory and Practice of Learning.* London: Kogan Page.

Jenkins, A., Breen, R. and Lindsay, R. (2003) *Reshaping Teaching in Higher Education: Linking Teaching with Research.* London: Kogan Page.

Jervis, M. L. (1996) Nursing education in universities – a perspective from biological sciences, *Teaching in Higher Education*, 1(1): 49–64.

Jones, B. and Little, B. (1998) Higher education curricula in the UK, in M. Henkel and B. Little (eds) *Changing Relationships between Higher Education and the State.* London: Jessica Kingsley.

Kelly, A. V. (2004) *The Curriculum*, 5th edn. London: Sage.

Klenowski, V. (2002) *Developing Portfolios for Learning and Assessment: Processes and Principles.* London: RoutledgeFalmer.

Knight, P. T. and Trowler, P. R. (2001) *Departmental Leadership in Higher Education.* Buckingham: SRHE and Open University Press.

Knight, P. T. and Yorke, M. (2003) *Assessment, Learning and Employability.* Buckingham: SRHE and Open University Press.

Kogan, M. and Hanney, S. (2000) *Reforming Higher Education.* London: Jessica Kingsley.

Kress, G. (2003) *Literacy in the New Media Age.* London: Routledge.

Kress, G. and van Leeuwen, T. (2001) *Multimodal Discourse: The Modes and Media of Contemporary Communication.* London: Oxford University Press.

Lave, J. and Wenger, E. (1999) Learning and pedagogy in communities of practice, in J. Leach and B. Moon (eds) *Learners and Pedagogy.* Milton Keynes: Paul Chapman/Open University.

Lawton, D. (1975) *Social Change, Educational Theory and Curriculum Planning.* London: University of London Press.

Lea, M. and Street, B. (1998) Student writing in higher education: an academic literacies approach, *Studies in Higher Education*, 23(2): 157–72.

Løvlie, L. Morenson, K. P., and Nordenbo, S. E. (eds) (2003) *Education Humanity: Bildung in Postmodernity.* Oxford: Blackwell.

Lucas, C. J. (1996) *Crisis in the Academy: Rethinking Higher Education in America.* London: Macmillan Press.

Lyotard, J.-F. (1984) *The Postmodern Condition: A Report on Knowledge.* Manchester: Manchester University Press.

MacFarlane, B. (1997) The business studies first degree: institutional trends and the pedagogic context, *Teaching in Higher Education*, 2(1): 45–57.

MacFarlane, B. and Ottewill, R. (eds) (2001) *Effective Learning and Teaching in Business and Management.* London: Kogan Page.

MacIntyre, A. (1985) *After Virtue.* London: Duckworth.

MacIntyre, A. (1988) *Whose Justice? Which Rationality?* Notre Dame, IN: University of Notre Dame Press.

McKenna, E. (1983) *Undergraduate Business Education.* London: London Chamber of Commerce and Industry.

McKenzie, T. (2000) Supercomplexity and the need for a practice and scholarship of self-reflexiveness in university research and teaching, *Staff and Educational Development International*, 4(3): 205–16.

Malcolm, J. and Zukas, M. (2001) Bridging pedagogic gaps: conceptual discontinuities in higher education, *Teaching in Higher Education*, 6(1): 33–42.

Malingham, R. and McCarthy, C. (eds) (2000) *Multicultural Curriculum: New Directions for Social Theory, Practice and Policy*. London: Routledge.

Marginson, S. (1999) After globalization: emerging politics of education, *Journal of Education Policy*, 14(1): 19–31.

Martin, E. (1999) *Changing Academic Work: Developing the Learning University*. Buckingham: SRHE and Open University Press.

Meredyth, D. (1991) The nerve and muscle of academia: the person-building techniques of the tutorial, *History of Education Review*, 20(2): 36–52.

Miller Smith, C. (2002) A business view of the graduate today, *Exchange*, 2: 8–11.

Mills, J. (ed.) (2002) *A Pedagogy of Becoming*. Amsterdam: Rodopi.

Moore, R. (2000) The (re)organisation of knowledge and assessment for a learning society: the constraints on interdisciplinarity, *Studies in Continuing Education*, 22(2): 183–99.

Morey, A. I. (2000) Changing higher education curricula for a global and multicultural world, *Higher Education in Europe*, 25(1): 25–39.

Muller, J. (2000) *Reclaiming Knowledge*. London: Routledge Falmer.

NCIHE (1997) *Higher Education in a Learning Society*. National Committee of Inquiry into Higher Education (chaired by Sir Ron Dearing). London: HMSO.

Newton, J. (2003) Implementing an institution-wide learning and teaching strategy: lessons in managing change, *Studies in Higher Education*, 28(4): 427–42.

Nowotny, H., Scott, P. and Gibbons, M. (2001) *Re-thinking Science: Knowledge and the Public in an Agony of Uncertainty*. Cambridge: Polity Press.

Nussbaum, M. C. (1997) *Cultivating Humanity: A Classical Defense of Reform in Liberal Education*. Cambridge, MA: Harvard University Press.

Oakeshott, M. (1989) *The Voice of Liberal Learning: Michael Oakeshott on Education*, ed. T. Fuller. London: Yale University Press.

Palfreyman, D. (ed.) (2001) *The Oxford Tutorial: 'Thanks, you taught me how to think'*. Oxford: Oxford Centre for Higher Education Policy Studies.

Parker, J. (2002) A new disciplinarity: communities of knowledge, learning and practice, *Teaching in Higher Education*, 7(4): 373–86.

Peters, M. (ed.) (1999) *After the Disciplines: The Emergence of Culture Studies*. Westport and London: Bergin and Jarvey.

Peters, M. and Roberts, P. (2000) Universities, futurology and globalisation. *Discourse: Studies in the Cultural Politics of Education*, 21(2): 125–39.

Peters, R. S. (1964) *Education as Initiation: An Inaugural Lecture delivered at the University of London Institute of Education, 9 December 1963*. London: University of London Institute of Education.

Platt, C. (2002) Nurses 'fit for purpose': using a task-centred group to help students learn from experience, *Teaching in Higher Education*, 7(1): 33–46.

Popper, K. (1975) *Objective Knowledge: An Evolutionary Approach*. Oxford: Oxford University Press.

Power, M. (1997) *The Audit Society*. Oxford: Oxford University Press.

Quality Assurance Agency for Higher Education (QAA) (1998) An agenda for quality: consultation issue, *Higher Quality*, 1(3).

Quality Assurance Agency for Higher Education (QAA) (2000) *Politics and International Relations Subject Benchmark Statements*. Gloucester: QAA.

Quality Assurance Agency for Higher Education (QAA) (2001) *The Framework for Higher Education Qualifications in England, Wales and Northern Ireland.* Gloucester: QAA.

Ramsden, P. (1992) *Learning to Teach in Higher Education.* London: Routledge.

Ramsden, P. (1998) *Learning to Lead in Higher Education.* London: Routledge.

Readings, B. (1996) *The University in Ruins.* Cambridge: Harvard University Press.

Reich, R. (1991) *The Work of Nations: Preparing Ourselves for 21st-century Capitalism.* London: Simon and Schuster.

Reich, R. (2000) *The Future of Success.* New York: A. Knopf.

Robbins, L. (1963) *Higher Education.* Report of the Committee appointed by the Prime Minister under the Chairmanship of Lord Robbins 1961–63, Committee on Higher Education, Cmnd 2154. London: HMSO.

Room, G. (2000) Globalisation, social policy and international standard-setting: the case of higher education credentials, *International Journal of Social Welfare,* 9: 103–19.

Rowland, S. (forthcoming) Intellectual love and the link between teaching and research, in R. Barnett (ed.) *Reshaping Universities: New Relationships between Research, Scholarship and Teaching.* Maidenhead: McGraw-Hill.

Rowland, S., Byron, C., Furedi, F., Padfield, N. and Smyth, T. (1998) Turning academics into teachers?, *Teaching in Higher Education,* 3(2): 133–41.

Salter, B. and Tapper, T. (1994) *The State and Higher Education.* London: Woburn.

Savin-Baden, M. (2000) *Problem-based Learning in Higher Education: Untold Stories.* Buckingham: Open University Press.

Schön, D. (1987) *Educating the Reflective Practitioner.* San Francisco: Jossey-Bass.

Scott, J. (1991) Women's history, in P. Burke (ed.) *New Perspectives on Historical Writing.* Cambridge: Polity Press.

Scott, P. (1997) The postmodern university, in A. Smith and F. Webster (eds) *The Postmodern University? Contested Visions of Higher Education in Society.* Buckingham: SRHE and Open University Press.

Sears, J. T. and Dan Marshall, J. (eds) (1990) *Teaching and Thinking about Curriculum: Critical Inquiries.* London: Teacher's College Press.

Short, E. C. (2002) Knowledge and the educative functions of a university: designing the curriculum of higher education, *Journal of Curriculum Studies,* 34(2): 139–48.

Silver, H. and Brennan, J. (1988) *A Liberal Vocationalism.* London: Methuen.

Silver, H. and Silver, P. (1997) *Students: Changing Roles, Changing Lives.* Buckingham: SRHE and Open University Press.

Silver, H., Hannan, A. and English, S. (1998) *The Experience of Innovators: A Report on the First Year.* Exmouth: University of Plymouth.

Slaughter, S. (1997) Class, race and gender and the construction of post-secondary curricula in the United States: social movement, professionalization and political economic theories of curricular change, *Journal of Curriculum Studies,* 29(1): 1–30.

Slaughter, S. and Leslie, L. (1997) *Academic Capitalism.* Baltimore: Johns Hopkins University Press.

Snyder, B. R. (1973) *The Hidden Curriculum.* London: MIT Press.

Squires, G. (1987a) *The Curriculum Beyond School.* London: Hodder and Stoughton.

Squires, G. (1987b) The curriculum, in T. Becher (ed.) *British Higher Education.* London: Allen and Unwin.

Stehr, N. (2001) *The Fragility of Modern Societies: Knowledge and Risk in the Information Age.* London: Sage.

Stenhouse, L. (1975) *An Introduction to Curriculum Research and Development.* London: Heinemann.

Taylor, R., Barr, J. and Steele, T. (2002) *For a Radical Higher Education: After Postmodernism.* Buckingham: SRHE and Open University Press.

Thomas, K. (1990) *Gender and Subject Choice in Higher Education.* Buckingham: Open University Press.

Tolley, G. (1983) Foreword, in D. Graves (ed.) *The Hidden Curriculum in Business Studies.* Chichester: Higher Education Foundation.

Tolley, G. (1990) Enterprise, scholars and students, in G. Parry and C. Wake (eds) *Access and Alternative Futures.* London: Hodder and Stoughton.

Tosey, P. (2002) *Teaching at the Edge of Chaos.* www.itsn.ac.uk/genericcentre/index.asp?id=16893 (accessed 20 May 2004).

Trowler, P. (1998) *Academics Responding to Change: New Higher Education Frameworks and Academic Cultures.* Buckingham: SRHE and Open University Press.

Vygotsky, L. S. (1978) *Mind in Society: The Development of Higher Psychological Processes.* London: Harvard University Press.

Walker, D. (2002) *Fundamentals of Curriculum: Passion and Professionalism,* 2nd edn. Hove, UK Lawrence Erlbaum Associates, Inc.

White, J. (1997) *Education and the End of Work.* London: Cassell.

White, J. (ed.) (2004) *Rethinking the School Curriculum: Values, Aims and Purposes.* London: RoutledgeFalmer.

Wraga, W. G. and Hlebowitsh, P. S. (2003) Toward a renaissance in curriculum theory and development in the USA, *Journal of Curriculum Studies,* 35(4): 425–37.

Wright, P. (1995) Learning through enterprise: the Enterprise in Higher Education initiative, in R. Barnett (ed.) *Learning to Effect.* Buckingham: SRHE and Open University Press.

Yorke, M. (2001) Assessment issues arising from subject benchmarking statements. LTSN Generic Centre. www.escalate.ac.uk.

Young, M. F. D. (1998) *The Curriculum of the Future: From the New Sociology of Education to a Critical Theory of Learning.* London: Falmer Press.

Subject Index

Page numbers in bold indicate key references.

ontological turn, 108
Oxford, University of, 82

participation, 14
pedagogical encounters, 144
pedagogical frames, 124
pedagogical relationship, 140
pedagogy, 5–6, 131
pedagogies
  critical, 35
  feminist, 35–36
performativity, 63, 82, 88–92
performative professionalism, 19
performative self-monitoring, 104
performative self-reflection, 103–104
portfolio assessment, 104–105
Principles of Undergraduate Learning,
  99
problem-based learning, 5
problem solving, 43, 82, 111, 131,
  138
professional doctorates, 146
professional education, 61
professional subject areas, **ch, 5**, 102
professionalization, **16–18**
programme specifications, 28–30, 51,
  108
see also benchmarking

quality, 14, 17
Quality Assurance Agency UK, 18, 28
see also benchmarking

reflective practice, 60
risk, 47, 49, 52
  educational, 46
Robbins Report, 13–14, 30–31, 45

scholarship of curriculum, 159–161
scholarship of teaching, 17
sciences and technologies, **ch5**
self, 63–65, **ch8**, 110, 126, 144, 149
self-reflection, 78, 103
self-reliance, 63–64, 101–102

situated learning, 60
skills, types
  communication, 76, 96, 98
  disciplinary, 56
  employment-related, 83, 94–95,
    100–103
  generic, 56, 58, 95, **98–100**
  generic intellectual, 18
  'high skills', 46
  key, 21, 74
  knowing, 92
  knowledge and understanding, 18
  personal transferable, 18, 99
  practical, 79
  subject-based, **94–98**
  team working, 23, 98–99
  transferable, 76, 94, **98–100**, 163
skills development, 23, 55
standards, 14, 16–17, 28–30
student experience, 6, 45, 89, 113
student markets, 72, 74
student voice, **112–114**, 126
subjectivities, 46, 108
success, **45–47**
Sussex, University of, 31

Teaching Quality Enhancement Fund,
  17, 20
  National Teaching Fellowship
    Scheme, 20
  Fund for the Development of
    Teaching and Learning, 20
  Learning and Teaching Support
    Network (LTSN), 20, 156
technologies, **89–91**

uncertainty, 47, 108

vocational turn, 45

White Paper (2003), 13
women's history, 73–74
women's studies, 86
work, 46, 56–58, 109, 113, 125

Author Index

The Society for Research into Higher Education

The Society for Research into Higher Education (SRHE), an international body, exists to stimulate and coordinate research into all aspects of higher education. It aims to improve the quality of higher education through the encouragement of debate and publication on issues of policy, on the organization and management of higher education institutions, and on the curriculum, teaching and learning methods.

The Society is entirely independent and receives no subsidies, although individual events often receive sponsorship from business or industry. The Society is financed through corporate and individual subscriptions and has members from many parts of the world. It is an NGO of UNESCO.

Under the imprint *SRHE & Open University Press*, the Society is a specialist publisher of research, having over 80 titles in print. In addition to *SRHE News*, the Society's newsletter, the Society publishes three journals: *Studies in Higher Education* (three issues a year), *Higher Education Quarterly* and *Research into Higher Education Abstracts* (three issues a year).

The Society runs frequent conferences, consultations, seminars and other events. The annual conference in December is organized at and with a higher education institution. There are a growing number of networks which focus on particular areas of interest, including:

Access	FE/HE
Assessment	Graduate Employment
Consultants	New Technology for Learning
Curriculum Development	Postgraduate Issues
Eastern European	Quantitative Studies
Educational Development Research	Student Development

Benefits to members

Individual

- The opportunity to participate in the Society's networks
- Reduced rates for the annual conferences
- Free copies of *Research into Higher Education Abstracts*
- Reduced rates for *Studies in Higher Education*

- Reduced rates for *Higher Education Quarterly*
- Free online access to *Register of Members' Research Interests* – includes valuable reference material on research being pursued by the Society's members
- Free copy of occasional in-house publications, e.g. *The Thirtieth Anniversary Seminars Presented by the Vice-Presidents*
- Free copies of *SRHE News* and *International News* which inform members of the Society's activities and provides a calendar of events, with additional material provided in regular mailings
- A 35 per cent discount on all SRHE/Open University Press books
- The opportunity for you to apply for the annual research grants
- Inclusion of your research in the *Register of Members' Research Interests*

Corporate

- Reduced rates for the annual conference
- The opportunity for members of the Institution to attend SRHE's network events at reduced rates
- Free copies of *Research into Higher Education Abstracts*
- Free copies of *Studies in Higher Education*
- Free online access to *Register of Members' Research Interests* – includes valuable reference material on research being pursued by the Society's members
- Free copy of occasional in-house publications
- Free copies of *SRHE News* and *International News*
- A 35 per cent discount on all SRHE/Open University Press books
- The opportunity for members of the Institution to submit applications for the Society's research grants
- The opportunity to work with the Society and co-host conferences
- The opportunity to include in the *Register of Members' Research Interests* your Institution's research into aspects of higher education

Membership details: SRHE, 76 Portland Place, London W1B 1NT, UK Tel: 020 7637 2766. Fax: 020 7637 2781. email: srheoffice@srhe.ac.uk
world wide web: http://www.srhe.ac.uk./srhe/
Catalogue: SRHE & Open University Press, McGraw-Hill Education, McGraw-Hill House, Shoppenhangers Road, Maidenhead, Berkshire SL6 2QL. Tel: 01628 502500. Fax: 01628 770224. email: enquiries@openup.co.uk – web: www.openup.co.uk

Related books from Open University Press
Purchase from www.openup.co.uk or order through your local bookseller

BEYOND ALL REASON
LIVING WITH IDEOLOGY IN THE UNIVERSITY

Ronald Barnett

A major work . . . provocative, unsettling and profoundly challenging. I think it should be prescribed reading for all vice-chancellors.

> Colin Bundy, Director of the School of Oriental and African Studies,
> University of London

Ron Barnett's latest book lives up to, and possibly exceeds, the high standards he has set himself in his previous books – which are now established as the premier series of reflective books on higher education.

> Peter Scott, Vice-Chancellor, Kingston University

Beyond All Reason argues that ideologies are now multiplying on campus and that, consequently, the university as a place of open debate and reason is in jeopardy. The book examines, as case studies, the ideologies of competition, quality, entrepreneurialism and managerialism. All of these movements have a positive potential but, in being pressed forward unduly, have become pernicious ideologies that are threatening to undermine the university.

Ronald Barnett argues that it is possible to realize the university by addressing the ideals present in the idea of the university, and so developing positive projects for the university. These 'utopian ideologies' may never be fully realized but, pursued seriously, they can counter the pernicious ideologies that beset the university. In this way, it is possible for the idea of the university to live on and be practised in the twenty-first century.

Beyond All Reason offers a bold optimistic statement about the future of universities and offers ideas for enabling universities to be 'universities' in the contemporary age. It will be of interest and value not just to students of higher education but also to vice-chancellors, administrators, academics generally and those who care about the future of universities.

Contents

192pp   0 335 20893 2 (Paperback)   0 335 20894 0 (Hardback)

QUALITY AND POWER IN HIGHER EDUCATION

Louise Morley

This book examines the power relations that organize and facilitate quality assurance in higher education. It interrogates power in terms of macro systems of accountability, surveillance and regulation, and uncovers the ways in which quality is experienced by academics and managers in higher education. Louise Morley reveals some of the hidden transcripts behind quality assurance and poses significant questions:

- What signs of quality in higher education are being performed and valued?
- What losses, gains, fears and anxieties are activated by the procedures?
- Is the culture of excellence resulting in mediocrity?

Quality and Power in Higher Education covers a wide range of issues including the policy contexts, new managerialism, the costs of quality assurance, collegiality, peer review, gender and equity implications, occupational stress, commodification and consumer values in higher education, performativity, league tables, benchmarking, increasing workloads and the long-term effects on the academy. It draws upon Morley's empirical work in the UK, on international studies and on literature from sociology, higher education studies, organization studies and feminist theory. It is important reading for students and scholars of higher education policy and practice and for university managers and policy-makers.

Contents
Introduction – The policy context of quality in higher education – How quality is assessed – Managing quality – The psychic economy of quality – Changing employment regimes – The micropolitics of quality – Reconstructing students as consumers – (E)quality – Desiring changes – References – Index

208pp   0 335 21226 3 (Paperback)   0 335 21227 1 (Hardback)

RESEARCHING HIGHER EDUCATION
ISSUES AND APPROACHES

Malcolm Tight

This book couples an authoritative overview of the principal current areas of research into higher education with a guide to the core methods used for researching higher education. It offers both a configuration of research on higher education, as seen through the lens of methodology, and suggestions for further research.

Contents

Case studies and tables are separately listed after the main contents pages – Part I: Recently Published Research on Higher Education – Introduction – Journals – Books – Part II: Issues and Approaches in Researching Higher Education – Researching Teaching and Learning – Researching Course Design – Researching the Student Experience – Researching Quality – Researching System Policy – Researching Institutional Management – Researching Academic Work – Researching Knowledge – Part III: The Process of Researching Higher Education – Method and Methodology in Researching Higher Education – Researching Higher Education at Different Levels – The Process of Researching – References

417pp   0 335 21117 8 (Paperback)   0 335 21118 6 (Hardback)

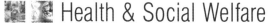